HOW EUROPE SHAPES
BRITISH PUBLIC POLICY

Janice Morphet

First published in Great Britain in 2014 by

Policy Press
University of Bristol
1-9 Old Park Hill
Clifton
Bristol BS2 8BB
UK
t: +44 (0)117 954 5940
pp-info@bristol.ac.uk
www.policypress.co.uk

North America office:
Policy Press
c/o The University of Chicago Press
1427 East 60th Street
Chicago, IL 60637, USA
t: +1 773 702 7700
f: +1 773 702 9756
www.press.uchicago.edu
sales@press.uchicago.edu

British Library Cataloguing in Publication Data
A catalogue record for this book is available from the British Library.

Library of Congress Cataloging-in-Publication Data
A catalog record for this book has been requested.

ISBN 978 1 44730 047 2 paperback

Cover design by Qube Design Associates, Bristol
Front cover: image kindly supplied by istock
Printed and bound in Great Britain by CMP, Poole
The Policy Press uses environmentally responsible print partners

For Robin, Sophie and Charlotte

Contents

Contents

List of tables and figures

Tables

Figures

Abbreviations

BIS	Department of Business, Industry and Skills
CEC	European Commission
CCT	Compulsory Competitive Tendering
CoP	Community of Practice
CPRS	Central Policy Review Staff
CSR	Comprehensive Spending Review
EAP	Environmental Action Programme
EEA	European Economic Area
EFTA	European Free Trade Area
EGTC	European Grouping of Territorial Cohesion
EIA	Environmental Impact Assessment
EPI	Environmental Policy Integration
ERDF	Europa Regional Development Fund
EU	European Union
FDI	Foreign Direct Investment
GATS	General Agreement on Services
GATT	General Agreement on Tariffs and Trade (until 1995)
GPA	Government Procurement Agreement
HMG	Her Majesty's Government
HMT	Her Majesty's Treasury
HOCL	House of Commons Library
IfG	Institute for Government
IMF	International Monetary Fund
LA21	Local Agenda 21
MP	Member of Parliament
MEP	Member of the European Parliament
NATO	North Atlantic Treaty Organisation
NPM	New Public Management
OECD	Organisation of Economic Co-operation and Development
OGDs	Other Government Departments
OMC	Open Method of Coordination
PASC	Public Accounts Select Committee of the House of Commons
PBR	Pre-Budget Report
PSA	Political Studies Association
RDA	Regional Development Agency
SA	Sustainability Assessment
SEA	Single European Act 1987
SEM	Single European Market (1992)
TENs	Trans-European Networks
TIA	Territorial Impact Assessment
UN	United Nations
UNCTAD	United Nations Commission for Trade and Development
WEF	World Economic Forum
WTO	World Trade Organization

Terminology

This book uses the term European Union (EU) throughout, although since its inception in 1957, it has legally been the European Economic Community (EEC) or known as the European Community (EC) or abbreviated as CEC from the French. The EU came into being as a result of the Treaty of the European Union (TEU) in 1992, which is also known as the Maastricht Treaty or just Maastricht. Although for some legal purposes, the EEC remains the appropriate term, it is easier from the point of view of the reader to use the single term EU, so that it what is used here.

The European Commission is referred to throughout the book as the Commission. There is little reference to the role of the European Parliament in terms of policymaking. This is not to underestimate its important and increasing role, but it is not discussed here in any detail.

The term Europe in this book title and the text refers primarily to the EU and does not extend to the wider geography that is Europe or the other European institutions including the Council of Europe, which comprises 47 members in comparison with the 28 in the EU.

Finally, this book uses the term British to include the policies, government and jurisdiction of the United Kingdom.

Directives bind governments as to the results required but leave the choice of means to them.

Regulations directly enter into the domestic law of all member states.

Decisions upon particular matters bind those governments or institutions to which they are addressed (Young, 1973, p xiii).

About the author

Janice Morphet has had a career in local and central government as an academic and a consultant. She has degrees in sociology, management, politics and literature. Her career started as a planner in London then moved to work in regeneration and project management. Janice's interest in the UK's membership of the EU and its interrelationship with British public policy developed while she was responsible for services that were opened to competition. This was extended through widening interest and application of sustainability in local government, when she was part of a small group of advisers representing British local government within wider European local government organisations. She has since been the chief executive of a unitary authority and a local government adviser in central government.

Preface

In 1994, I attended a reception in the European Parliament on the evening before the first meeting of the Committee of the Regions. As part of the support to the UK local government delegation, there was a hopeful feeling among our group. Local government had been through a difficult time since Thatcher became Prime Minister in 1979, and although she had gone, there was still a sense that local government was undervalued and fighting to fulfil its role. The Committee of the Regions was a new affirmation of the role of sub-national government, which might help to change this position in the UK. The reception room was crowded with all the other delegations and there was a good buzz of conversation in the air. After about 30 minutes or so conversing in our group, I looked around to find that the UK delegation was the only one left in the room. All the others had disappeared. Where had they gone? Had we overlooked some other event? On enquiring, I found that all of the other delegations had agreed to have joint pre-meetings and briefings over dinner. They had planned to meet up with old friends and to make new alliances. No one had asked the British delegation to join them and we were insufficiently experienced in working in Brussels to make our own arrangements to do this. This was a timely reminder of the way the UK operated and how separate we were.

The UK's attitude towards the EU has interested me since the 1980s. I have always found it hard to understand why, when the UK has decided to pool many of our policies and powers with other member states, we appear to have little public engagement in policy discussions and decisions. Worse, any attempt to discuss the development of UK policy within this context is always taken as being from a pro- or anti-EU position. The EU is a sectarian issue in the UK. It is only possible to discuss EU policy and objectives with other Europeans or people from the UK who engage in this world. This is very different from people from other member states who are better informed and engaged in these processes. Why is it that journalists attend the press conferences of other member states after meetings to find out what has really happened? Why do we need to read the newspapers or watch the TV of France or Germany to hear about current policy debates? And why are politicians from the EU member states or officials from the Commission ridiculed on television? Why is it that our MPs are largely unaware of the way in which the EU works and display this ignorance in media discussions?

This book cannot answer all of these questions, but it is an attempt to discuss why the UK takes this position, why it continues to happen and the consequences of this lack of understanding. The role of the EU in shaping British public policy is largely submerged but does not need to be. The UK is involved in all decision-making processes in the EU despite the appearance by politicians of absence, distance and, at worst, victimisation. This means that the UK's politicians are disengaged from much of the legislation that they are implementing – perhaps not surprising when it was probably agreed five years before they came into government. They have little interest in current negotiations because it will be another minister that will put this decision into effect. Without an EU narrative, the implementation of policy becomes an exercise in immediate ideological spin.

Thus, the role of Europe in influencing British public policy is considerable but it is rarely, if ever, discussed. Most books written about Europe and the UK are about the struggles over time together with the inevitable political history that has involved all of the key political leaders in the UK over the last 50 years. Other literature deals in detail with the development and operation of aspects of Europe – the EU, Court of Human Rights, European Court of Justice – and is concerned with the struggles between the integrationists and the intergovernmentalists and the extent to which all of this is leading to a Europeanisation of policy, legislation and institutions across Europe. In the UK, we have been involved with the EU since its inception, which is now over 50 years, and the UK has been a member of the EU for 40 years. European Union membership remains something that is done to us, not an agreement to pool our sovereignty for our own benefit.

Many thanks are due for this book. The invitation to consider writing it came from Ali Shaw of the Policy Press at the Policy and Politics Conference in Bristol in 2010. I had asked Janet Newman my 'Emperor wore no clothes' question – 'Is localism a trope for subsidiarity?' – in a session during the conference and Ali thought that this was worth exploring. Ali's encouragement was supported by Emily Watt, the commissioning editor, and the result is here. So, great thanks to Janet, Ali and Emily. I should also thank all of those whose work I have read but not met. Reading is always a stimulating process, but, of course, the faults and omissions are my own. My purpose is to encourage readers to think about the UK's position in the EU, and when they are next at a reception in Brussels, let us hope that they will not be on their own at the end of the event.

Janice Morphet
Wandsworth, February 2013

CHAPTER ONE

Introduction: the UK's relationship with the EU

Introduction

Britain's relationship with the European Union (EU) is frequently characterised as being simple. In ways never really explained by the media and politicians, the EU is perceived to have 'taken away' Britain's sovereign powers and has the ability to determine much of its legislation. The history of how this process has occurred is never discussed and, unlike other countries in Europe, no UK newspaper or broadcast media has a regular slot for the daily work of the European Council or Commission to inform or educate such debate. The European Parliament fares better with a share of the BBC Democracy Live website, but its substantive discussions rarely appear in the print media.

Neither the British public nor other parts of civil society have the knowledge and, thus, the ability to converse about current European policy issues as they do on other domestic or international topics. Megaphone diplomacy seems to be the order of the day – popularly characterised through headlines in newspapers. When discussing EU policy processes on television or radio, Members of Parliament (MPs) demonstrate that they do not understand how the EU works. This is remarkable after 40 years of membership and 50 years of a relationship. It is also a position that may be English rather than British. Being unable to engage in policy debates, discussions on emerging legislative programmes and spending decisions suggests a sense of hopelessness, or even fatalism, at achieving any kind of influence. Or is it the collective burying of the national head in the sand? This suggests that if Britain is not seen to engage in the processes of its successive and continuing pooling of powers within the EU, then it cannot be held accountable for the outcomes of these decisions.

What is the reality of the relationship between Britain and the EU? This book will explore this through its provenance and subsequent engagement. This extends from the original opaque presentation of the implications of EU membership during negotiations and subsequent referenda (Camps, 1964; FCO 1970, George, 1991), the continuing fractures at the heart of government when centralising formal negotiating positions (O'Riordan and Rowbotham, 1996; Jordan, 2008) and a failure to maintain public day-to-day engagement in a joint institution within which Britain has invested much of its sovereign powers (Bulmer and Burch, 2009).

After 40 years of membership, does the EU shape British public policymaking? Or does the UK shape its own policy through its collective engagement within the EU? Since 1972, when the UK joined, the EU has had considerable influence on the domestic legal framework. Some of the influences are well known, such as those in employment and environmental law, and agriculture and fisheries policy. Others, such as transport, are partially understood (Banister et al, 2000; Stevens, 2004). Some policies may have been attributed to the EU but derive from external treaty obligations, such as those on opening up the public sector to competition or 'privatisation' agreed with the World Trade Organisation and its predecessor. A recent example of this in the UK is the introduction of competition into the provider side of health services (Lipson, 2001; Pollock and Price, 2007).

Beyond this, EU membership has had a significant effect on the structure and functions of governance in Britain. The application of the principle of subsidiarity has influenced the implementation of devolved governance for the nations of the UK and a general power of competence for local authorities. It has also led to the separation of the Courts, changed the mix of responsibilities of government departments and introduced a programmatic form of government expenditure. In many cases, the stimulus for these changes is buried deep inside Whitehall and not discussed, even at Westminster. Rather, they have been implemented through the camouflage of different party-political ideologies that are used to set the tone for policy and legislation. They are frequently hidden in plain sight.

Examples of these policy meta-narratives include privatisation, the Big Society and localism and they are frequently attached to general election manifestos, particularly at times when power seems likely to shift between parties. Without a continuing narrative on the way the UK works within the EU, the machinery of government becomes the main technology for implementing change. Unlike the EU, the UK government moves in steps, not flows.

Britain's position on the powers that it has pooled and agreed within the EU needs to be considered so that it can be taken into account when assessing domestic policy development and delivery. While some attempts have been made to estimate the extent to which British legislation is European in origin, both specifically and in its wider framing role (Miller, 2010, 2011b), there is no tracked assessment available as in other countries (John and Bevan, 2011). Beyond this, there is little consideration of the ways in which Treaty agreements, which set out the intentions that frame EU policy and legislation, have influenced governmental change. Given the extent of the powers that Britain has pooled with its partners within the EU, it is remarkable that there is not more daily discussion of how this is working in practice and which policies need to be promoted to support national needs and interests. On the other hand, the UK has also influenced the workings of the EU, including the development of the Single European Market (SEM), trade, Trans-European Networks (TENs), the Open Method of Coordination (OMC) and foreign and territorial policy.

Policy impulse and progression in the EU

The EU comprises several key institutions and it operates through the interrelationships between them. Member states pool their powers in specific policy areas and these are then set in binding treaties and other intergovernmental agreements. Setting the policy agenda that provides the impulse for action can occur in a number of ways, which include external agreements such as trade or environmental treaties, globalised policy fashion, internal progress towards agreed ends or specific national concerns. The member states empower the European Commission to propose the ways in which their pooled powers should be used and agreements implemented. The Commission is at the heart of the EU. It has the power of initiation in these pooled areas and proposes policies, legislation and other actions. These are then discussed and agreed by the member states in the Council of Ministers (Naurin and Wallace, 2010; Miller, 2011b) and with the European Parliament, which increasingly has co-decision power on a widening range of issues.

Disputes between the member states and Commission are taken to the European Court of Justice (ECJ) for determination. Member states can agree to take joint action in subsets within the EU, such as on defence cooperation between France and the UK. At the operational level, there is an agreed administrative code that has no legal basis but is adopted between the Commission and member states (Shapiro, 2004; Heidbreder, 2009).

The Commission does not have direct powers of delivery; this is undertaken by the member states. Delivery can occur in two key forms – through treaties and, second, through legislation. Treaties and their protocols contain overarching principles that are adopted and applied in framing governance by member states. An example of a

Treaty principle that has progressed in importance from the Single European Act (1986), to the Treaty of the EU (1992) to Lisbon Treaty (2009) is that of subsidiarity, and this has had a major influence on state structures in the UK. Another example of a Treaty principle that has grown in importance over time is that of cohesion. Beyond this, the methods of policy delivery may be prescribed through decisions or regulations, but are more frequently left to the member states to determine through the implementation of directives. Each member state needs to submit compliance statements to the Commission on the achievement of all three. Failure to implement EU law can result in the Commission progressing action against a member state, and the member state being taken to the ECJ (Stevens, 2004).

The EU policy lead includes both specific and general applications. Where there is no specific power for the EU on an issue, member states make their own policies (Miller, 2011b). Decisions about implementation of policy are each subject to pre-agreed approaches. In some policy areas, such as taxation, unanimity of member states is required before action can be taken. On others, including those on the SEM, which are the most central and far-reaching powers, a system of qualified majority voting (QMV) pertains. Also, on each issue, there is a role for the European Parliament, which has increased over time. In other areas of policy, OMC can be used (Heritier, 2001a; Armstong 2004a, 2004b; Borras and Jacobsson, 2004). This was introduced during the period of the Blair government and is an approach that enables agreements to be made on issues where there is no formal Treaty framework, which has been used for social policy issues.

Policy shaping

Much of the discussion about the relationship between the UK and EU is set in the context of direct effects and actions that have been central to delivering specific policies and programmes. It is in these micro-relations between the UK and EU that the culture of engagement is exemplified. However, this represents only part of the story and can overlook the influence of the EU on the UK government's overarching strategy and substantive programmes, which is submerged and disguised for the purposes of domestic consumption. That is how Europe is shaping the UK's public policy agenda.

Policy shaping is an indirect process that operates through influence and social constructions (Rochefort and Cobb, 1994). It can be intentional, creating frameworks for problem interpretation (Goffman, 1974) through their context and potential solutions. These frames could be ideological, legal, institutional or cultural, and can be combined in hybrid forms. Policy frames can be mobilised in the interests of organisations or individuals and used to define what is inadmissible or 'other' in the approach to problem definition and solution. Policy shaping can also be unintentional, where acculturation or habituation leads to the perception of expected signs and signals that are then used to frame and shape policy problems and approaches to their solution (Stead, 2012).

The relationships between the EU, particularly the Commission, and the member states are set within both these formal and informal frameworks (Daviter, 2007). The formal frames are primarily focused on the negotiation of Treaties or Intergovernmental Conferences (IGCs), which are then delivered through specific policy programmes and legislation. Since 2000, softer mechanisms have been used as part of this repertoire of formal engagement (CEC, 2001). Through these formal set-piece approaches to EU policy development, Rhinard (2010) argues that the Commission has the potential to frame the agenda in ways that promote integration either directly through agenda-setting or indirectly through negotiation and trade-offs between nations and issues. These are important processes and they have been used on occasion to achieve specific UK outcomes, such as the rebate or the SEM, as Thatcher's diaries illustrate (Thatcher, 1995). On the other hand, as discussed later, much of the UK's engagement with the EU is more detached. The UK has become a fence-sitter in negotiations (Borzel, 2002), a receiver of policy (Bulmer and Burch, 2009) and a routine, but not always complete, implementer of legislation (Jordan, 2004).

However, the strategic directions for the EU set by Treaties are implemented over the subsequent 10- to 20-year time periods also create a framing context for UK domestic policy narratives. This flowing character of policy development in the EU provides time for more specific domestic policy narratives to be developed within the UK. Those who have negotiated these EU treaties as politicians or officials are long gone once the point of delivery is reached. Those responsible for delivery have no organisational context or institutional memory to draw on or a public narrative to support implementation. The UK's approach to policymaking is seen as being short-term (Jenkins, 2011). The main strength of this approach is said to be the ability to provide responsive flexibility to political agendas and events (Hallsworth, 2011). It is this short-term flexibility that is used to translate long-made EU delivery commitments into current political deliverables. In some cases, where the rhetoric is unable to cover the delivery agreements or there is no prepared depth of argument with key stakeholders, policies can hit the choppy waters of professional and public opinion.

Through the pooling of policy sovereignty within the EU, its role in policy shaping has become an important strategic construct in the development and implementation of UK public policy. Its key influence is left unseen, rather than through directives and regulations transposed into EU law (Miller, 2010), which emerge at the end of the process. It is the direction, discussion and thrust of EU policy development prior to EU Treaty agreement that has this underpinning role in shaping British public policy. Ideological and political narratives have to be extended or reshaped to incorporate these overarching frames. The core executive spends much of its effort in developing delivery disguises that can be used within government and in the public domain. Ironically, a more open position on the role of public policy that is pooled within the EU might have led to the UK being able to focus on its own agenda for strategy and priorities, rather than using its energy in creating camouflaged policies.

The provenance of Britain's position

The provenance of Britain's membership of the EU is key to understanding its present relationship. Cultures and habits that were established after 1945 have become part of the UK's institutionalised genetic code of internal engagement and external performance in relation to the EU. After 1945, in the post-colonial world, Britain maintained its position in the key decision-making global bodies, including the United Nations Security Council and as a leading member of the North Atlantic Treaty Organisation (NATO). The interrelationship between these global roles and membership of the EU is a tension that Britain has yet to resolve. In the immediate post-1945 period, when the EU was being set up, both the experience of the war and the development of the Cold War had a significant influence on the British psyche (Kynaston, 2007), while even projects such as the Channel Tunnel aroused fears of possible invasion (Pick, 1993).

The end game of a political and economic union was always explicit in the development of the EU. Initially, it provided a post-colonial transition for France and Belgium through the creation of a replacement that had the same amount of influence, if not more (Camps, 1967). From the outset, the member states of the EU have wanted it to be a power equal to the US in economic terms. There has always been the intention to create a supranational legal structure with the influence that accompanies this (Camps, 1967).

Britain's initial view of membership of the EU was influenced both by its immediate past and its emerging position (Wall, 2008). The EU was regarded as a 'good thing' by Churchill, as a means of strengthening European cooperation and reducing the potential for future war. Although invited to participate in discussions, Britain saw the formation of the EU as a post-war action, that is, looking back rather than looking forward. Britain had a growing concern about its loss of a world role and its changing relationship with the US (Cannadine, 2003). The creation of the European Coal and Steel Community, the first step in creating the EU, was considered to conflict with the Labour government's proposals for the nationalisation of steel, energy production and supply (George, 1998; Young, 1998). The development of the joint European agenda after 1950 was overlooked by Britain (George, 1998). Britain also had strong ties to the Commonwealth, where its main trading links were, but as these loosened, there were concerns about the performance of the economy. However, it quickly became clear that the trading status agreed between the founder EU states, set in an EU that was conducted in French government processes and language, could be disadvantageous to British trade interests.

In terms of achieving political union, the debate inside the EU was about the 'union of states' (French) and 'union of peoples', which was set out in the Bonn Declaration 1961 (Camps, 1964). As part of the early negotiations on British entry, Ted Heath, later to become Prime Minister, stated in a Western European Union speech in 1962 that the UK accepted the commitment to political union and the logical extension to fields of foreign policy and defence and had an open-minded approach to longer-term institutional development (FCO 1970). On the other hand, in the domestic context, sovereignty was always played down as an issue: 'There was little inclination to paint the positive advantages of transcending sovereignty but moving to a new kind of relationship among states' (Camps, 1964, p 424).

The past drivers and continuing influence on Britain's perception of the EU and its relations with it remain trade and the economy. While Britain signed the Treaty of Rome 1957 in 1972, which included the political objectives that have been there from the outset and have continued through subsequent treaties, particularly in 1987 and 1993, these have never been espoused by any UK political party. Instead, constitutional reform has been achieved by stealth, as demonstrated by the Labour Government 1997–2002 the Coalition government on subsidiarity in 2011.

Overall, Britain's attitude towards EU membership has always been defensive, rather than shaping, and a matter of practical politics (Camps,

1964). At the outset, Britain wanted to be inside the EU in order to influence it, but also saw it rather like a Commonwealth, where membership of a wider trading body was not accompanied by binding legislative structures. Britain was strongly encouraged to be on the 'inside' of the EU by the US, which was concerned to focus Britain on European trade after the post-1945 Lend Lease deal ended. Europe had higher annual growth (Sanders, 1990) and this was seen to be developing further as trade was increasingly liberalised throughout the 1950s and 1960s. Thus, Britain was losing its economic support in the US and its traditional trading advantages. Overall, the UK approach was slow, apprehensive and somewhat dismissive. From the outset, Camps (1964, p v) describes it as 'the British search for an accommodation with the European ... Community'.

Despite early resistance by elements in Britain as well as in France, Britain made an application for membership without making fully transparent the issues that would accompany pooling some of its sovereign powers. The potential for the EU to become a new power in its own right was not discussed openly in the UK despite the clear political agenda of the founding members. Would this lead to a post-national position of a single state or a new form of intergovernmental entity? These issues are still alive in discussions within the EU and the UK today. Glencross (2011), for example, questions whether citizens can have democratic engagement outside a member state in the current structure, although Held (2006, 2010) argues that this is an open question. While the member state is a way of legitimating a supranational authority, it is not a substitute for it, although it could be developed further (Beardsworth, 2011). Despite the anti-US position of France, Jacques Delors, when President of the Commission, looked to the US model, where states have their own legislature but US citizens also vote directly for their President (Grant, 1994; Young, 1998). He also introduced an EU flag and anthem. Democratic legitimation remains a continuing issue within the EU and an interpretive lens for assessing EU actions.

In the EU, the pooling of some national powers both aggregates decision-making and fetters individual action. There can only be 'one vote' on any decision, and if this is in the EU, then it cannot be at home. However, there remains in all member states, not least in Britain, continuing issues about how to 'sell' these decisions domestically. Each member state is part of the EU and each democratically elected government participates in decision-making and votes as if it were doing so for itself. When pooling power, politicians have to develop a way of putting this into an overarching narrative or focus for domestic consumption. Over their period of membership, most member states have developed a national political discourse that supports the pooling of powers, and that what then follows from this process is beneficial and in the national interest. Some governments have found to their cost that they have misinterpreted what they have agreed to do when methods of implementation and reporting have run counter to national norms and cultures (Borzel, 1999; Evers et al, 2009).

In Britain, the 'strength through pooling of powers' narrative has never been offered. Rather, the EU is promoted as a 'club', which has rules that have to be kept in general. There is little communication of the process of joint decision-making and that decisions, once agreed, are legally binding. This is despite the UK being challenged on compliance in the ECJ and being required to pay fines or refund payments. The implementation of programmes in different policy areas has been viewed as being 'aspirational' (Haigh, 1996), rather than as commitments. Britain has little language or discourse that enables a discussion about the utilisation and implications of pooling powers with the member states of the EU and how to pursue its own interests in these processes. In the UK, all major decisions taken within the EU, particularly from Treaties, are encased in programmes of domestic policy, locally determined and delivered. When this is not the case, for example, on the application of EU policy to air quality, waste, recycling and bathing water standards, or where there is late communication and or failure to pass on jointly agreed standards, such as recycling, this has left other scales of government facing major implementation costs (Jordan, 1999; Knill and Lenschow, 1998). To overcome this, 'operational' implementation requirements for employment or environment law are submerged into delivery. It also explains why some policies seem to have no genealogy, for example, the creation of the separate Supreme Court or the separation of the Home Office and Ministry of Justice.

The European project is long-term and delivered through formal mechanisms. It is now possible to see that this has moved beyond an internal focus and is global in its reach. This is illustrated by the effects of the euro crisis on other global markets and the role of the International Monetary Fund (IMF) in supporting a solution. Beyond this, Morris (2010) argues that the EU is now a key player in changing the functions and roles of world institutions. This has the power to make Europe greater than the sum of its parts. If this is the case, then is this threatening to Britain's role as a major power? Britain frequently attempts to exploit its pivotal role between the US and Europe, particularly in financial matters. However, this is an area where the development of the SEM into financial policy (2010–20) may increasingly have an influence on the UK's role (CEC, 2005).

The EU's economic role is critical for Britain – both for its global position and its market. The EU now represents the largest internal market in the world and has the potential to develop further, both through economic growth within member states and expanded membership. The EU represents the greatest market for British goods and 54% of the UK's goods (in 2010) and 49% of its services (in 2009) were to other EU countries (Thompson, 2011). If the EU economies falter, UK business interests are likely to suffer. Much of the UK consideration of the EU market is focused on the role of the private sector, but there is also a less formal but more subtle set of approaches that has secured greater EU economic integration. The development of the SEM in combination with the application of the Government Procurement Agreement (GPA) between the EU and World Trade Organization (WTO) in 1980 and the WTO Uruguay Round agreements (1986–94) to further open the public sector to competition has generated new areas of business that can be quickly transferred across member states. The French energy company EDF now supplies British nuclear energy and Siemens, from Germany, is building trains to operate in Britain – both examples of markets opened as a result of this process. The UK has also benefitted from the opening up of these markets through finance, student transfers, and budget air lines (Aughey, 2007).

The founders of the EU always included economic and monetary union on the agenda, even if not specified in the first phases of its development (Young, 1973). The defining role of the market and financial services remains a key point of tension for Britain, not least as it defines its ability to have global influence. The UK has an individual seat on the United Nations Security Council and at the IMF. In time, this may be threatened by changes in EU competencies, a falling position in the world markets or a break-up of the UK through Scotland's independence (Salmond, 2012; O'Donnell, 2011b). Outside the EU, Britain has adapted to the changing focus of post-colonialism. It has retained links with the Commonwealth (Murphy and Mole, 2013) and extended this experience to the absorption of migrant workers from all over the EU. It has responded to crises in other parts of the developing world through increases in its own aid budget and absorbing human rights refugees. It has restricted the number of migrants into Britain but managed to do this in such a way that these ties are not lost. Britain has also become adept at dealing with migratory waves from the widened EU, yet its understanding of its relative relationships with its EU partners and the EU construct has remained underdeveloped.

Finally, an example of the crisis in Britain's role is when a new American President takes office. There is always a concern about which European leader has the opportunity for the first meeting. In 2009, President Obama met the Chancellor of Germany before the British Prime Minister, despite his role in responding to the international financial crisis in 2008. This pivot role between the UK and US that has been chosen by Britain can also undermine its role in Europe. It serves to link the UK with the US, particularly in France, where anti-neoliberal views against the US are strong. The appearance of linked neoliberal ideologies between the UK and US surfaces in other member states. In Germany, for example, an anti-US approach is expressed through the management of debt, both in the economy and as part of domestic practice. Germany has focused its business interests to the East rather than to the West. The growth of the German economy after the economic crisis in 2008 has been based on manufacturing and exports, which was criticised in the earlier years of this century. Further, once described as the 'sick man of Europe', Germany has led the solutions to the eurozone crisis as the main funder. After 50 years of engagement, Britain's chosen role as a pivot or hinge between Europe and the US does not necessarily represent the perceived view of this role within either the EU or the US.

A culture of denial?

Despite Britain's pooling of powers within the EU and the Commission's power of initiation, discussions on how to use the wider powers that are then generated at the EU level have not entered the British political lexicon or discourse. It seems that once the powers have been pooled, the main consideration in Britain is delivery. The way in which the UK works with the EU is set in a hierarchical relationship. Central government's core executive is comprised of the *troika* of the Cabinet Office (CO), the Treasury (HMT) and the Foreign and Commonwealth Office (FCO), and this leads all key EU policy development (Stevens, 2004). This is where detailed discussions about the development and content of Treaties are held, and they only reach Parliament when in a near-final version. The institutional arrangements for the core executive are set out in the *The cabinet manual* (O'Donnell, 2011a) and they are not transparent on EU policy negotiation.

Below this, operational government departments and devolved nations are responsible for the implementation of UK policies agreed within the EU. Senior civil servants in operational departments will engage with the *troika* on policy and then pass down the policy requirements to operational civil servants and agencies (Bulmer and Burch, 2009). Over time, the *troika* has become less experienced and focused on delivery, increasingly interested in inputs rather than outcomes. The Blair government (1997–2007) attempted to change this (6 et al, 2002, 2010) but there has been a subsequent retreat into 'system stewardship', which does not engage with delivery (Hallsworth, 2011). Since devolution, the UK nations have been treated as government departments in this process (Page, 2010). When ministers from Scotland request to attend EU meetings, they do so on behalf of the UK and do not advance separate positions (Happold, 2000; Thorp and Thompson, 2011).

Once specific policy powers have been pooled in the EU, Parliament spends less time in discussing the principles. It is also argued that there has been a bureaucratisation of administrative power across the EU and an increase in administrative over political power (Rose and Miller, 2010). This has been led by specialist civil servants and influenced by policy communities and networks, specialist advisers, think tanks, and trade associations (Loughlin, no date; Knill and Liefferink, 2007; Naurin, 2007; Stone, 2008; Hagemann, 2010). It has been argued that the role of British politicians, like those in the rest of the EU, has been reduced, while the role of the detailed negotiators in the delivery of legislation has been increased (Heidbreder, 2009; Bulmer and Burch, 2009).

It is also the case that implementing policy is seen to be less important and less likely to concern politicians and senior civil servants than determining its principles (Bulmer and Burch, 2009; Blair, 2010; Hallsworth, 2011). Borzel (2002) argues that the UK is a fence-sitter when engaging in policy discussion and development. She illustrates this through the UK's position on environmental policy: 'when Britain joined the EC in 1973, it failed to take environmental directives very seriously since they could easily be incorporated into existing legislation' (Borzel, 2002, p 207). However, it came as a shock when the costs of implementation became apparent, for example, for urban waste water. This lack of engagement reduces knowledge, which, in turn, can reduce understanding and result in additional costs. Borzel (2002, p 209) notes that the record of fence-sitters in the implementation of EU legislation is frequently worse than the foot-draggers.

In the UK, Parliament has established a scrutiny role for EU legislation and policy through Parliamentary select committees. These were initially implemented in 1980 and have increased in power as their roles have been extended. The work of the select committees can form part of the government's process for consideration. Parliamentary select committees can review matters at any stage – pre- or post-delivery. However, they do not form part of the mainstream decision-making by the government. Indeed, they are set up to be apart as a scrutiny process. Parliamentary select committees have no executive power. The select committees for the scrutiny of all European affairs have been operational since 1974 and have changed little over this time, although they were regrouped in 2011 (Baines, 2004; Wright, 2004).

The Lords and the Commons Committees have had different terms of reference, with those of the Lords being far wider than those in the Commons. Although the committees have been regarded as being effective, particularly in the House of Lords, they are limited by late involvement in treaty and legislative developments and a lack of executive power. Further, there has been reluctance from ministers and civil servants to engage them earlier in the processes for fear that the UK's negotiating position would be fettered (Baines, 2004). The restrictive terms of reference and the more mechanistic approach of the Commons select committee has meant that it has been poorly attended.

Other key issues have continued to influence Britain's relationship with the EU. First, the processes for progressing legislation and implementation were always different in the British model. The British, familiar with *episodic* government processes, focused on ministerial meetings and key events and did not recognise or engage easily with the *flow* model of negotiation and discussion in the EU (Camps, 1964; Kuus, 2011a, 2011b). Britain also has an approach that agrees policy positions in the UK before negotiation of any treaty or policy. Information is circulated around Whitehall to all departments and then a central position is agreed. This is frequently described as being a model that is envied by other member states, where EU information flows within government are less well-oiled (Bulmer and Burch, 2009). However, it may also be seen as evidence of a fractured and competitive position in government, where no one department may step out of line in negotiation for fear of breaking the agreed position. In an organisation that has a continuous negotiating style, such as in the EU, fixed positions may be a disadvantage (O'Riordan and Jager, 1996a).

The culture of Whitehall thus remains a key issue. The EU is seen to be external and there is little recognition of the areas where sovereignty has been pooled and what skill sets and cultures are required for effective engagement. Page (2004, p 41) argues that the view in Parliament is that 'the limits of the [EU] competence have been eroded to the point at which it could be said that there was nothing on which the [EU] could not legislate'. In the past, there has been a legacy of assuming that EU treaties give rise to policies that are aspirational rather than commitments, and this affects their integration into consideration. This is further compounded by their separation between the core executive and those government departments that are responsible for delivery. A failure to grapple with delivery in an integrated way may result in an undermining culture of apathy and rejection. The notion of 'variable geometry' has been used as an argument by the UK to allow it to adopt an 'a la carte' free-rider approach to the EU, which has also served to undermine engaging in solid negotiating positions (Jamet, 2011). Undertaking negotiations that are considered unlikely to be binding when agreed serves to reduce the importance of the process – even more so when this judgement subsequently proves to be incorrect.

At the heart of this culture of denial is the primacy of EU legislation. It was always clear that UK membership was bound by Treaties, and, hence, EU legislation would take precedence (Page, 2004). Parliament was concerned about this during the discussions on membership and agreed that if it could participate in the development of discussions on legislation, it would be satisfied (Kitzinger, 1973). Once Britain became a member of the EU early on, it is said to have exhibited 'exemplary' behaviour as a partner (Sanders, 1990), including implementing regulations and directives. However, the narrow operational approach to delivery can lead to an underestimate of the potential scale and scope of policy on wider issues.

This culture of detachment from the EU expressed by UK civil servants could be born out of self-interest. No civil servant wants to admit that the power and role of their department is diminished by Britain's pooling of power within the EU. This serves to undermine their role of being the main source of policy advice. On the other hand, the silo nature of Whitehall and the hierarchical structure of the core executive have reinforced the centralised method of controlling negotiating positions. This represents the division of power between government departments and the ways in which the relative pecking orders maintain the control of processes (O'Riordan and Jager, 1996a). If the UK civil service has incorporated its dealings with the EU within its own culture and not changed its approach over 50 years, then this suggests a lack of focus in dealing with a changed EU (Wall, 2008; Bulmer and Burch, 2009).

Without a clear strategy and public engagement in EU policy issues, it can be argued that Britain has developed a 'victim' mentality in relation to the EU. In part, a position has been developed that leaves the explanation of decisions arising from UK agreements within the EU until the last possible moment before implementation. This is a promoted view of 'powerlessness' to act in the face of 'bullying' behaviour by 'other' unnamed politicians and civil servants that is now readily accepted by the media and public. However, the UK has the same opportunity as all other member states to influence policy and to achieve objectives. As Thatcher's (1995) memoirs demonstrate, this needs long periods of negotiation, use of influence and generating a willingness to operate within the EU rather than stand outside. On the other hand, when EU legislation has been implemented, there has been a temptation of civil servants in Brussels for which Brussels has become a byword to get a 'free ride' for their own agenda through a process known as 'gold-plating' (Miller, 2011a; HoC, 2012). 'Gold-plating' is defined as 'exceeding the requirements of EU legislation when transposing Directives into national law' (CEC, 2011a, p 7). This can be effected in a number of ways, including:

- extending the scope by adding in some new way to the substantive requirements or substituting wider UK legal terms for those used in the directive;
- not taking advantage of any derogations that keep requirements to a minimum (eg for certain scales of operation or specific activities);
- retaining pre-existing UK standards where they are higher than those required by the directive;
- providing sanctions, enforcement mechanisms and matters such as burdens of proof that are not aligned with Macrory principles (eg as a result of picking up the existing criminal sanctions in that area); or
- implementing early, before the date given in the directive (taken from BIS, 2007, p 28).

This has led to some policies being 'blamed' on the EU (Hood, 2011). Successive governments have sought to outlaw 'gold-plating', with the latest approach being one of 'copy out' or direct word transposition between the directive and UK law (Miller, 2001a; Cable, 2010). There can be problems in this method, not least as it undermines the member states' role in interpreting the requirements of the directive to meet domestic circumstances (Miller, 2011a). Copying out also makes the UK appear to be supine and passive in the application of EU legislation.

Camouflaging the EU's influence on British public policy

Although it is frequently possible to find the relevant documents that provide the background and shape of likely future EU agreements, these are more difficult to locate when there is no indication that these issues are in play. An example of this is the British response to Europe's key budget plan after the economic crisis of 2008 – *Europe 2020* (CEC, 2010a). This is available on the Treasury website, and its key themes appear in UK budgets (HMT, 2010), growth White Papers (HMG, 2010, 2011b) and transport policy papers (DfT, 2012a) without either the provenance of the priority or the British response to them being mentioned. One version of this narrative bears similarity with the Hans Christian Anderson fairy story of the 'Emperor's New Clothes' – people see what they have been habituated to expect will be there, not the reality (Berger and Luckmann, 1966).

Despite being concerned to maintain an independent stance from the EU and to avoid greater integration or Europeanisation, the irony is that it is the actions required as a result of UK agreements within the EU that have been the most systematically implemented and regarded as being the most successful. In 2010, the Political Studies Association (PSA) and the Institute for Government (IfG) polled PSA members on which public policies had been most successfully implemented since 1980. However, most of the policies identified at the top of the list have been located in EU decisions, as shown on Table 1.1. When asked about the reasons for this success, the role of EU legislative requirements was not identified and success was seen to be related to political interest in the policy (Rutter et al, 2012a).

Devolution, the UK and the EU

In discussing the influence of Europe on Britain, it is also now more difficult to consider Britain as a unitary state. The continuing development of devolution since 1999 has led to further powers being devolved, including taxation (Scotland Act, 2012). The main issue that will face the governance of Britain in the period to 2020 may be the future of the union in the aftermath of the referendum on Scottish independence. Furthermore, the governance of England and the UK may need to be disentangled to provide an assembly or parliament for England (Jenkins, 2011; Lodge et al, 2012). This also has a potentially significant influence on Britain's membership of the EU.

The introduction of devolution in the UK is directly related to the application of the principle of subsidiarity. This has challenged the central state within the UK. First introduced in relation to the environment in the Single European Act 1987, this has now been extended to all EU responsibilities through the Lisbon Treaty 2009. Spatial differentiation through locality or economic success has been

Table 1.1: Most successful Westminster policy interventions since 1980

Rank order	Issue	European provenance/ principle	Direct or indirect
I	Minimum wage	Social cohesion	Indirect
2	Devolution	Single European Act 1986, Lisbon 2009/subsidiarity	Direct
3	Privatisation	Directive 77/62, SEA 1986/ competition	Direct
4	Northern Ireland peace process	Social cohesion; subsidiarity	Direct through funding programmes
5	Sure Start	Social cohesion; public health	Indirect OMC
6	Human Rights Act	ECHR	Direct
7	Independent Bank of England	TEU 1992	Indirect
8	NHS investment	TEU 1992 for public health; SEA 1986 for health services	Direct
9	EU integration	TEU 1992	Direct
10	Trades union reform	Single European Act 1986	Indirect
11	Smoking ban	TEU 1992/social chapter	Direct
12	Council house sales	Single European Act 1986/ competition	Direct

Sources: PSA, IfG and the author

a concern of the EU since the UK's membership in 1972, when the approach to differential funding for lagging regions was introduced as a key programme of structural funds. Second, criticisms of the EU's lack of a democratic mandate has encouraged it to develop direct working relationships with sub-state governance, and its economic and social policies have been delivered primarily through regional and local governments. This was reinforced in principle when the Committee of the Regions was established in 1994 (Morphet, 1994). At the same time, EU enlargement following the opening of Eastern Europe had the effect of reforming the role of targeted structural funds and moving towards edge-to-edge processes across all places and all states in the EU, and embodied in the principle of cohesion. Following the Lisbon Treaty 2009, the EU's adoption of the principle of territorial cohesion has expanded the scope of existing policy interests.

These increasing relationships between the EU and sub-state governance have had a considerable influence on the constitution of Britain. This is rarely discussed and is not on the core executive's agenda. These influences have included the development and implementation of devolution in the nations of Britain and the continuing nature of this process. Since devolution was introduced in 1999, further powers have been passed to all three nations and to the directly elected Mayor in London. Within English local government, this has been extended from signing the Council of Europe's agreement on local authorities in 1997 to the introduction of a general power of competence in the Localism Act 2011. Powers for parish councils have been extended in successive legislation from 1999 so that parishes now have the same powers as local authorities. The process of devolution continues through the government's proposals to see directly elected mayors in major cities (HMG, 2011b). Other constitutional changes have included the separation of the Supreme Court from the House of Lords and the developing role of human rights and administrative law.

The issue of access to and delivery of EU funding has also been important in the UK. It has encouraged the development of direct relationships between territories and the EU. This has not been welcomed and, in England in particular, there have been centralised strategies deployed to siphon local funding through regionalised government agencies. The completion of the subsidiarity process has led to these structures being abolished by the government, including Regional Development Agencies. Bottom-up approaches to the delivery of EU funding are part of the new programmed approach (BIS, 2012), (CEC 2011f).

For Wales, Scotland and Northern Ireland, the EU has an important relationship that is different from that with the UK government. Knowledge of EU policies and their implications is more widespread and the media reports more EU news on a daily basis. In nations other than England, the EU is seen positively. In England, the EU is seen not as a source of governance, but as a source of funding. The support that has been provided to the whole of England through transport and other projects is not recognised and the relationship with the EU is seen to be more take it or leave it. This has left England more isolated and without a clear strategy.

Conclusions: nature or nurture – what is the genealogical and cultural legacy of 50 years of this approach?

After 50 years of these conflicted views on EU membership, has there been a lasting impact on the genealogy of the relationship or is this a cultural legacy that could be overcome by changing approaches? Campaigns to promote the UK's membership of the EU demonstrated that it was possible to generate a more positive approach if there was national coordinated and focused leadership (Kitzinger, 1973). It may not be possible to repeat this. The lack of public education and promoted engagement with the EU, which goes beyond town-twinning to policy engagement and reporting, remains a key issue. This lack of public education on the implications of joining the EU has been an issue from 1961 onwards (Camps, 1964). Britain has always seen the EU as a restraint on freedom, rather than as an opportunity through alliance – we 'backed into' the EU.

Despite the difference in political stance and rhetoric towards the EU since UK membership, Camps's view in 1967 still retains some resonance: 'In the end all British governments seem likely to reach much the same conclusions about the main thrust of British policy' (Camps, 1967, p 194). Where Prime Ministers have engaged proactively, including Thatcher (1995), Major (1999), Blair (2010) and Brown (Seldon and Lodge, 2010), this has frequently been undertaken out of sight and in ways that their own officials with responsibility for providing government negotiating lines on more detailed policies and legislation might not agree.

Since the UK has been a member of the EU, there has been a lack of development and growth about the role and progress of the EU. Britain seems to be standing still at the point of entry, absorbing EU processes into domestic culture (Bulmer and Burch, 2009), rather than learning from experience. It is as if Britain is frozen in time and cannot shift its position in relation to the EU. The UK's relationship with the EU has been set as passive aggression rather than engagement. This has become a cultural consensus and a normative style of habituated behaviour that has not been influenced by decisions and outcomes in practice, seeing these as 'one-off' examples.

British politics have been transformed by Europe, but not in ways that are generally understood (Geddes, 2004). Within political and policy discussions about the EU, there has always been a *sectarian* undercurrent – a need to adopt a pro- or anti-EU stance in order to discuss it. There have also been times when any discussion about the EU has been off-limits for civil servants, such as in the mid-1990s, when key business that affected the UK was being transacted. A second cultural legacy is a lack of transparency in negotiations, coupled with the third, which is that the discussions between the UK and the EU are seen as being episodic in style. These discussions relate to specific policies and commitments rather than being seen as continuous and part of a flow.

Lastly, a post in the Commission is not seen to be a career-enhancing role for a UK civil servant or politician, as it is in other member states (Borzel, 2005; Borzel and Risse, 2012). On the contrary, a period spent in Brussels is seen to be career-damaging and being 'out of the loop'. Brussels is not in Britain's political 'beltway'.

CHAPTER TWO

Mechanisms of policymaking

Introduction

Policymaking is at the heart of the discussion of the influence of the EU on the UK. Public policy is the expression of any government's activities and its response to political objectives, events and external relationships. The consideration of policymaking processes is important for this book as they comprise the sites where interactions and disagreements can occur. Policymaking can be influenced and developed in different ways and this chapter provides some context to these processes. The objective here is to examine the provenance of specific policies and how they reach implementation.

This is an area where there is a considerable literature, which sets out a number of approaches. Some are theoretical; some discuss the means or technologies of implementation; and others are based on practice, locating policy development and modes of operation within different explanatory frameworks and traditions. These approaches may also be set in knowledge silos and the approach taken to investigating policy processes may influence the outcomes (Capano and Howlett, 2009). Policy analysis sets the success or otherwise of specific policies within the *real* or more practical politics of negotiation and decision-making within organisations (Rhodes, 2011).

Policymaking is critical for any government or intergovernmental organisation. Policy is a way of expressing political direction and strategy (Pollitt, 1984; Mulgan, 2009). On the other hand, Letwin (2012a, 2012b) argues that policy is delivered through strategy, as it is only democratically elected politicians who can determine and agree policy. The former approach is taken here. It is assumed that policy derives from the political decisions and choices of any organisational governing body while those who serve it implement this policy. Policy is subject to influence both from inside and outside the organisation and this will be for a variety of ends, whether personal, political, charitable or profitable (Newman, 2005; Mulgan, 2007).

Policymaking is an art rather than a science. All policy implies change as that is at the core of its function (Hogwood and Peters, 1982), and this is the case even where the policy is to maintain the current position. The effectiveness of any policymaking is in its provenance, reinforcement and delivery (Hill, 1981, 2006). To be effective, a policy has to attain acceptance by those on whom it is targeted and appear to achieve a defined outcome, which may be solving a problem or a progressive move forward (Barratt and Fudge, 1981a) Policymaking has to be considered within a governance context – where wider sets of interests are included in the process of developing, delivering and owning policy in order to increase its effectiveness (Heritier, 2001b). Campaigns can be formed around maintaining a policy, defending it or seeking to amend it (Mulgan, 2007).

Policymaking is a multifaceted process that may be undertaken in silos or in a more coordinated way (6 et al, 2002, 2010; Hood and Peters, 2004). All policies are intended to have outcomes, but these can be generated as unintended consequences (Popper, 1944; 6, 2011). Organisations or individuals might find ways to continue the actions that the policy was designed to influence or to undertake new activities through opportunities opened up in the process (Margetts et al, 2012). Also, individual behaviours may change in ways that were not anticipated (Halpern, 2004). Policies have owners and promoters (Laredo, 1998; Bulmer and Burch, 2009) who are adherents to strategic objectives or specific policy outcomes. These may be pursued as single issues and through individuals or coalitions of interest, and can operate at all scales.

Policymaking can be undertaken in a variety of ways. It can be developed in the context of formal or legal powers or in more flexible informal styles, and, in practice, both are frequently used together. Policies can be influenced by treaty obligations (Putnam and Bayne, 1987), soft power relations (Nye, 2004; McClory, 2011) and events (Hallsworth, 2011). Policymaking can be bureaucratised (Page and Jenkins, 2005) or developed through cooperative methods that may not need legislation (Heritier, 2001a; Armstrong, 2004a, 2004b; Haahr, 2004). Policies can be adapted and developed from those used by others through a process of policy transfer (Dolowitz, 2003) or policy networks (Hay and Richards, 2000). Those who have specific interests, expertise or influence can create policy communities (Loughlin, no date; Keating et al, 2009), which seek or maintain ownership of policies that operate within the institutional settings and on their margins (Jordan, 1990). Policies can be mobile (McCann, 2011), created through assemblages (McCann, 2010) or spread by 'gurus' and international figures (Ward, 2011). Policies can be subject to 'bandwagon' effects (Halpin, 2011), where policy fashion is generated through expected outcome panaceas. Within these contexts, there are approaches to evidence-based policymaking (Davies, 2004), where pilots or trials are used to review effectiveness before full implementation (Cabinet Office, 2003), or policy can be influenced both by the prospect or the outcome of scrutiny (Sweeting and Ball, 2002; Baines, 2004) and freedom of information legislation (Flinders, 2000).

If the key task of government is to deliver its political objectives through policymaking, then these interventions need to be seen to have some 'public value' (Moore, 1995) in a government's contract with the electorate. The government's control over the processes that deliver these outcomes might be seen as a central requirement (Bevir and Rhodes, 2003; Page and Jenkins, 2005), although others have argued that 'steering rather than rowing' (Osborne and Gaebler, 1993) or 'system stewardship' (Hallsworth, 2011) creates a tight–loose framework that sets a direction but is less concerned about controlling delivery. Others, such as the New Public Management School (Hood, 2000, 2002; Pollitt and Boukaert, 2000; Blair, 2010), argue that unless there is a clear process of targets and accountabilities in government, delivery can lose focus, become 'producer-focused' (HMG, 2007) and lapse into 'hobbying' – doing those things that are easier and most enjoyed rather than those that are more difficult or of less interest.

There are debates about the difference between inputs (resources put into achieve policy delivery), outputs (defined measureable differences as a result of a policy) and outcomes (changes in behaviour and culture that cannot necessarily be measured in the short term but are the real focus of policy). The period 1997–2007 in Britain marked a prioritisation of outcomes in government, but the tide has now turned, with a focus on inputs (Hallsworth and Rutter, 2011). An emerging view is that the civil service manages the system of policymaking while not expecting to manage the associated delivery (Hallsworth, 2011; Parker and Pickard, 2011). This approach has been challenged both by the Parliamentary Public Administration Select Committee (PASC, 2011a, 2012) and by the heads of the home civil service, who have suggested introducing contestability into civil service advice to ministers (Heywood and Kerslake, 2012; Maude, 2012).

Strategy and policy: the 'So what?' question

All policy depends on a strategy, even if that is continuing to do what has been done before (Moore, 1995; Mulgan, 2009). Without this, policy can look like strategy, but it may have no sense of purpose, focus or outcome (Jenkins and Gold, 2011). Also, without strategy, those making policy have no common point to work towards or 'golden thread' to hang on to (Micheli and Neely, 2010). Policymakers will view any strategy through the prism of their own specific interests. The diversity in interpretation of strategy can be the subject of policy itself (HMG, 2010). Without strategy, there is neither a sense of direction or framework within which action can be located, nor a narrative that can be communicated to all concerned. 'Getting the story straight' is a key mechanism for policy delivery (Rhodes, 2011).

Even 'business as usual' can convey continuing norms and a strategy that may have deteriorated over time but remains recognisable and able to be communicated. Without strategy, policy can be unfocused and there may be few ways of assessing whether it has been achieved. Given that policy commands the distribution of resources and has strong opportunity costs associated with the choices that are made, policy has to answer the 'So what?' question, that is, 'What demonstrable difference does it make?' At the same time, the delivery of strategy may only be as good as the cultural context within which it is placed; without leadership and organisational reinforcement, prevailing 'culture can eat strategy for breakfast'.

Policy provenance and impulse for change

What are the impulses for policy continuity and policy change? The dynamics of change may be related to past experience or history (Howlett and Cashore, 2009) and institutional factors, such as the influence exercised by existing players. Specific policies can become resistant and persistent despite efforts to change them (Capano, 2009). Major change will frequently arise from external factors (Sabatier and Jenkins-Smith, 1993; Thelen, 2004), but may also result from events, such as general elections or a public mood swing on specific issues. Managing this public mood is a key component in the success of any policy, regardless of its scale. The requirements of external change may be harnessed to achieve other policy changes through a process of 'gold-plating' (Miller, 2011a) or policy-free loading, while policy spillovers may result in unintended consequences (Alter, 2000; Barzelay and Gallego, 2006).

Studies that examine the nature of policy change are profuse and frequently take a causal factor as a means of explaining either the persistence of policy or why it changes (Zittoun, 2009). Change can be managed as an incremental process (Lindblom, 1959, 1979), characterised as continuous progress through a variety of small steps. Change can also be managed in major steps, using catastrophes or set-piece events as their drivers (Kuhn, 1962; Hall, 1993). Change can also be managed within a falsifiability framework (Popper, 1944), where there is a constant search for improvement through contestation, and, once found, these changes may be in large or small steps. This supports New Public Management approaches, with their search for efficiency and effectiveness as their driver (Hood, 1998, 2000). Evidence-based policymaking takes analysis as its impulse for action. Other approaches consider that change has to be centralist and 'top-down', while others suggest that more effective change can be delivered through addressing cultures (HMT, 2004, 2005), achieved through behavioural insight (Halpern, 2004; Thaler and Sunstein, 2008; John et al, 2011; Brown, 2012). Some policy changes may occur through external events, such as the global financial situation, or in response to a pandemic. Changes may also be caused by public opinion or media pressure.

The issues that promote policy change are problematised so that it is possible to set them in terms of alternative solutions. The problems also frame the assessment of the likely effectiveness of any solutions that can be examined against other factors, such as cost, ease of implementation and public acceptability. Understanding the provenance of policy and how it sets the agenda is an important component in considering the potential for influence on this process. One approach is to consider who frames policy by setting its context, the rules of engagement and the acceptability of outcomes (Goffman, 1974; Rhinard, 2010). This framing process can also set the priority for an issue to be considered (Cairney, 2012) and this influence over agenda prioritisation can be persistent over time (Baumgartner and Jones, 2002) or be captured by specific interests (Thurber, 2004). Issues can also come to the top of the agenda and be catapulted into a priority position. This may be due to events or public mood. In some cases, issues emerge as political priorities without much public preparation. On other occasions, a policy window might emerge, when it is possible to promote a policy as a free-rider on another initiative (Kingdon, 2003). Some policies are promoted by entrepreneurs, who attempt to influence the prioritisation of problems to improve the potential role of their solution.

There is a developed literature that considers three types of approach to policy development, adoption and change: multiple streams (MS), punctuated equilibrium and advocacy coalition frameworks (ACR) (Real-Dato, 2009; Cairney, 2012). The role of ACR suggests a more proactive externalised interest group approach to policy. Punctuated equilibrium suggests that policy agendas are stable over long periods, either because they have been captured by ideology or interests or because there is bureaucratic inertia, but that this position can be punctured by elections or external pressures (Baumgartner and Jones,

2002). The MS approach explores the role of those who are engaged in agenda-setting and the extent to which they can exploit policy aporia or entrepreneurial opportunities to promote their issues. These three approaches are politicised in a variety of ways. The role of joint-working can be organisational rather than through democratically accountable politics, while policy networks and communities can be captured by external interests. As Real-Dato (2009) demonstrates, there are problems with all three approaches, which are all partial and selective in their explanations of causation and boundary frameworks.

Others use specific metaphors or analogies to characterise the process of policy change. Bertelli and John (2011) make a financial analogy, suggesting that once in government, political parties see policies as capital. They then consider policies within a risk and reward system in the same way that companies may consider their business or the launch of new products. In this model, policies are driven by politicians seeking re-election and other factors are not seen to be of much, if any, importance. Issues such as the date of the general election, the independent spirit of ministers or where ministers are mouthpieces for entrepreneurial departments all need to be managed to create a whole, but this is seen primarily to be a political task. The only sanction available in this model is the appointment or dismissal of ministers, although 'machinery of government' changes could also threaten departments if they are promoting unwelcome policy lines or underperforming. Bertelli and John (2011) also suggest in this model that the role of the annual programme of legislation, announced in Britain through the Queen's Speech, is focused on the external presentation of policy, which will assure the electorate of the outcome of change, rather than politicians or civil servants necessarily having an expectation that these policies will be successful. In developing these programmes, governments have to problematise issues and set programmes of action against them as technologies to achieve solutions (Rose and Miller, 2010). However, tying stated outcomes to specific programmes may or may not work in practice.

In addition, it is also possible to use another financial analogy and consider policy changes as being responses to impulses. Impulses are stimulants of change, which may be specifically promoted or unintended. These may range over a variety of sources (Pollitt, 1984; Capano and Howlett, 2009) and may also be subject to differentiated party politics (Zohlnhofer, 2009; Bertelli and John, 2011). Where winning the next election is the most important goal, any policy programme content may be subject to those who hold political 'vetoes'

(Tsebelis, 2002). Table 2.1 sets out a range of issues that may be the provenance of a policy impulse.

Table 2.1: Provenance of policy impulses

• Institutionalism
• Existing policies – 'what works'
• Political ideology
• Manifesto (in response to other parties)
• Intermediate elections, eg, local elections, by-elections
• Formal commitments, ie, treaties, eg, United Nations, European Union, World Trade Organisation
• Informal external pressure, eg, Organisation for Economic Cooperation and Development, World Economic Forum
• Events (major and minor)
• Media
• Public pressure/petitions
• Evidence
• Fashion
• Emulation
• Criticism
• Fear
• Foibles

Source: Author

Policy may progress in a continuous or punctuated/episodic form. The continuous form can be planned and work towards a strategic end or can be incremental in response to the past rather than responding to the future (Hill and Smith, 2004a). Episodic change can also be planned through set-piece events, such as the annual Budget or legislative programme in the UK. This episodic approach can also be described as 'punctuated equilibrium' (Baumgartner and Jones, 2002; John and Margetts, 2003; John and Bevan, 2011), where some policy changes are seen to be more dramatic because they are set within a culture of policy continuity.

The driver of policies in the 'punctuated equilibrium' model is seen to be derived from forces associated with political success and re-election. In tracking these relationships, Bertelli and John (2011) also found that governments were likely to be more radical in their policy programmes once in government in comparison with promises set out in their pre-election manifestos. This suggests that once in government, there are more considerations to be included in policymaking than those that are entirely political. There may also be specific reasons for not sharing all that might be done once in office with the electorate prior to an election. The 'honeymoon' period, or first 100 days after an election, can be used by governments to promote and implement less popular policies (Zohlnhofer, 2009). This is also known to civil servants, who will work with opposition parties prior to general elections in order to prepare to implement their manifesto proposals and to develop ideologically consistent strategies that can be used to implement continuing commitments, for example, to implement EU legislation.

The shifting of responsibilities between departments or ministers in 'machinery of government' changes has been a consistent feature of managing 'in government' changes. A ministerial reshuffle in government is an episodic mechanism that creates instant change and action. It is also a way of implementing changes when more continuous methods are not culturally acceptable. These changes may be driven by political expediency – to respond to political problems or public demands (Davis et al, 1999). They could also be driven to improve efficiency, although March and Olsen (1984) suggest that this is a form of ministerial rhetoric to carry political change. Pollitt (1984) suggests that the three main drivers for this type of change are political expediency, administration or external necessity, whereas Hogwood (1992) indicates that changes in the machinery of government may give the appearance of activity when none is planned. What does seem to be clear is that there are few, if any, principles for establishing the machinery of government or changes that are made within it (Davis et al, 1999). These changes may also be cyclical and represent an acceptable repertoire for the remixing of responsibilities within any nation state. Changes in the machinery of government remain a prime ministerial prerogative, although the political considerations between different factions within the political party also fetter these choices.

Increasingly, governments have central policy teams or units to advise Prime Ministers (Truswell and Atkinson, 2011). These central teams have been seen as the embodiment of the power of the core executive (Rhodes, 1995; Smith, 1999). Prime Ministers have increasingly appointed central policy units to strengthen their own hands in these processes. In the UK, Prime Ministers have used these institutions to reinforce their leadership rather than be managed by a set of departmental 'robber barons' or back-bench rebellions in the House of Commons.

The global context can also provide an impetus for policy change (Pollitt, 1984). At the global governance scale, different governments loosely package responsibilities for similar issues in ministerial portfolios, for example, home affairs, the environment, foreign affairs and so on (Zohlnhofer, 2009; John and Bevan, 2011), but each nation state will choose different bundles of policy areas to sit together. This broader packaging is important to civil servants who need to maintain links with

European, Commonwealth or international agendas and colleagues over time (Alexander et al, 2011). This close working may survive institutional reforms, such as devolution (Keating et al, 2009; Clifford and Morphet, 2012), agencification and privatisation.

Mechanisms of policymaking and their influence

The generation of government policy is subject to influence from interests and by cultures and styles (Parker and Bradley, 2000; Cowles and Risse, 2001). These might be characterised as approaches that are centralist, relying on 'top-down' command and control, and others that are more decentralised (Wollman, 2000; Breuss and Eller, 2004; Miles and Trott, 2011). Decentralised approaches work in a number of ways, such as the inclusion of locally derived policies at the national level or initiatives and services that are determined locally.

Given these overarching thematic approaches and the practical development of policy content, how is policy made? Literature on policymaking tends to follow specific analytical and theoretical pathways, which frequently develop through comparative case studies of similar issues in different countries or different issues within the same country (Bache and Jordan, 2008; Nadin, 2012; Stead, 2012). The key approaches are discussed here and include: policy networks; policy transfer; policy communities; policy mobilities; and evidence-based policymaking. Others take an institutional approach, examining the role of government bodies, agencies and other influencers in the policy process in a core executive model (Rhodes, 1995; Smith, 1999). Some take a more interpretive account, from policy to source, tracking and evaluating what has occurred (Bevir and Rhodes, 2003). Finally, there are theories that are related to international relations, where external agreements, legislation and treaties or informal influence can have a significant influence on policy (Welch and Kennedy-Pipe, 2004; Costa and Jorgensen, 2012). Each of these approaches has something to offer in the understanding of policy but none provides a complete picture. These approaches need to be understood in their influence on existing processes and as change agents, which can disrupt systems of policymaking. Policymaking relationships between Britain and the EU operate in all these ways.

Influence in and on policymaking

Much of the work on policymaking has been undertaken on who influences policymaking agendas and content. This interest can be from specific communities, business, trade associations or scales of government. Some of the biggest influences in changing policy in the UK have been major campaigns based on coalitions of interest, such as those for the countryside and fuel protests for the Labour government in 1998 and 2000 and health, forestry and planning for the Coalition government in 2011/12. Interest mobilisation (Jordan, 2003; Jordan and Halpin, 2006) can create policy 'bandwagons' (Halpin, 2011) that take on wider forms of professional or organised interests and turn these into a public confirmation of importance or at least an acceptance that the resulting policies are needed.

There are a number of factors that are significant when considering the way in which policies are adopted or are influenced. These can include formal institutions and mediating points, political and organisational cultures, differential empowerment of actors, potential for veto, learning, convergence and divergence, collective identity, and mimicry (Cowles and Risse, 2001). All of these have some social or group context within an organisational or interest environment. As discussed later, this occurs even when policies emerge from external and formal sources as well as those that are evolved through more informal mechanisms.

1. Formal processes of policy development: treaties and protocols

Domestic policymaking is frequently propelled by international treaties and related protocols that, once signed, are binding on signatory states in their implementation and adherence. These treaty obligations can comprise a variety of forms, including general objectives or specific obligations. In some cases, such as treaties generated by the World Trade Organization (WTO) or the EU, convergence to the agreed outcome may imply that each signatory has to undertake different policies and actions in order to reach a compliant position. Treaties are frequently seen as 'coercive' tools and are described as if the signatories were in some way subject to the agreement but not party to the process. They are frequently treated as separate forms of policymaking, yet they can create significant frameworks for policy development and delivery, which might be as wide as a general approach to achieving more open exposure of the public sector market to the private sector or more detailed obligations in relation to wheat or bananas.

The process of developing any treaty usually takes place over a number of years, with the engagement of different actors at each stage of the process, frequently with a fixed secretariat in each of the signatory states or organisations to retain continuity. These processes become institutionalised and, frequently, the greatest tensions can be between the specialist officials and politicians within a single state rather than between states. The process of treaty negotiations and international summits is based on policy exchange. Putnam and Bayne (1987, p 260) have identified four types of policy coordination that are attempted through these processes:

- mutual enlightenment, that is, sharing information about national policy directions;
- mutual reinforcement, that is, helping one another to pursue desirable policies in the face of domestic resistance;
- mutual adjustment, that is, seeking to accommodate or ameliorate policy divergences; and
- mutual concession, that is, agreeing on a joint package of international policies designed to raise collective welfare.

Beyond this, there is less consideration of the way in which issues enter this formal policy agenda. Summits and treaties have their origins in wider debates that precede them. Once a treaty negotiation has started, its direction is set and it is the detail that is subject to intense negotiation. Opening up competiton in the public sector can lead to major changes in institutions and governmental practices. In some cases, such as the WTO, it is trading groups, such as North American Free Trade Agreement or the EU, that are responsible for the delivery of agreements. This is undertaken through internal processes of harmonisation of legislation, which has the consequence of the convergence of practices. Bulmer et al (2007) illustrate this in respect of the liberalisation of the telecommunications industry within the EU. Negotiation for content and direction within treaties is highly contested, with 'red lines' or areas that will not be agreed by one particular country. This is an approach frequently used by the UK (Phinnemore and Nugent, 2010). It is also used as a means of signalling areas where trade-offs and bargains can be made between participants. They may also lead to policy convergence between states over time as a consequence of agreeing and implementing treaties (Bennett, 1991). Convergence may also occur as different organisations or states 'emulate' each other (Bennett, 1991) or adapt policy initiatives to make them fit local circumstances.

2. Policy transfer

Policy transfer can occur when politicians or officials are seeking responses to specific issues or problems or can be used as carriers or justifications for policy approaches. It is primarily viewed as a harder-edged process that is specific and has a power relationship between the sender and receiver of the policy being transferred. Sometimes, policy transfer can be conceptual, such as 'privatisation', 'marketisation' or 'choice', and transmitted into practice through culturally specific processes and institutions. This concept has been extended by Dolowitz and Marsh (1996) to include both voluntary and coercive forms of behaviour. Cairney (2012) states that policy transfer can also use the trope of 'lessons learned'. Although the literature on policy transfer focuses on the international scale, it is also clear that it occurs between localities, within localities or states, and between sectors.

Within an EU context, this includes the transfer of a policy objective or specific delivery mode that has some binding qualities. These might include policy priorities or regulatory methods. In some cases, member states can implement European legislation in ways that imply a policy transfer or fixed mode whereas the implementation needed might be more flexible than this might suggest. On other occasions, the application can be more specific and seek to replicate what has been delivered elsewhere. In the UK, the sectarian approach to the EU has meant that policy provenance from the EU is politically problematic. However, since the election of the Coalition government in 2010, UK politicians have frequently offered policy examples from other EU member states to demonstrate the likely efficacy of their own policies. This allows for policies developed within EU member states in response to agreed EU commitments to be exemplified at one remove. Policy examples used in this way have included schools systems and pension policies from Sweden (Mulholland 2012; Hutton, 2011), youth policies from Finland (Pitts, 2005; Symonds, 2012) and city policy from Germany (Clark, 2012).

Some policy transfer is unintended and occurs through viral marketing, where ideas and ways of doing things are passed between networks and now more formally captured through social networking sites such as Linked In, Twitter and Facebook (Shirky, 2011). There has also been an increasing use of e-petitions to influence policymaking (Miller, 2009) and the use of crowd-sourcing for evidence – photographs taken on mobile phones and then uploaded and shared within seconds have been used to force public authorities into action. This was particularly used in 2012 to demonstrate the gap between official statements of the length of time taken to pass through immigration control at London Heathrow airport and the experience of those in the queues who could broadcast their experience immediately.

The application of policy transfer to explain or analyse policy development and change has both widened and deepened. As Benson and Jordan (2011) indicate, the application of policy transfer theoretical and analytical models has incorporated more activities but has also generated studies within sub-areas of interest, such as Europeanisation and transfer through governance networks (Blanco et al, 2011). Policy transfer has not generally been considered in a domestic context, although it can be equally applicable. Much of the basis for attending conferences is to hear about the 'message from government', including additional information that may embellish more widely available policy material, giving attendees a policy edge.

There are also critics of policy transfer as a mechanism for policy development. McCann (2011) suggests that it is insufficiently engaged with the identity and motivation of agency, that is, the social construction of those engaged in the transfer process. Second, McCann criticises the literature for focusing on the national scale and for not considering sub-state policy transfer. Much policy transfer focuses on the international and formal processes while the use of policy transfer within the state is generally covered by the policy networks and communities literature.

A centralised approach to policy transfer within states may also be part of legislative programmes that do not operate at the international scale. The presupposition that a power relationship in the policy transfer process also under-represents the obligations that countries have within treaty obligations – to the WTO or EU – which have been freely entered into. Another consideration can be the role of quasi-voluntaristic approaches, which emerge from membership of the Organisation for Economic Co-operation and Development (OECD), United Nations (UN) and the use of the Open Method of Coordination (OMC) for agreed issues within the EU. Here, the organisations are not able to make binding decisions that compel action by the individual state, but membership is clearly influential in transferring policy priorities, objectives and constructs through the use of soft power means of influence, such as the publication of comparative indicators. Policy transfer can be buttressed by external reporting or benchmarking, whether this is applied unwillingly or as a useful exterior mechanism to cover interior change (Hood, 1998).

3. Policy networks

Policy networks have been defined as a 'limited number of participants, frequent interaction, continuity, value consensus, resource dependence, positive-sum power games and regulation of members' (Marsh and Rhodes, 1992, p 23). They spring from the use of the governance model (Bevir and Rhodes, 2003; Rhodes et al, 2003) and are used as a means of understanding how policy is made in the 'real world' (Blanco et al, 2011). Policy networks assume a common framework of interest and an exchange of experience and research across localities or countries, where comparative experience of policy development, acceptance and success in delivery can be used as a means of informing policy development (Adam and Kriesi, 2007) and also create arguments for acceptance of particular approaches.

Policy networks have a less formal role in developing policy, but their cultural cohesion may make them influential in both development and delivery. They can be seen as a strategic-relational model (Hay, 1998), which 'seeks to apply a theory of collective strategic action to the social practise of networking' (James, 2010a, p 369), with the objective of achieving some common agendas. In this version, networks are intentional in the way in which they operate and the issues that they select for common action. They have processes for recruiting new members and can adapt over time (Hay and Richards, 2000). They can be used for a range of policy issues and may be of particular relevance when a more open or formal approach may be problematic or challenging. Policy networks can operate in the back room and their hidden nature can allow the inclusion and possible incorporation of interests and influences. In this style, they imply a common objective and recognition of the benefits of joint actions through shared information, resources (Hay, 1998) and tactics. The policy network also has to be 'read' and 'managed' if it is to be effective and it can encourage compliance through elite access and grey information. Such groups can take on a 'task and finish' character, which underpins their instrumental role for all network participants. They manage change, containing the voices and influences that might destabilise or undermine the process.

Policy networks that can be considered effective may have some common characteristics, including stability, insularity and resource dependency (Peterson, 2009). Policy networks have the benefit of being able to incorporate policymakers into confirmation and ownership of policymaking, adaption and adoption while, at the same time, allowing for local differentiation. They also provide locations where policy-related problems can be shared and potential solutions discussed. Public officials in policy networks can find sympathetic colleagues with whom to share problems and triumphs and can also use colleagues as exemplars to reinforce their own positions in the policy debate. For those network members who come from other sectors, networks provide both a means to be informed of policy thinking and also to influence the approaches being taken through soft measures. For both the private and voluntary sectors, the ability to network either personally or through social media is now seen to be a critical attribute in demonstrating influence and a key attribute of 'emotional intelligence' (Goleman, 1998). On the other hand, policy networks may be enclosed spaces within given frameworks and may be unlikely to suggest or promote paradigm shifts in policy development and delivery.

Political policy networks are also important between politicians, such as the links between the Labour government of 1997–2010 with Australia, Canada and the US (Mulgan, 2011). Here, successful policy ideas have been adapted and adopted within contexts that have cultural similarities. In the case of Australia and Canada, they have demonstrated post-colonialist maturity. They are further reinforced through exchanges of key policy personnel. Hence, a further issue to consider is who has the credentials and credibility to be part of a policy network? Does the closed nature of policy networks exclude problems and experiences from other states? This may lead to cultural vacuums and the exclusion of ideas through insularity. This is becoming a key issue in the West's understanding and potential emulation of perceived distinctive success factors central to the development of the Brazil, Russia, India, China economies (Morris, 2010).

Policy networks also have their own genealogy and can widen out or narrow down depending on their culture (McGuire and Agranoff, 2011). Kahler (2009) differentiates between networks as structures and networks as actors. Networks as structures can be established formally or can emerge informally. Groups of local authorities or organisations can decide to work together as networked groups in order to exchange experience, information or policies. When new policy initiatives are introduced, a common approach is to establish a network to support development as part of the delivery mechanism. Networks are now easier to facilitate using social media, which allow members to view discussions and be influenced by them without contributing directly (Margetts, 2010; Shirkey, 2011).

Networks can be powerful through their ability to bargain externally, not least as they can promise to 'deliver' a group of like-minded people (Kahler, 2009). Networks can also be powerful in the level of access they may provide or use exclusion to maintain social solidarity and a sense of loyalty through selective membership of a tribe (Elkins, 2009; Tett, 2009). Policy networks can act as critical masses that form a sense of solidarity and reduce the concerns of participants (Granovetter, 1978). Within policy networks, individuals or areas of activity can become reference groups (Merton, 1968), which are recognised as leadership centres or touchstones of credibility. Building on reference group activity may offer more external confidence for the policy pursued. However, this approach might increase centralised homogeneity and discourage decentralised decision-making systems that exaggerate difference because of rivalry or result in separate policies that encourage divergence (Alesina and Wacziarg, 1999). It might also encourage trade-offs within the network (Jamet, 2011).

The EU has increasingly become a site of policy network investigation and study (Blanco et al, 2011). Within the EU, a policy network could derive from specific member states that have a known interest or competence on a specific issue, such as the Nordic or Dutch members on the environment or Germany on the manufacturing industry. However, these points of reference might also be used as exemplars to be rejected, such as the British approach to privatised services, and can become examples to the network of practices to be avoided and cited in a negative way.

If networks are about learning, they may also become Kuhnian paradigms (Kuhn, 1962), where adherents may take a normative view expressed through policy convergence and its takes a paradigm shift for change to occur (Hall, 1995; Currie et al, 2011). Some networks may have 'entry requirements' that are prized, and adherence to networked norms become a requirement at the point of membership. These policy networks may have gained important power-broking positions and, as a group, be able to destabilise those individuals and organisations that seek to challenge them. Specific actors may have powerful roles in representing the rest. The reinforcement of policy network ideas are also spread by international consulting firms (McNutt and Pal, 2011), businesses and civil servants.

Are policy networks particularly useful in solving difficult, wicked or persistent problems? Ferlie et al (2011) suggest that the literature evaluating the role of networks points this way. Wicked problems often focus on policy failure, but how far can policy networks be used to overcome them? In some cases, a policy network might be used as a means to criticise prevailing orthodoxies or groups with a controlling interest. They may also be used to demonstrate where there are systemic failures in approach or delivery.

Where civil servants and politicians need to inject policy ideas into the political system, they frequently use think tanks to engage with networks .Think tanks can be viewed as external to and, to some degree, independent of the prevailing policy discourse. They are regarded as a means of generating new ideas. Think tanks can be issue-based and seek to influence all political parties on their agendas. They can be politically aligned, and can change this political alignment over time. Think tanks can be used by governments and the civil service to generate ideas that appear to be external and as mechanisms to generate policy turns. Ministers can be seen to alight on external 'good ideas' promoted by organisations that are credible sources, whether politically or thematically.

However, the role of think tanks can also be criticised. Pautz (2011) describes them as knowledge regimes and argues that there should be a re-evaluation of how we define and consider their role. There is also their provenance to consider: 'Who funds them?', 'What is the experience of the staff – former civil servants or politicians?', 'How are issues for discussion and research identified?' Pautz (2011) argues that think tanks are set up to further the ideas and interests of the funders rather than being independent. Think tanks are part of a managed landscape of policymaking and where civil servants want to inject ideas into policy discussions that can counterbalance those of ministerial special advisors (SPADs) (Truswell and Atkinson, 2011), they can have a key role. Further, when the civil service is uncertain about the outcome of the next general election, it can develop symbiotic relationships with think tanks to feed ideas into all political parties.

Policy think tanks can act as a policy network and become an alternative source of credible thinking and policy approaches (Pautz, 2011). Think tanks are frequently made up of former civil servants or government advisers, so their role is incorporated within the government machine rather than standing at a distance from it. This can also extend to the externalisation of advice (James, 1993; Stone, 2000; Maude, 2012). This assumes that the organisational loyalties of former civil servants persist after they have left the civil service in a Jesuitical model. Over-recruitment into the civil service fast stream generates organisational spillover as those leaving join other organisations. Most think tanks close to government are made up in this way and their leading staff have been engaged in activities of this type in both directions. Former UK civil servants and advisers are in leading roles in UK think tanks, including Centre for Cities, the Policy Exchange, the Institute for Public Policy Research (IPPR) and Demos. Junior staff or interns frequently move on to political or civil service roles (James, 1993; Stone, 2000).

How far can policy networks influence government policy? The UK civil service has been increasingly criticised for its ability to deliver – 'the finest minds' do not necessarily mean the finest outcomes (Hallsworth, 2011; Hallsworth and Rutter, 2011).Yet, the civil service is an elite policy network with the survival of a generalist group being an important factor in its institutional memory (Letwin, 2012b). Pressured to focus more on delivery, although regarding policymaking as its main function, the civil service has consistently sought to externalise delivery and implementation through the creation of agencies or privatisation. This retains power at the centre and reinforces a mode of delivery that mirrors forms of colonial administration.

The extent to which policy networks can influence government may depend on whether civil servants are members of them (McGuire and Agranoff, 2011). As noted elsewhere, this may also be related to the membership of former civil servants, who can be relied upon to share common goals, values and norms. They may open or steer agendas and act as early warning systems for potentially rogue or outlying members. They can also act as a litmus test for ideas and attract potential opponents so that they are easier to incorporate or manage. On the other hand, as Newman (2005) points out, networks can also be used to open up new issues and lines that are outside the control of central policymakers and this can be enhanced through social media.

There may also be power dependency within the networks, particularly if one of the members is also responsible for allocating resources to group members or their affiliate organisations (McGuire and Agranoff, 2011). Policy networks can be effective where there is a common drive to achieve problem-solving, but this may perhaps be disturbed where there is a competition for funding (Ferlie et al, 2011). However, as Hay and Richards (2000) demonstrate, policy networks can have an organised influence on outcomes. This makes core executive approaches to policymaking closed (Smith, 1999), inward-looking and inclined to be self-referential.

4. Policy communities

Policy communities are similar to policy networks and are described by Heclo and Wildawsky (1974) as policy 'villages', which are the locations of bargaining relationships within government that can be open to influence (Richardson and Jordan, 1979). They are groups with shared interests but not necessarily from the same sector. Indeed, lobbying industries and those working in organisations wanting to influence government policies come to know about 'administrative parishes' (Jordan, 1990, p 475). Here, 'Ministers and civil servants devolve the bulk of decision making to less senior officials who share power with interest groups when they exchange access for resources such as expertise' (Cairney, 2011, p 211) and 'street level bureaucrats' effectively make power when there are too many initiatives thrown at them to implement at the same time (Cairney, 2011, p 214). They can also be the location of the application of soft governance tools introduced into the EU in 2000 (CEC, 2001).

Policy communities can set boundaries within states or domestic policy communities, unlike policy transfer, which is generally defined as being between states. They start with 'a process by which knowledge of policies, administrative arrangements, institutions in one political system (past or present) is used in the development of similar features in another' (Dolowitz, quoted in Benson and Jordan, 2011, p 366). Policy communities are comprised of experts who can signpost to others in the community and can reinforce exemplary approaches (Kingdon, 2003). Policy communities can also identify first-movers, who, in the search for innovative solutions, are hunter-gatherers, boundary-spanners (Williams, 2012) and policy tourists.

Experiences of others, whether these are innovators or pilots, are also seen to be useful in successful policy communities and aid viral development of policy salience. This approach has a number of attractions to government, not least when organisations are encouraged to compete for pilot front-runner status (Cabinet Office, 2003). Those that are successful are used as peer exemplars, which are more likely to be credible in the sector. Those organisations that are not successful will have made some commitment to the policy principle in the bidding process. Where local authorities are in these groups, policy communities are set up or positively encouraged to support learning and policy innovation. Other opportunities can be created through 'peer to peer' discussions (Wolman and Page, 2002) at the 'margins' of other meetings or through car park conversations that occur spontaneously.

Policy communities can be developed further through the use of communities of practice (CoPs), which are online spaces where individuals probably unknown to each other can share documents, views and problems. CoPs are continuing groups engaged in some common endeavour (Eckert, 2006), although they may be used as specific common work communities for task and finish activities. They are seen to be means of common learning (Wenger, 2000) and can help with problematisation and sense-making, particularly in the development or delivery of new policies or government policy shifts. They are seen as non-threatening safe havens where those at different levels of policy competence or development can find information or knowledge that has developed over time and where there is a mix of experience between members.

5. Policy mobilities

Policy mobility is a relatively recent approach to considering the ways in which policies are generated. It has developed through a critical approach to policy transfer and its perceived hierarchical nature. Policy mobility takes a networked approach (Bevir and Rhodes, 2003), 'which incorporates actors and interests that are often implicitly and explicitly assumed to be located elsewhere' (Cochrane, 2011, p x). One of its main concerns is the way in which globalised policies influence what occurs at the local level. It addresses this through the relationship between geographies and territories and the individuals that carry policies between them (Ward and McCann, 2011). These networks promote 'good practice', which is carried by individuals (McCann and Ward, 2011), and this is the object of the mobility.

Policy mobilities provide an insight into the notion of informal policy transfer within a globalised network, partly based on face-to-face contact, but also through the use of new media. Those who perform this role may be brought in as experts, but also act as social hubs for transferring ideas and examples that reinforce their views through social media such as Twitter. This approach is concerned with the guru or external expert. The other, in the form of an external expert, can be useful in providing ideas that are separate from those in governance and can also be a way to test out the acceptability of ideas before they are adopted. In a globalised world, an external 'expert' may have more resonance than an internally generated idea.

Is the policy mobilities approach a successful model? Do cities or localities that are more inward in their approach fare less well, Do externalised reference points make any practical difference to success factors/performance, however assessed? Focusing on the individuals who are carriers or transporters of these policies, their values and objectives (McCann, 2011), creating a global ideas aristocracy, brought in to provide specific insights into issues, but mainly to give international or external reinforcement to a local initiative. These individuals may be introduced by central government, as in the 'personality' reviews used frequently by the Treasury during 1997–2007 and reinstated by the Coalition government (eg Freud, 2008; Dilnott, 2011; Hutton, 2011).

The openness of ideas and their provenance may mean that policy mobility is more easily seen and understood than before. In the 1960s, much consideration was given to the US approaches to locational poverty (Harrington, 1962). Other policies that have been mobile include place-making (Florida, 2009), local taxation from Canada (McLain and McMillan, 2003) and infrastructure planning from Australia (Morphet, 2011). Policy mobilities are based on policy performativity, by taking 'successful' policies as a shield to cover the introduction of change.

Policy mobility is a useful concept in a world that is more concerned with territories, where places are the generators of change rather than industry or politicians. The role of policy mobility is reinforced through notions such as 'world-class cities' against which formal and informal benchmarking can be undertaken (Flowerdew, 2004; Florida, 2009). The selection of policies or approaches to promote and emulate is also critical (Robinson, 2011; Ward, 2011).

One approach has been to consider how policies take hold and are then reinterpreted, without 'interrogation', in specific geographies through assemblages or territories that conceptualise place and identity (Allen and Cochrane, 2007). Brenner et al (2010) consider how ideologies such as neoliberalism take an overarching and framing character across a range of states and then transfer these ideas into localised contexts. The implications of the internalisation of these reforms can frame subsequent institutional approaches. Policy mobilities may be similar to policy communities and networks, which may be focused around specific issues or engaged in promoting preferred ends.

6. Evidence-based policymaking

Evidence-based policymaking is a central model, although one that is frequently more difficult to use in a short-term political culture. It can be described as a necessary underpinning to 'getting a grip on the problem' (Osborne and Hutchinson, 2004) and to create a results-oriented approach, although there is always a tendency when dealing with challenges, issues or problems to consider the inputs rather than the outcomes (Osborne and Gaebler, 1993). Evidence is not an end in itself. However, the increased focus on evidence-based policymaking has, it is argued, engendered a new and vigorous debate about the role of evidence and Boaz et al (2008, p 247) argue that the use of evidence in organisations and policymaking has started to produce a 'tangible shift'.

Evidence has a number of roles. It can measure the effectiveness of public interventions, such as campaigns to change modes of travel, improve literacy or enabling more people to move back into work. Evidence can be viewed as single tests of data or they can be combined to consider the effects of synergistic interrelationships for areas, organisations or people. All evidence is 'owned' or sponsored and this process of 'ownership' will mean that the questions that are addressed through the evidence or even they way that it has been collected are likely to reflect the main interests of its 'owners'.

Evidence-based policymaking is most prevalent in medicine, and has increasingly been used in the development of public policy in three main ways. These are to identify what needs to be done, what has worked here or elsewhere, and whether this approach solves the problem or improves the outcome. The identification of what needs to be tackled has been a long-standing feature of public policy. In some cases, evidence has been used to identify issues where attention is required, for example, shorter life expectancy or poorer air quality. This approach may also be used to identify areas where there are multiple problems that may not be the responsibility of one agency.

In identifying what has worked elsewhere, there is a view that public interventions need evidence of their likely outcomes before major investment is made. Pilot projects are a means of testing approaches before the wholesale commitment of funding, although pilot projects are frequently not then translated into general use. This may be because they do not fully achieve the outcome expected or because the underlying issues or conditions have changed (Davies, 2004). There may also be political pressure to implement an initiative without waiting for the results of pilots. Finding examples of what has worked is not confined to England. Experiences and approaches from other countries are also considered (Cabinet Office, 2003). As Collins (2009, p 15) comments, in central government, 'rarely is a policy enacted … without an appeal to evidence of some kind. That said it is usually the policy that comes first. The idea tends to lead the search for evidence rather than the other way round'. The last main use of evidence is during an examination after the event. Have the interventions worked and what can be learned for next time? This stage of evidence-gathering is less developed, although audit and scrutiny has increased. Performance and outcome assessment are based on this approach.

7. Not making policy? Muddling through, incrementalism, unintended consequences and adaptation

Policymaking can also be responsive to problems rather than being politically led. Lindblom's (1959, 1979) approach to 'muddling through' or disjointed incrementalism is seen to be a safe way to progress that limits risk and is more acceptable to organisations and individuals. This is short-term and no strategic objectives are developed. It is about survival and responding to circumstances. Unintended consequences can limit the control of events (Marks, 1993; Pierson, 1996). When changes in institutional or organisational arrangements are introduced, such as performance management, new behaviours are formed (Smith, 1995). These unintended consequences can be closed off at the next opportunity but then further behavioural responses to these may occur, for example, in closing taxation loopholes. Risk-management processes can only mitigate potential outcomes rather than prevent them and much risk analysis does not factor in 'unknown unknowns'. As a response to this, the focus may be shifted to managing blame in the case of failure (Hood, 2011). Adopting well-defined goals and objectives may lead to difficulty and Kay (2011) argues for the principle of 'obliquity', where problems are solved through adaptability and agility – trying things, learning and changing rather than single answers.

8. Policy as fashion

Many policies are considered and adopted because they are fashionable – that is, they are seen to demonstrate that an institution or organisation is at the leading edge of thinking and practice on a particular issue. Policy fashions can spread internationally, such as New Public Management (Pollitt et al, 2001; Richardson, 2000), although their interpretation and delivery will be localised. Fashion is an economic term and without it, much of the consumer-based economy would not flourish. However, in policymaking, the 'new' is not always acceptable and may be used to reject change. The openness to change in organisations is related to culture and experience. In organisations that are traditional and internally focused, particularly those where promotion or advancement is dependent upon immediate supervisors or managers, change can be limited. In organisations that recruit externally as well as internally and where employment is related to performance, there may be more openness to change.

Conclusions

Models of policymaking focus primarily on inputs, who is influenced in the process and the degree of coercion involved. There is less focus on the outcomes, apart from evidence-based policymaking, although policy effectiveness is incorporated into policy transfer. Policies are used because of their perceived political and delivery success. There is also a degree of fashion in selecting policy methods and borrowing from one field into another (Kingdon, 2003). Methods used by the private sector can appear as radical paradigm shifts when adopted by the public sector.

What is clear from all these approaches is that policymaking is a social undertaking. Policy practitioners prefer to operate in groups to ensure that policies are accepted and that potential problems can be considered before implementation. In this culture, the cost of development is shared, also reducing risk. What each of the policy network, policy community and policy transfer models suggests is the importance of the frame of reference and the pool of social contacts that make up the process. Which individuals are trusted or heard may be as important as groupings of peers. Policy transfer between states is described in some cases as coercive, but this overlooks these underpinning relationships.

Policy transfer processes might occur through 'imitation', 'emulation' or 'transfer' (Westney quoted in Laguna, 2010, p 6), but are based on policies that are in operation in one jurisdiction. In comparison, policy networks and communities develop policies that fall into their areas of interest through incorporation, adaptation or innovation as well as transfer. This can explain why some policies transfer more quickly than others. Policy transfer is fostered by Internet search engines and social networking, but, as yet, these are rarely considered in this literature. Policy professionals are frequently 'hunter-gatherers' or operating as 'discipline tourists' in the hunt for a new concept that can be applied. Although *Nudge* (Thaler and Sunstein, 2008), *Black swan* (Taleb, 2007), *Sprit level* (Wilkinson and Pickett, 2010) and *Obliquity* (Kay, 2011) are all populist versions of more serious work, it is the power of the social media that has seen their incorporation into policy lexicons rather than through research-based literature. 'Policy assemblages' capture the 'peer-to-peer' process of gathering information for policymaking within a digital world (Benson and Jordan, 2011; Prince, 2010). Policymaking is difficult to control (Hallsworth, 2011).

The context of policymaking, who is involved and its institutional setting and attendant cultures are all important (Laguna, 2010). The promotion and reception of policies (Bulmer and Burch, 2009) are also dependent on these factors. Policymakers select from repositories of ideas and salient communities of influence. As reader reception theories indicate, the engagement between the receiver and material is governed by a range of factors (Iser, 1980; Goffman, 1974). In policymaking, this includes a social element. Policymakers graze for new ideas but need to ensure that they are anchored into culturally acceptable provenances before promoting them. The literature on policymaking is well developed; it is set within its own taxonomies but it does not provide much assistance on the origins of policies and the drivers for change. Inevitably, political agendas are driven by difference from the rest and what went before. The repertoire of policies used and their development is considered further in Chapter Three.

CHAPTER THREE

British public policymaking

Introduction

The mechanisms of British policymaking can be considered within ideological, theoretical and realist frameworks. The theoretical approaches have been more overtly influenced by anglophone countries – the US, Canada, Australia and New Zealand – rather than elsewhere in Europe (Pollitt and Bouckaert, 2000). These approaches have been focused on the development and adoption of New Public Management ideologies (Hood, 1995, 1998; Newman, 2001), networked/relational schools (Bevir and Rhodes, 2003) and, more recently, choice-based architectures (Greener, 2008; Dowding and John, 2009) and behavioural insight (Halpern, 2009; Dolan et al, 2010). These have all drawn from policy experiences that have been influenced by international exchanges of staff and cross-country learning (Margetts et al, 2012). This has been primarily driven at the political level by the Labour Party. Before 1997, it drew on Clinton's experience in the US (Cole, 1998; Freeden, 1999; Deacon, 2000) and this was then passed on to the Labor Party in Australia (Frankel, 1997; Deacon, 2000). Both Canada and New Zealand had also been engaged in public sector reform experiments, particularly focused on integrated working, which were also used as exemplars (Hewison, 2001; McLain and McMillan, 2003).

The ideological dominance of a neoliberal economic model, with its focus on efficient welfarism, has been antithetical to some EU states, which have regarded the UK as being too strongly influenced by the US (Cerney and Evans, 2004; Clarke, 2004). However, the focus on realist performance management, which has been a dominant feature of British public policy since 1997 (Newman, 2001; Cutler and Waine, 2002; Harrison, 2002; Hood, 2002), has also been influenced by Organisation for Economic Co-operation and Development (OECD) benchmarking practices (OECD, 1996; Pollitt and Bouckaert, 2000; van Thiel and Leeuw, 2002). This comparative approach based on external evaluation of performance and outcomes has spread into Europe, although not as New Public Management. Rather, it has been influential in the role of OECD country reviews and the development of the Open Method of Coordination (OMC), which has been developed

—
47

as a soft governance method within the EU since 1999 (CEC, 2001; Heritier, 2001a; Radaelli, 2003; Haahr, 2004).

Setting British public policy agendas

UK policymaking agendas are characterised as being responsive, flexible and short-term, rather than strategic. The dominant process of central policymaking in Britain is episodic. These episodes are created through relying on set-piece events such as general elections, the Queen's Speech (John and Bevan, 2011) and 'machinery of government' changes (Davis et al, 1999; Hazell and Morris, 2009), commonly associated with ministerial reshuffles to instigate changes of policy direction. This includes a low use of strategy and devaluation of delivery (Jenkin, 2012). Although politicians lead policymaking, it is the role of the civil service to advise them (O'Donnell, 2011a). Policy is delivered through a variety of mechanisms, primarily at sub-state levels through agencies, local authorities and nations. Policy and delivery are susceptible to fashion and influence from other countries. Delivery mechanisms range from direct means such as legislation to the use of soft power through behavioural insight (Nye, 2004; Thaler and Sunstein, 2008; Dolan et al, 2010; John et al, 2011).

Political leadership is expected to show public value in government (Moore, 1995). However, the relationship and, on occasion, struggle for leadership in policymaking between politicians and civil servants is well documented (Crossman, 1979; Lynn and Jay, 1990a, 1990b; Ianucci, 2005; Carswell, 2012; Letwin, 2012b). This struggle for policy dominance is frequently seen as being more significant than successful implementation (Jenkins and Gold, 2011). Since 1999, when devolution was introduced, this tension has grown more complex in Britain and represents a turn in practice (Cairney, 2011). This has led to confusion about the role of the UK and particularly England in policymaking processes.

British public policy: the role of internal and external influences

Britain is frequently described as a centralised state, where Westminster and Whitehall are the main drivers of policy. Within this, there have been concerns over the role of the executive in relation to Parliament (Flinders, 2002; Forman, 2002). The increasing role of Parliamentary select committees has been seen as critical to the slow rebalancing of power between Parliament and the executive since they were established in their current form in 1980.

In Britain, discussions on policymaking in government have grown. Policy priorities are contained in party manifestos and then delivered through legislation (John and Bevan, 2011). The role of political ideology has always been more important in setting policy agendas than the details that support their implementation (Russell, 2012). Less attention has been given to the extent to which policy agendas in Britain are external in their character but then 'wrapped' in political ideology for their delivery, rather than being initiated by British politicians (Rutter et al, 2011). Where this is the case, these agendas are translated and mitigated primarily by the civil service, which supports ministers in their work. Before general elections, civil servants work with opposition parties to develop delivery approaches to new policies as well as aligning previously committed policies to prevailing political ideology (Riddell and Haddon, 2009).

Approaches to practical policymaking in British government have primarily been structural rather than methodological or procedural. Using the approach of policy mobility (McCann, 2011), 'personality reviews' of policy – such as Barker (2004, 2006) on housing, Eddington (2006) on transport, Freud (2008) on benefits and Hutton (2011) on pension reform – demonstrate that this is a consistent approach across all governments and parties, creating an 'externalised' impulse in government to achieve internal policy change. Units are also set up to develop, review or promote policy approaches such as 'evidence-based policymaking', joined-up government and outcomes- or customer-focused approaches (6 et al, 2010; Lewis, 2011). These are primarily driven through government departments and have not been focused on outcomes (Lewis, 2011). Finally, 'tsars' have been appointed to take a role in specific policy areas. This practice was introduced by the Labour government during 1997–2010 and has increased in use by the Coalition government since (Levitt, 2012).

The next sections consider the ways in which British public policy is developed using the range of means available, including both episodic and flow models of change. Episodic approaches are bundled groups of policies that may herald significant changes in direction and rely significantly on 'machinery of government' processes. These approaches are useful mechanisms to introduce change that may be unwelcome within the civil service or government or when there are external commitments to deliver policy. Flow methods of policy development promote change within existing frameworks but are implemented in the normal course of business. Flow change styles are more prevalent when service delivery is involved and there is a public interface.

1. Internal mechanisms: electoral cycles and the machinery of government

A key internal structural approach to practical policy development is through the use of electoral cycles. The Parliamentary term is five years whilst, the precise length of the Parliamentary term has been in the hands of the Prime Minister, who has been able to call an election when it has seemed to offer the greatest advantage. The role of annual set-piece events in the Parliamentary calendar, such as the Budget, the Pre-Budget Report and the Queen's Speech, in signalling and setting these agendas is considerable. As noted in Chapter Two, the role of these events in offering policy punctuations is also an important structuring feature (Baumgartner and Jones, 2002).

Parliamentary cycles become important for policy horizons and delivery. However, this can lead to short-termism and a failure of longer-term decision-making, which Dyson (2011) describes as 'strategic inertia', caused in part by a government's lack of popularity and re-election campaigns being exploited by operational tribalism and competition. Although the Labour and Conservative parties had agreed to accept the spending programmes they inherited as commitments from 1996 onwards, this broke down in 2009 after the Conservatives refused to adhere to Labour's spending priorities and programmes in the wake of the global financial crisis.

The second internal structural component of the development and management of British central government policy is through the use of the machinery of government. This includes changing either departmental or ministerial responsibilities or both. Within the lifetime of governments, changes are achieved through cabinet reshuffles, which may be planned or precipitated by external events such as a minister resigning over personal misdemeanours. These reshuffles provide an opportunity not only to change the government's ministerial team, but also to change the alignment of responsibilities within government. Cabinet reshuffles are also ways of moving ministers who are not seen to be sympathetic with their current brief or who cannot get along with their civil service teams, who also provide an annual review of their minister's performance. Some ministers are moved frequently and others stay with briefs over a period of time and their subsequent careers can be linked with such issues as disability, foreign affairs or one of the UK nations.

Both the use of electoral cycles and the 'machinery of government' approaches to external presentation of internal policy changes are episodic in their nature. They are demonstrated through events that are visible and enable changes to be managed in ways that are less challengeable by both politicians and civil servants (Hazell and Morris, 1999). They turn change into a procedural task. The civil service maintains its cellular approach and generalist staff on the basis that it can quickly adapt to these changes. In practice, these changes can vary in the extent to which they influence departmental structures and portfolios. Some departments are frequently joined together and split apart. The Department of Work and Pensions maintains two separate structures and information technology (IT) systems despite having been created in 2001, while the Department of Communities and Local Government had a common personnel system with the Department of Transport despite being in merged and demerged arrangements since the 1970s.

2. Internal mechanisms: the role of policy units

Internal policy development and change has primarily been achieved through the role of policy units and external think tanks. The initial development of specific approaches to policymaking was first adopted by Conservative Prime Minister Ted Heath in 1971 as the Central Policy Review Staff (CPRS) coincided with the UK's membership of the EU. The CPRS was seen as a 'think tank' inside government. Its foundation arose from Heath's paper on changes in the *Reorganisation of central government* (HMSO, 1970). This set up a government departmental structure that was seen to be more efficient and a central unit to consider strategy to support the Prime Minister in ways similar to those available to ministers within their own departments (Blackstone and Plowden, 1990).

In comparison with other states in the EU, some countries such as Finland have responded by considering their approaches to both domestic and EU-focused policy development and delivery by cutting across existing ministerial silos and being policy- or issue-focused (Bouckaert et al, 2000; Peters, 2004; Page and Jenkins, 2005). In the UK, civil servants are generalists, compared with lawyers in France. In the Nordic system, ministries are small and most delivery is through agencies and their links to municipalities (Pollitt and Bouckaert, 2000). In France and Germany, the approach of the civil service is more rule-based and, as a result, has been seen to be more difficult to reform (Knill, 1999; Cole and Jones, 2005; Hood and Lodge, 2005).

Strategic planning is not an acknowledged role in current UK domestic government (Hay and Richards, 2000; Mulgan, 2009) and it is an issue that is being investigated by a Parliamentary select committee (PASC, 2012; Letwin, 2012a). Strategy for defence and foreign policy is acceptable, not least because the external world understands longer-term positions and can respond should sudden changes be made. Even here, there are current concerns in the UK about who is responsible for this external strategy (Jenkin, 2012).

Before the general election in 1997, constitutional reforms were referred to as a programme by the Labour Party. However, after the election, they were neither presented as a single policy package nor an overarching narrative (Radaelli, 1998; Jones and McBeth, 2010; Shanahan et al, 2011). This may be to invoke a narrative arc suggests some conclusion and either this has not yet been considered or, more likely, it is seen to be too difficult to reveal to the public media or, indeed, mainstream politicians. Change is effected without public engagement and diversions are frequently used to draw attention away from key changes, such as through the passage of Parliamentary Bills. In effect (and discussed later), these reforms are more likely to be a policy response to the application of the principle of subsidiarity adopted in the Treaty on the European Union (TEU) in 1992, but each element of this reform programme has been dealt with individually to reduce the negative impacts of any wider strategic reveal.

The contemporary reasons offered for these changes are based on Whitehall's alleged weaknesses in strategic planning. In the early 1970s, the civil service was criticised for its homogeneity, silo allegiance to single departments and hierarchical culture (Fulton, 1968; Kellner and Crowther-Hunt, 1980).

Civil servants are recruited from a variety of backgrounds as generalists. Their expertise is in how Whitehall and Westminster work, rather than in any specific policy area. This differs from practice in other European states, where civil servants tend to be lawyers or economists (Page, 2010). Ministers have increasingly introduced special advisers to support them, although there has always been an ambivalent attitude towards them by politicians and civil servants. The CPRS was an internal approach to providing policy advice. The popular naming of the CPRS as the 'think tank' suggests a role that is external and not directly involved in decision-making. Despite its intention to be politically neutral, it was this lack of political engagement that reduced the interest of ministers while it had a better relationship with the rest of the civil service (James, 1988).

The CPRS could provide a mechanism for promoting policy issues that did not have an existing life within political or civil service priorities. In particular, it took client-based approaches to social policy from McKinseys and the Lincoln Institute in the US (Lewis, 2011). This was a means to ensure that external issues were introduced into cabinet consideration in a seemingly unforced way. It was also an opportunity to develop a 'flow' approach to changes in government policy rather than be dependent on using other episodic techniques of agenda change. Blackstone and Plowden (1990) point out that most of the CPRS were civil servants at the beginning of their careers, but who ended up as Cabinet Secretaries (eg Robin Butler), or political researchers, who ended their careers as government ministers (eg William Waldegrave).

The CPRS also had to work with the Prime Minister's Policy Unit, set up when Wilson became Prime Minister in 1974. The role of providing policy advice to the Prime Minister was already an overlapping, interlocking and contested process. Opposing internal policy advice units could operate in a 'wild west' style of policymaking – who could shoot first to be the last (policy) man standing. Establishing a collective mechanism to provide all ministers with advice would support the CPRS's coordination role, but the essence of success was seen to be influencing modes of behaviour in secrecy and avoiding being sucked into the Whitehall 'consensus' (Blackstone and Plowden, 1990).

The establishment of the CPRS also coincided with Britain's entry to the EU. It assumed that part of its role would be to support ministers who had to spend a lot of time at the EU meetings, although this was only seen as extending to agriculture. It was also used to develop the coordination of European policy for the Cabinet Office (James, 1988). The CPRS also considered issues that were emerging on the EU agenda, including the management of nationalised industries (Blackstone and Plowden, 1990). As the role of the CPRS was to help ministers anticipate future issues, it was a useful device that could allow the insertion of EU policy issues into debates without any real questioning of their provenance – they could always be ascribed to someone in the think tank. The *Reorganisation of central government* White Paper (HMG, 1970) also allowed for a realignment of departments to EU portfolios, such as the establishment of the Department of the Environment (Haigh, 1987; O'Riordan and Rowbotham, 1996). The wider implications of joining the EU were understood but not visible. A change from a system where individual ministers and their departments developed policies to one where this responsibility was pooled with the EU had to be considered within a different framework. Further, adoption of EU legislation and its implementation would need a central steer to ensure compliance.

Following the CPRS, other central policy units began to emerge, such as the Efficiency Unit in 1987. Like the CPRS, this became a way to introduce externalised change, including competition into public services (Rhodes, 1994; Stewart and Walsh, 1992), once it was clear that this would be agreed as part of the General Agreement on Tariffs and Trade/World Trade Organization (GATT/WTO) round that commenced in 1986 (see Chapter Six). The role of potential privatisation was contentious (Jenkins and Gold, 2011), with the first executive agencies being established in 1988, although the creation of new agencies may have been an attempt to reform the civil service in the face of a potential attack on its role, size and competence (Chapman and O'Toole, 2010).

In addition to fulfilling the need for potential exposure to competition, the establishment of executive agencies also widened the gap between policy and delivery, leaving the potential for operational management in the hands of those with experience whilst senior civil servants remained as policy advisers to ministers (Talbot, 2004a, 2004b; Pollitt, 2006). This separation of policy from delivery also protected civil servants from the potential of being exposed to competiton from the private sector. However, it is also clear that, then and subsequently, the management of executive agencies has largely been in the hands of those who have had senior experience in the civil service, thereby creating management by extension rather than an arm's length model (Mabey and Skinner, 1998; Smith, 2006). It was also a mechanism for improving the status of any government department which increases as contacts with the public decrease.

Executive agencies were expected to concentrate on the 'how', leaving the 'what' to ministers and civil servants. This approach to policy delivery had advantages for ministers and civil servants, who could distance themselves from failure, although it also meant that when the levers were pulled from the centre, little could be achieved (Blair, 2010). There were other disadvantages in agencification. It is difficult for any operational organisation not to build up its own experience about priorities and the 'what' agenda, not least as it is receiving feedback from its stakeholders and users. Agencies also became useful means for the UK to engage with the delivery of EU policy, such as in the environment (Fairbrass and Jordan, 2001). This meant that EU-agreed policy could also pass directly from discussion, to agreement and then to implementation without touching the sides of departmental policymaking approaches.

3. External influences: events and organisations

Policy influences will also be external. There are a number of ways in which Britain's membership and relationship with international organisations influences government objectives and subsequent policymaking (Pollitt, 2004). The role of and influence on domestic policymaking is primarily focused on the larger outcomes of a globalised approach, whether this is marketisation (Shaw et al, 1995), McDonaldisation (Parker and Jary, 1995; Mahony et al, 2002) or contractualisation (Pollitt, 2004). Globalisation of government agendas and discussions has been influential in setting priorities and then translating into specific policy actions. Governments also have to respond to external events, such as the 2008 financial crisis and energy shortages.

The main concern of governments is to attempt to claim the credit for those successful aspects of policy that they implement, regardless of provenance, and demonstrate their domestic 'fit' into a broader agenda. Not all government business neatly fits into Parliamentary terms or cycles. Where Britain is a member of international organisations, such as the WTO or EU, different time frames and programmes will cut across UK electoral cycles. Yet, these external agreements include commitments that have policy and delivery consequences. Even where the UK belongs to organisations as a voluntary member, such as the OECD, opinions and advice have considerable influence on domestic economic and social policy. Recent examples where this has occurred include the Localism Act 2011 and policies such as that for housing (Andre, 2011; OECD, 2011a) and education (Martens, 2007; Ozga and Lingard, 2007; Braconier, 2012).

The level and type of influence on policy exercised by external organisations will depend on the structure of their institutions and the UK's relationship with them. These are linked together through a lattice of policy networks and communities. The first to consider is the *quasi-informal* and these include the major economic groupings such as the G8 and G20, where the UK comes together with other countries to consider the state of the world economy. There is an overlapping membership between the G8 and members of the UN Security Council, which has led to development aid policy being a focal point. The President of the European Commission has attended all G8 meetings since first invited by the UK in 1977, and in 1997, it was widened to include other international organisations, such as the OECD. The regular summit meetings discuss key economic themes, such as energy, which are translated into policy and legislation through other bodies that are formally constituted, such as the EU or NAFTA.

The second type of international grouping that has influence on UK policy agendas is that derived from membership of *opaque informal* organisations. These operate in key areas, such as the World Economic Forum (WEF) held annually in Davos and now with other meetings held throughout the year. These meetings are mechanisms for an interchange between business, governments and international institutions and are constituted through a range of formal sessions and fringe and informal meetings on the margin (Graz, 2003). Although the agenda and programme are transparent, being available through a variety of media, their role in shaping wider economic and public policy is less understood. The WEF can set agendas for action through the promulgation of ideas, informal discussion and private one-to-one meetings. It is in these fora that the agendas for international institutions and governments can be set through informal agreements (Hay and Rosamund, 2002). They can also create a 'fashion' for governmental priorities. These are high-level policy communities that are penetrated and influenced by multiple sectors, and captured in an annual lobbying event to which physical and social access is restricted.

The third organisational type that exercises influence on UK policy are those that are *formal*, that is, where the UK has either entered into treaties on membership (eg the EU) or has agreed that the decisions made by these organisations are binding, such as the WTO. In these cases, once joined, the UK has agreed to pool some of its powers and agreed to implement the decisions made by the organisations as a result of the initial and/or subsequent binding treaties. These policies and legislation are developed and implemented through the methods of policy transfer between nations and directly apply in ways that reflect the power relationships between the parties engaged in the transfer process.

The fourth type of relationship is *quasi-voluntaristic* and includes organisations such as the UN and the OECD. The UK's membership is formal, but any actions are taken on a case-by-case basis. As far as the UN is concerned, engagement in any military action is voluntary, but has to be sanctioned through formal agreements. The UK also belongs to other UN bodies that have binding commitments, such as the World Maritime Organisation. The UN has also led on other treaties that commit action on the part of its members, such as the Kyoto climate change protocol. The OECD has a different role. Here, the UK submits its economic and social policies for examination and comparison. As a result, the UK economy is reviewed regularly in detail, with special reports on areas of concern, such as inequality, regulation and green growth (OECD, 2011c, 2012a, 2012b). The OECD also provides advice on best practices across a range of issues, such as transport, energy, agriculture, IT and effective governmental practices. It is a soft power mechanism and uses policy mobilities to promote case studies and practices. It can set informal expectations but then judge their application (OECD, 1996; Helgason, 1997; OECD, 2011a).

In less formal ways, other organisations seek to influence government agendas, such as quasi-independent bodies including Chatham House for Foreign Policy, the Kennedy School of Government and international consultancies (Saint-Martin, 1998; Riddell and Haddon, 2009). All operate by influencing individuals through events and short-term appointments so that, as institutions, they are able to have a global web of intelligence and influence. Other key influences on public policy are external organisations, lobbyists and civil society. The growth of lobbyists in and around government has been an issue of concern (Jordan, G., 1998). The Coalition government's programme (HMG, 2010) included action on lobbyists, including registration. Despite the legislate role of keeping government and civil servants advised about current developments in policy and sector interests, there have also been concerns that this is a development in Machiavellian marketing (Harris and Lock, 1996).

Role of the civil service in policymaking

The role of the civil service is to support the government through advice and deliver its agenda through legislation and policymaking (Smith, 1999; Burnham and Pyper, 2008). Civil service roles are governed by the Civil Service Code and the Constitutional Reform and Governance Act 2010. Through these, civil servants are expected to behave with integrity, honesty, objectivity and political impartiality (O'Donnell, 2011a). Political advice is provided by special advisers, who are temporary civil servants.

According to Page (2010, p 407), the civil service has four main features: 'political neutrality, generalism, life-long career paths and a strong policy advisory role'. In agreeing to political neutrality, civil servants give up their politics for neutrality as part of a public service bargain (PSB) and that shapes the relationship between civil servants and politicians (Hood, 2000, 2002; Salomonsen and Knudsen, 2011). In some countries, leading bureaucrats have to be members of the ruling party, for example, in Germany and the US (Hood, 2002). Despite not having a political tie between civil servants and elected politicians, there may be an alignment of purpose. Retired senior civil servants describe their periods at work as "when I was in government" (former senior civil servant, December 2011); in the UK system, civil servants are never 'in government'.

The ownership of policy advice by the civil service in Britain has been a central feature of policymaking, although this has now been challenged through the potential introduction of contestability (Heywood and Kerslake, 2012; Maude, 2012). Incoming ministers have made attempts to establish clear leadership on policy agendas through the appointment of their own advisers, but they are frequently counterbalanced by think tanks, which are populated by former civil servants and advisers. Attention has been paid to policy development and its link with delivery by Prime Ministers, including Thatcher (1995) and Blair (2010), who both saw the connection in practice. However, the periods in office of both of these Prime Ministers has been followed by counterbalancing periods of more passive, low-energy, 'management by events' approaches.

In the consideration of the relationship between civil servants and politicians, there is always an issue about how far administrative roles are politicised (Pollitt and Bouckaert, 2000; Pierre, 1995). The British civil service is seen to be independent. However, where senior political and civil service careers are intertwined, there may be greater unanimity of purpose, not least where politicians and civil servants have known each other from school and university (Kellner and Crowther-Hunt, 1980). Alienation between civil servants and politicians may come further down the organisation, where these links are not so close. Lowe (2005) argues that the role of political special advisors (SPADs) has served to maintain neutrality in the civil service. Although increasing the role of SPADs was initially resisted, they are now regarded not as 'grit in the oyster but sand in the machine' (Blick, 2004, p xvii), who are taken on board as irritants but gradually absorbed into the system. As a result, some of the civil servants' policy advisory role may have declined. Their role of policy implementation (Page and Jenkins, 2005; Page, 2010) has also come under challenge, as Permanent Secretary and Chief Operating Officer posts at the head of government departments have been filled by former local authority chief executives (eg Departments of Transport, Education, Justice, Communities and Local Government, Her Majesty's Revenue and Customs, Department of Environment, Food and Rural Affairs, Home Office).

Civil servants and ministers do not always agree. When Labour came to power in 1997, there was a major fear that the civil service would continue to follow the priorities of the previous government, either intentionally or on autopilot. What the incoming government found, however, was that there were separate agendas. The Labour government then spent over 10 years attempting to influence, manage and ultimately control the civil service through performance measures, described as thermostatic controls by Hood (2002), and by appointing external managers. Hood (2010) argues that this kind of close management of civil servants by politicians can partly be ascribed to politicians wanting to pass the blame to civil servants. On the other hand, ministers are expected to resign if their civil servants do not perform or deliver (Rutter et al, 2012b). This position is reversed in local government, where politicians rarely resign but officers do, and this practice is now more frequently the case when central government agencies fail to perform. In this latter case, ministerial distance provides some protection and is seen as a benefit of agencification (Talbot, 2004b).

The civil service has been pressurised to change by successive governments. The Conservatives (1979–97) wanted to inject efficiency into the civil service. As part of an earlier plan to evade change and downsizing at the centre while responding to competition, the civil service had developed the Next Steps agencies in 1998 (Jenkins, 2008; Jenkins and Gold, 2011; Gains, 2004b), which reduced the headcount of civil servants in direct roles, and although many civil servants were transferred into other organisations, they maintained their culture and ethos, as well as their employment conditions. The application of the agency principle has also been a key element in managing distance and, beyond this, 'blame' (Hood, 2011).

More recently, there has been a focus on the role of strategy and delivery to ensure that politicians are not diverted from their main policy priorities. In addressing the issue of strategy in England, Mulgan (2009), a former adviser to Blair when he was Prime Minister, suggests that linking a political position to delivery in a linear model is no longer appropriate. Instead, he argues that governments need to be clear about what they want to achieve and where they intend to engage their attention to do this but are more fluid in their methods. They also need to be able to set a direction, focus actions and learn from what they are doing (Mulgan, 2011). They will also need to use resources and to manage the rest of the political agenda, including the appearance of 'unknown unknowns', if they are to deliver their agenda. The development of strategy is also associated with leadership and together these are said to provide the foundation of economic success (Nizzo, 2001; Charbit, 2011).

However, as Bevir and Rhodes (2003) point out, the Labour Party came late to considering the civil service's role in policymaking and was already two years into their agenda before proposing changes in the *Modernising government* White Paper, (Cabinet Office, 1999). Blair's concern was to keep the civil service 'on side' and although expecting obstruction, he found 'inertia' (Blair, 2010, p 19). The main concerns of the Labour government were those of coordination and the costs unintended consequences of the silo-based approach to government (6 et al, 2002) and a lack of focus on outcomes. Policy was seen to be an input-driven process without any consideration or monitoring of policy success. The frequent revolve of civil servants also meant a lack of learning – policies were not never seen through to delivery and, as a result, accountability for policymaking was poor (Bevir and Rhodes, 2003; PASC, 2011a). The culture also did not support institutional memory so that previous experience could not be used to improve policy development and delivery (Pollitt, 2000). This was in contrast with other parts of the state, for example, local government, where delivery was paramount (Lyons, 2007; Morphet, 2008). Where ministers responded by opening up the civil service to those with more delivery experience, including former local authority staff, these 'outsiders' were supported by long-serving civil servants who maintained the existing culture by managing agendas around them.

During the period of the New Labour government (1997–2010), and particularly during the Blair period to 2007, a change was made in the PSB. This switched ministers into more managerialist roles and made civil servants responsible for delivery. This approach was based on the local government model, where politicians in the Blair government had considerable experience. Although the Labour government initially viewed local government as its Achilles heel when it came to power in 1997, the government's expectations of delivery were based on local government practice (Morphet, 2008). The government pressurised the civil service to have a more interventionist approach, but Hood (2000) called this process one of 'half hearted managerialism'. This was a difficult role change for the civil service, as it perceived this responsibility as a reduction in status, and has been one that has been rejected subsequently (Rutter et al, 2011).

The focus on public management reform in the civil service in the UK and Europe is also culturally bound. France and Germany are not supporters of New Public Management, with its focus on efficiency and its imitation of the private sector. Page et al (2005) found that New Public Management was seen as a 'passing fad' in other countries, despite the insertion of performance management into OMC processes (Radaelli, 2003). Further, they found that it has made no difference to the core requirements for recruitment of civil servants in either the UK or Germany. Rather, the civil service has 'gone through the motions' of competency-based change (Radaelli, 2003, p 859). Since the UK general election in 2010, there have been attempts to reverse this position, where civil servants are to be responsible for advice at the input stage and not responsible for determining the outcomes (Hallsworth, 2011; Rutter et al, 2011; Letwin, 2012b). UK civil servants have reverted to a view that their role is in providing policy advice to ministers rather than its delivery. Hallsworth and Rutter (2011, p 101) argue that civil servants should accept that policymaking is 'messy' and 'ad hoc', but, at the same time, they should develop an approach that is more resilient to pressures from ministers on civil servants.

Over time, the civil service has enhanced and protected its position through adherence to this policy advice role and by gradually divesting itself of responsibilities for delivery through the establishment of agencies, devolution and localism. If there is operational failure, there is some distance between the minister and the organisation delivering on the front line. Civil service responsibility for policy options and advice may always be in the 'here and now', having short-term horizons for the future, while the corporate memory of government may be about recycling policy manoeuvres rather than learning from experience of the ways in which policy failures can be averted. Further, the institutional memory of the civil service is of its own culture and mores rather than that of the departments and policy areas that they support. Progress and promotion rests on the future agenda rather than delivering successfully in the past.

Policymaking is the main function for civil servants. Any influence or policy derived from other bodies can lead to strategies of denial, incorporation or contempt. Assessing the quality of outcomes is a contested process, so focusing on the policy *process*, that is, the inputs rather than the outputs or outcomes, can be safer (Rutter et al, 2011). This might be a response to the New Labour focus on outcomes and a return to more comfortable approaches (Burch and Bulmer, 2009; Jenkins, 2011), but also indicates a preferred style of operation, which is less accountable.

The UK civil service remains more concerned with its methods of policy control and fears that the reality of delivery will subvert policies in practice. Hallsworth (2011) sets out an internalised approach that rejects attempts to professionalise and rationalise a policymaking process. It indicates a danger of politically led policies that are not generated through the civil service process and sees outside influences as being single responses to particular headlines. Hallsworth promotes the notion of civil servants 'as a counter balance to ministers' (Hallsworth, 2011, p

9) and that opening up policymaking to the outside world can reduce options: the solution is a 'discerning openness' (Hallsworth, 2011, p 9). This is seen as best achieved through a 'combination of the political mobilising of support, presenting a vision, setting strategic objectives and the technocratic (evidence of what works, robust policy design, realistic implementation plans). The two poles are largely represented by Ministers and civil servants' (Hallsworth, 2011, p 12) and any problems with this are seen as primarily internal and resolved by righting this balance and constructing an 'effective relationship' between ministers and civil servants. However, Letwin (2012b) has argued that delivering ministerial decisions cannot be defined as politicisation, but is rather the administrative role of the civil service.

Much of this civil service concern is about how to maintain control at a time when political policy is to reduce centralised control through initiatives associated with the application of subsidiarity principles. Maintaining policy leadership is now expressed as managing through 'system stewardship' (Hallsworth, 2011), which provides a sense of containment and control, albeit at a higher level, while others are responsible for delivery. The system described takes little account of external influences, such as the private and voluntary sectors, the EU, or wider global interests. This suggests an inward-looking approach. There is also no overarching strategy (Jenkins, 2012).

However, there is also another set of literature that sees the civil service as potentially in decline or facing upheaval and challenge. Foster and Plowden (1996) described these challenges or 'hollowing out' as coming from external changes, including devolution and areas covered by EU treaties, although Pyper and Burnham (2011, p 195) argue that these areas of policy are at least 'shared' and do not represent an underlying change of role.

Devolution: the changing context of policymaking

Since 1999, devolution has been a major factor in policy delivery and is now changing into policy leadership. Although at the time of devolution, the civil service considered that there would be problems, the political alignment between England, Scotland and Wales enabled political and official channels to deal with any issues that had not been considered. Parry (2008) argues that the relationship between the centre and the nations, or 'devolved administrations' as they are known in Whitehall, is to view them as departments of state rather than having any independent role (Page, 2010; McQuaid, 2011).

The government, structure and institutions of the UK have changed since the introduction of devolution in 1999. The governments of Scotland, Wales and Northern Ireland have developed separate policy and delivery agendas, although, over the period, they are beginning to show some similarity in effect, if not in name or timing (Cairney, 2011; Morphet, 2011). The proposal to hold a referendum on Scottish independence in 2014 has promoted consideration of the role of England and that of the union, including the external role it might play (Jenkins, 2011). Suggestions for a more overtly federal structure in the UK are emerging. The outgoing head of the home civil service has stated that the application of the subsidiarity principle in the UK is an issue that has not been given enough attention and would cause difficulties in the future (O'Donnell, 2009, 2012b).

The failure at the centre of the civil service and government to recognise the changing nature of the UK is a continuing tension. Since devolution, there is an increasing need to consider policymaking in this context, particularly when the domestic policy agenda is no longer set out and delivered as a common approach across the UK. Policymaking in the UK is now devolved, apart from some specific reserved matters such as defence and taxation. In each of the four nations, policymaking is led by ministers and supported by civil servants. Hallsworth et al (2011, p 4) argue that the 'strength of policy making is integral to the strength of government as a whole and that of the country at large. When policies fail, the costs (whether monetary or otherwise) can be significant'.

Much of the policymaking and implementation of EU legislation is now undertaken in Scotland, Wales and Northern Ireland. In 2014, the UK will also have a single funding programme that will be devolved to the nations and sub-national groupings of local authorities (BIS, 2012), including in England. This represents a major shift away from overt centralised policymaking. Coordination between the four nations of the UK is undertaken through meetings between ministers and separate meetings between civil servants (Poirier, 2001; Trench, 2001a; Carter, 2002; Scott, 2001). In 1999, as devolution was implemented, the Labour Party was in the majority in the UK government, most local authorities in England, Scotland and Wales, as well as the new devolved governments. In this period, much of the policymaking could be achieved through political coordination and direction. By 2012, however, each nation had a different political party or parties in power and the level of coordination is dependent on more formal channels of inter-ministerial meetings organised by the Cabinet Office and more informal discussions and arrangements between civil servants, ministers and other key actors in each of the four governments.

Although there is much debate about the role of the central state and the potential problems of fragmentation after devolution in Britain (Allmendinger, 2003; Keating et al, 2009), there has been far less discussion about policymaking in the UK for those issues that have been devolved. Further, there is little discussion on shared policymaking with and within the EU as part of the internal politics (Wall, 2008) and mechanics of the process (Bulmer and Burch, 2009).

The introduction of devolution has developed the existing role of territorial policy communities within Scotland and Wales. Although Keating et al (2009) suggest that these may have emerged post-devolution, Loughlin (no date) argues that devolution was path-dependent on policy communities within Wales. These policy communities have a role in developing coherence within the state that can withstand pressure for convergence outside it, although there is evidence that policy communities also incorporate policy practices and initiatives from elsewhere (Morphet, 2010a). These policy communities may have been developing since the failed devolution referendum in Scotland in 1979 and have been a mechanism for building the capacity of separate institutions that would be both in favour of devolution and confident in practice.

Although Scotland always retained a separate legal system and has acted independently in policymaking, the transition at devolution confirmed that, in addition to separate legal practices, there would be a transfer of responsibility for the interpretation and application of EU policy and legislation (MacCormick, 1999). This also extended to Wales in the devolved policy areas. While the separation of public policy approaches between Scotland and the UK before devolution was high, there was also an opportunity to blame 'down South', particularly during the Thatcher period, when there were no Conservative MPs in Scotland (Bradbury, 2002). Up to this point, the main European policy focus in Scotland and Wales had been on structural funds, which supported projects. Although arranged through programmes, the delivery was episodic and mainly localised. The transposition of EU legislation into policy practice is more procedural and requires governance arrangements to be in place and potentially greater coordination in delivery than had been the case hitherto.

In Wales, Loughlin (no date) argues that there were significant changes in policymaking. Although sectoral groups for business and the voluntary sector were close, the introduction of the Welsh Assembly policymaking process meant that those who sought to influence it had to shift their frames of reference. The Government of Wales Act 2006 extended the devolved responsibility for implementing EU policies in the same way as in Scotland. EU matters have also been devolved in Northern Ireland since 2007. The UK has responsibility for negotiation, coordination, delivery and compliance. In England, the same ministers undertake these two tasks almost indivisibly, as they hold both offices. The UK approach to EU policy delivery is coordinated through the post-devolution inter-ministerial processes set up through the Cabinet Office. However, like the outcome of agencification, the distance between negotiation and delivery has been extended and thus the ability to influence delivery experience and outcomes into these negotiating positions is reduced. The governments of Wales, Scotland and Northern Ireland have become three more government 'departments' to add into the negotiation process, rather than reflecting any other position (Bulmer and Burch, 2009; Page, 2010). Devolution has devolved implementation to its nations but not a role in EU policymaking within the UK.

This leaves an interesting issue for policymaking at the centre in England. Ministers who have responsibilities for the UK also have responsibilities for England and there is no separation. This mixture of responsibilities is reflected in the uncertainty of language between the UK and English position when issues are discussed by ministers and civil servants. The devolution of law-making powers to Wales in 2014 intensifies this position. Loughlin and Sykes (no date) also point out that there could be a perceived coalition of interest between those on the 'Celtic fringe', who have had common cause in the past and may now have shared interests in developing acceptable and parallel processes as devolution matures. It could be argued by the devolved nations that England receives some priority consideration in any EU negotiations. This may be because the English position is not identified and is seen to be synonymous with the UK's. In contrast, Wales, Scotland and Northern Ireland all have clear national and political strategies for their future, which each have a leading role for the EU within them. In the years before devolution, the EU was seen as an important ally to the nations of the UK and as many member states are equal or smaller in size with the devolved nations, they became submerged comparators.

As yet, there has been little research on the changing role of English policymaking post-devolution and, as Hazell (2006) indicates, that may be problematic. The development of policies focused on England may be seen to be a downward step in status for the civil service. Since 2011, civil servants in some departments have been seconded to local authorities or city regions and this transfer of power and responsibilities, which has commenced through sub-regional and localism subsidiarity policies, seems likely to continue. At the same time, the role of the British Irish Council (BIC) has become more explicit. Founded as part of the Belfast Agreement in 1998, the BIC comprises the four nations of the UK, the Republic of Ireland and the states of Jersey, Guernsey and the Isle of Man. In 2011, it established a permanent headquarters and staff in Edinburgh. Modelled on the Baltic Sea Council, it may become a new European Grouping of Territorial Cohesion (EGTC) in due course (Layard and Holder, 2010; Holder and Layard, 2011) (see Chapter Eight).

The outcomes of devolution on shaping British policymaking are as yet unclear, but the development, delivery and responsibility for policy since devolution has changed. This is a continuing process with the offer to directly elected city region leaders and mayors in England of forming a national cabinet (Cameron, 2012). Page (2010) argues that devolution has brought fewer changes than expected and this may be a view from the centre (Rutter and Hallsworth, 2011). As Peters (2004) indicates, governing in a decentred state is not a new issue and is something that federal states have to accommodate. However, if policymaking remains in the hands of the centre on both reserved and EU matters, then is the UK a decentred state? Second, if central government policymaking has to be informed by delivery (Mulgan, 2009; Letwin, 2012b) where does this interaction occur in the British state?

Conclusions

Policymaking in the UK is split between the four nations and the UK as a whole. Those policies that have been devolved are those that are also pooled between the UK and the rest of the EU. This aporia at the heart of government may suggest the *real politik* of policies that are not owned and delivered by the civil service. The civil service maintains its role at the centre of the UK following devolution. Civil servants are rejecting processes of policymaking that are programmatic because they do not reflect political reality. This may be too simplistic a view of policy development and needs. Maintaining that policy is more responsive to events may suggest short-termism and a desire to retain control.

The need for the UK to be active in European policymaking processes is a view expressed by those outside the UK who take an integrated view in assessing its response to policymaking within this wider setting. Working within the EU, taking multiple negotiating points over a range of policies each set within different programmes requires different skills from those exercised in domestic policymaking (Peters, 2004). It also needs an approach that can demonstrate some domestic or national interest while engaging in a pooled approach (Kassim et al, 2000).

CHAPTER FOUR

Shaping policy in the EU

Introduction

Policymaking in the EU is concerned with the development and implementation of treaties and other intergovernmental agreements. Like other member states, the UK is part of this strategic decision-making and policy agenda-setting process. The final decisions on treaties are made by member states in the European Council of Ministers, which has a rotating chair, or through co-decision between the Council of Ministers and the European Parliament. The areas of co-decision have increased in each treaty. Practical policymaking within the EU is led by the European Commission where it has the power of initiative, following which it is considered over a long gestation period by member states, the European Parliament, the Committee of the Regions, European Economic and Social Committee and trade and sector bodies.

This chapter will consider the provenance and impulses that shape policymaking in the EU, including the formal and informal influences on the process. It will consider the cultures of policymaking, which encompass both integration and intergovernmentalism. The chapter goes on to consider Europeanisation and institutionalism as both intended and unintended responses to these policy initiatives. Much of the discussion about European policymaking is about its provenance and impulse through debates about agenda-setting (Pollack, 1997; Kingdon, 2003). It is assumed that agendas within the EU are made from 'above' by the Council of Ministers or 'below' by working groups of experts, and in both instances, the Commission has some advantage in the framing of the issues (Princen and Rhinard, 2006). There are also wider externalised influences on the EU agenda, such as formal agreements by the World Trade Organization (WTO) or informal pressure through Organisation for Economic Co-operation and Development (OECD) country reports (Ozga and Lingard, 2007; Mahon and McBride, 2009). In addition to the Commission's internal influence through its power of initiation, it is argued that it has a leading role in framing these external agendas, and together they enable the Commission to shape the EU agenda (Rhinard, 2010).

The EU derives many of its competencies from its role in negotiating trade agreements on behalf of EU member states in the WTO and its predecessor the General Agreement on Tariffs and Trade (GATT) (Woolcock, 2010; Dur and Elsig, 2011). This agenda is allied to that of the internal single market. As with any policymaking process, it is not seen to be neutral or free from political interest (Hill, 2006; Cairney, 2012). As this chapter considers, EU policy is primarily viewed as a force for further EU integration or as a mechanism to achieve greater influence through intergovernmentalism. Whichever side is taken, it is assumed that all the processes of the Commission and other EU institutions such as the European Parliament and European Court of Justice are in favour of greater integration, as set out in the Treaty of Rome 1957 (Brack and Costa, 2012). As intergovernmentalism and integration are seen to be on a common spectrum, discussion of the way these concepts are used in an analysis of EU policy shaping is from one end or the other (Moravcsik and Schimmelfennig, 2009). This frequently places the intergovernmentalist position as the critic of integration (Rosamund, 2000).

This integration objective that was set out in the Treaty of Rome is ignored or denied by UK politicians and the UK has primarily been intergovernmentalist and fears the integrationist approach (see Chapter One). In both cases, there are debates about the role of supranationalism, the superstate or a new political construct created by the EU and how it can function (MacCormick, 1999). This has been tested through the eurozone crisis (2010–12). These issues are discussed in this chapter as they create a key context within which to examine the way in which Europe influences and shapes British public policy.

Treaties are developed into programmes of legislation and initiatives. These may result in Europeanisation, where there is a similarity in legislation, institutions, initiatives and political cultures in all member states. The literature on each of these issues – integration, intergovernmentalism and Europeanisation – tends to be separate and siloed, which reduces the ability to consider these three issues in a more discursive way. A key consideration in this chapter is how far the development and character of EU policy and its narratives has had an influence on the policy and institutions of its members, including the UK. The exponents of Europeanisation and integration theories frequently suggest that there is a convergent pattern, so that all EU member states will eventually become more similar in their institutional and legal structures (Cowles and Risse, 2001; Kassim, 2005). On the other hand, Bulmer and Burch (2005) and Risse et al (2001) have found that although there is evidence of the influence of EU membership through the adaptation of governance, institutions and policymaking methods, these adaptations are mediated by the form of each member state rather than converging into a single approach.

Policymaking in the EU differs from that in the UK in several ways. In Chapter Three, UK policymaking is characterised as being responsive, flexible, short-term and episodic, and not strategic in its nature. In the UK, policy advice is provided by generalist civil servants who are primarily short-term and internal in their focus (Page, 2010). In contrast, the EU's long-term objectives are set through the treaties agreed by member states and all its legislative and policy activities are focused on achieving these ends, primarily through specific, fixed-term programmes. EU policy implementation is indirect as it relies on interpretation and delivery by member states. Each state has a different starting point and culture, so the routes to common ends will vary. The EU policymaking approach can be seen as episodic in that it works through key events such as Inter Governmental Conferences (IGCs) and treaties, but because it has an overarching objective, as set out in the Treaty of Rome, it incorporates these events into its policy flow.

EU policymaking is planned and programmatic in its character (Simmons et al, 1974; Rotmans et al, 2001). It moves towards the achievement of agreed objectives through fixed-term programmes to achieve longer-term goals. This approach may be due to the scale and complexity of achieving common policies and outcomes across 27 member states within a common time frame. The European Parliament is subject to direct elections and although this is not the case for the European Commission, its Commissioners are appointed for fixed terms (Tallberg, 2003). In member states, there are pressures on the political leaders that are approaching national elections, which are on fixed terms in most member states and therefore predictable. This can have an important influence on agreements, public stances and the ideology of those elected to represent their countries. The use of five- or seven-year EU policy programmes that transcend these electoral cycles creates a programmatic predictability within which politicians in member states can operate.

Between the member states' civil services and the Commission, a European Administrative Space (EAS) has been developed. It is based on the application of the principles of the European Court of Justice (ECJ) as a common set of standards of administrative law (Shapiro, 2004; Heidbreider, 2009). The EAS is made up of *acquis communataire* but the operational rules have been codified to ensure compliance in candidate member states, and they have been adopted by all member states (Cardona, 1999; Nizzo, 2001). The term 'EAS' was invented as a metaphor for a 'non-existent model and collective term' (Meyer-Sahling, 2009, p 10). Heidbreider (2009, p 16) argues that it is the 'non-binding quality of un-coordinated voluntary standardization' that makes this approach attractive to member states because it creates venues for cooperation without a formal transfer of competencies.

Theories, claims and wider explanations of policy development within the EU

The role of the EU in developing policy is based on its legal competencies derived from the *acquis communataire* – a cumulative set of legal powers that each member state has to adopt and accept in full at their point of entry. These powers are developed through treaties and then translated into action programmes, which comprise legislation and other initiatives. In some cases, the EU is responsible for negotiating international agreements, such as those made by the WTO and United Nations (UN), and is then required to deliver compliance with these agreements (see Chapters Six and Seven). Other legislative programmes are developed to promote internal objectives (see Chapters Eight and Nine).

At its heart, as expressed in the Treaty of Rome, the EU has always had the objective to develop political and economic union. The EU has been working to progress this through deepening integration between member states and widening the range of sectors within which pooled decision-making is made at pan-European level. The initial reasons for greater integration in Europe remain political stability and economic growth. Dinan (2010) argues that these have both served Europe well and continue to be important. This process is gradual but consistent. This role has been reinforced by the citation for the award of the Nobel peace prize to the EU in 2012.

Before a treaty is agreed, much of the content has already been developed through IGCs, such as that of Nice 2001, where fundamental changes to the founding treaties are considered. Another method of developing policy is through the use of extended bilateral arrangements, where two or more countries agree to progress joint action or policy pooling on new areas currently outside EU competence. This may be on defence through the establishment of joint army commands (eg between the UK and France), through joining financial policymaking (eg between France and Germany) cooperation on criminal matters (thr Prium Convention).

The *EU governance* White Paper (CEC, 2001) introduced softer methods of working. These included pilot actions and less formal agreements. A third key way of developing joint approaches included in this White Paper is through the Open Method of Coordination (OMC) (Heritier, 2001a; Radaelli, 2003; Haahr, 2004), where issues not part of the EU's competence are nevertheless discussed and decisions are taken about common action in a voluntaristic rather than legal context. Topics in this category of action, which can lead to EU competencies, include social and youth policies. There may also be agreements between states without any of these formal devices through inter-ministerial agreements, such as those for planning (Duhr et al, 2010). These new softer approaches have been applied in the context of the Sixth Environmental Action Programme (EAP), but, as noted in Chapter Six, these have been evaluated as not being effective and the seventh EAP will return to more traditional legislative methods.

Policy provenance and impulses in the EU

As in any political machinery, policies represent what those in power wish to achieve. This will influence legislative time and priority (Goetz and Mayer-Sahling, 2009), funding decisions, and the outcome of future elections. However, no government can determine all the priorities that they set as some will be derived from external agreements or events, such as previous treaties or global economic issues. The policy impulses in the EU, like in the UK, come from external and internal drivers. These are also subdivided into formal and informal influences, which are considered in more detail in the following.

1. Integration

Integration theory is used by both those who promote European integration and those who argue against it. George (1991, p 19) suggests that the attraction of integration theory is 'partly the neatness with which it appeared to explain what was actually happening in Western Europe: events fitted the theory'. Haas (1958, p 16) defines the process of integration as a situation or culture 'whereby political actors in several, distinct national settings are persuaded to shift their loyalties, expectations and political activities towards a new centre, whose institutions possess or demand jurisdiction over the pre-existing national states'.

The key approach to integration theory is related to political and policy processes that support EU development. These can be closely aligned to either chronological stages in the development and growth of the EU (Diez and Wiener, 2009) or discussions on the value of integration as an objective. Pollack (2010) applies different theoretical constructs to the periodisation and genealogy of the EU's development and growth and uses these to characterise the dominant form of policymaking. These theoretical approaches may represent contemporaneous dominant policy issues rather than illuminate the debate between integration and intergovernmentalism.

The internal agenda of the EU, and particularly of the Commission, is seen to be dominated by an integrationist position. This can be viewed as being both a retrospective and prospective standpoint, creating a 'golden thread' for policy. Retrospectively, Commission policy is focused on achieving the founders' aims for closer integration in the Treaty of Rome. It may also be viewed as prospective, concerned with what the EU might achieve in the future. In this, the potential role of the EU as a super- or supra-power is at the forefront. The founding policy impulse to achieve a more integrated Europe is still seen to drive the EU's actions, although critics question whether the Commission's actions are ahead of the member states' views. Those who see integration driving the Commission suggest that there are a variety of devices that are used to promote policy to achieve these ends. A key approach is the 'elasticisation' of policy competencies that seek to extend the role, reach and remit of existing policy principles and agreements. This is most commonly seen through the Single European Market (SEM), which was initially assumed by the UK to be narrowly confined to trade. However, the definition of trade has expanded into wider areas such as employment, migration, environment, transport, regulation and now finance, which all make up the trading system. This 'elasticisation' is coupled with a second approach of 'filling in' policy gaps. This has been developed through bilateral working between member states, which can then be expanded into common practice for all. OMC or other cooperative methods can be used to develop common approaches that can then be formalised. Territorial and structural funding programmes can be used to develop integrationist objectives through cross-locality working (Smith, 1997; Midelfart-Knarvik and Overman, 2002; Rodriguez-Pose and Fratesi, 2004).

The integrationist view may be given more strength through the EU's external role. The EU is an international organisation and has a role in negotiating on behalf of the EU with the WTO. It attends meetings of the G8, G20, OECD and UN. The EU's position in global bodies can be seen to enhance its role externally. There are differing views on whether this has reduced the integration objective internally (Taylor, P., 2008) or is an essential feature of it (Meunier and Nicolaidis, 2006; Rhinard, 2010).

One key consideration in the discussion about EU integration is whether this is a central focus of the Commission rather than of the member states. Although officials join the European Commission from member states through direct application and open competition, those who are successful frequently have some previous experience within their own national governments and might be expected to come at least with their own domestic perspectives and objectives. However, those who apply for jobs in the Commission might be those more interested in or supportive of longer-term integration and be self-selecting. There may also be assumptions that a socialisation of officials occurs over time and they will become more integrationist in their approach (Brack and Costa, 2012). Hooghe (2001) examined the orientation, objectives and values of senior officials and found that the officials represented a range of views and positions. However, organisational values were higher when politics and budgets were under consideration, as in most other bureaucracies. Hooghe also found that once the leadership set the agenda, officials complied in their efforts to achieve it.

Commission policymakers are also defined as 'hunter-gatherers', suggesting that they do not have a monopoly of technical expertise but are open to engaging with others from member states or specific sectors as part of the policy development process. Hooghe's view is that the Commission does not represent a unified whole but is made up of different groups focused on their own policy agendas, as in other governmental organisations. Further, this difference has been extended through enlargement and growing the EU's competencies so that the Commission now has more variation within it (Brack and Costa, 2012). Risse (2003) argues that Commission officials have absorbed some of the growing sense of Euro-scepticism in member states such as the Netherlands and Finland and have learned to present different views in Brussels and at home. On the other hand, the Lisbon Treaty 2009 has also attempted to implement a more unified approach through the permanent head of the Council of Ministers and a High Representative for the EU's growing international competencies.

In another series of studies, Kuus (2011a, 2011b, 2011c) has detected other forces at work within the Commission and its policymaking processes. These are through an examination of the role of proximity and the daily management of business within the European quarter of Brussels. Here, Kuus found some key components of technical expertise that supported the integrationist approach to policy. First, although the Commission is multi-lingual, the default language of policymaking is French and without a good knowledge of this, it is seen to be difficult for any individual to have influence. Second, most officials come from three key backgrounds as economists, political scientists or lawyers. Third, there is a degree of social integration through family and other recreational activities that reinforces ties and values within this policy community.

Not all approaches to integration suggest a unified outcome. Taylor (2008, P.) argues that integrated approaches can recognise difference, differentiation and coexistence and that these can be seen through centralised objectives and direction being delivered through decentralised and devolved mechanisms in line with subsidiarity (Haahr, 2004; Jessop, 2004). However, Piris (2010) underlines the method of integration through a union rather than as a single state. The use of models to describe the state is always undermined by close examination and inevitable simplifications. The EU may be a federal state in the making (Glencross, 2009), or is it closer in comparison with the US as a 'decentralised unitary state', albeit without a directly elected president?

How far is integration a requirement of long-term viability and success for Europe? Does the EU have to keep rolling forward to prevent failure? The achievement of economic success is predicated on achieving the political and economic union that has been a continuing objective since 1957. When reviewing the Euro financial crisis in 2011. Politicians in France, Germany and the UK stated that this success can only be achieved through greater economic and political union (Barroso, 2012; Miller, 2012). This suggests that the principle of integration as an objective and shaper of EU policy will continue.

2. Intergovernmentalism

The EU also has international standing because of its combined population and economic role. The EU's international role is therefore important for intergovernmentalists. This is characterised as national self-interest, within the context of international relations. Here, it is argued, member states pool their powers because the net benefit of doing so is greater than would be the case if they acted alone. In this way, the EU can be seen as a political construct that is an alternative to an integrated structure. Intergovernmentalism is a common framework for other organisations, such as the UN, North Atlantic Treaty Organisation (NATO) and OECD, and can be used for formal or informal purposes. Membership of an intergovernmental organisation does not imply a convergent position towards integration. Apart from negotiation of trade treaties through the WTO and bilaterally, the EU has also focused on environmental issues, which have been led by the UN (Bretherton and Vogler, 1999). The EU may also wish to encourage the rest of the world to tackle particular issues, such as development aid.

However, external roles can also drive more integrationist policies. In trade, after negotiation, the EU is responsible for implementing legislation and for checking compliance within its geography. Rhinard (2010) argues that the mechanisms for policy implementation can involve agenda-setting and trade-offs with other policy areas. Despite the expectation that staff in the Commission will be primarily integrationist (Hooghe, 2001), Delhousse and Thompson (2012a, 2012b) have found that there is a significant presence of those in favour of intergovernmentalism. However, even this group favours greater pooling of powers by member states, particularly in areas such as foreign and security policy and energy. The greatest number of intergovernmentalists were from the UK, making up 20% of this group, although representing 5% of Commission staff overall.

Is intergovernmentalism a theory of a type of European integration (Diez and Wiener, 2009), or is it a theory of international relations? Sanders (1990) suggests that the approach of member states is based on the assumption that the world in anarchic and that it is not possible to put an overarching authority in control to 'police' what goes on. This is based on a Hobbesian view that nation states are driven to protect their security and to enhance their own positions. The assumption that intergovernmentalism is a theory of integration leads to a consideration of the extent to which it delivers an integrated outcome (Cini, 2007a) or is a 'baseline' for more integrated approaches (Moravcsik and Schimmelfennig, 2009).

Other ways of examining intergovernmentalism may be to consider decision-making on an issue-by-issue basis to see whether the degree of alliance or joint decision-making varies over time or on specific issues. In this case, the role of intergovernmentalism may take the form of international relations theory. While membership of the EU is a primary one for many member states, others with a role in global institutions make take a different view, including the UK and France.

The main divergence in approaches in intergovernmental and integration theory is through the use of neo-functionalist theories (Rosamund, 2007). However, these theories give partial explanations rather than being overarching and can be captured within their own constructs. Intergovernmentalism suggests that it is the member states of the EU that have driven forward policymaking over time rather than the Commission. As the Commission only has the power of initiation in policy areas that have been previously agreed by the member states, these two positions are not incompatible. There is some evidence that this has been the case at the point of negotiation for membership, when aspirant member states have had a particular interest that they have wished to promote. When the Nordic countries became members, they wished to maintain and enhance the environmental policies that they had agreed between them and to see these adopted as minimum standards across the whole of the EU's area. This was ahead of other parts of the world and similar trading blocs and could have been seen as anti-competitive. However, the incorporation of this priority within the EU developed its role in leading on the adoption of international environmental standards.

Analysis of the role of intergovernmentalism has primarily been within specific policy areas and studies can offer results that seem at odds with sovereign states acting within an intergovernmental context. Where results demonstrate that national interests have not been achieved, this can be explained as a longer game or as a trade-off. As Pierson (1996, p 127) states, 'at any given time, the diplomatic manoeuvring among member states looms large, and an intergovernmentalism perspective makes considerable sense. Seen as a historical process, however, the scope of member state authority appears far more circumscribed'. The role of member states and any significant victories in policy development will enter the institutional memory. However, as Pierson (1996) points out, over time, the institutional memory also learns how to bypass or reduce the effectiveness of individual state manoeuvres so that specific member state tactics become less effective and new ones need to be devised.

The principle of intergovernmentalism emphasises the individuality of interests of member states. The perception of the benefit of policy to individual sovereignty will be a consideration in any negotiating process. Further, deferred gains may be an issue to consider in negotiation (Putnam and Bayne, 1987; Nye, 2004) and how these interact with each other in the EU. It is possible for a member state to have a highly developed view of its own interests and sovereignty on specific policies while also being successful in achieving them as a pan-EU policy. This can be achieved through the culture and style of negotiation. Some member states can better achieve their own national goals by deploying joint and apparently 'externalised' methods.

Conversely, member states that attempt to pursue their own interests or who are less determined to achieve specified ends may do less well, even if their objectives are closer to those being proposed. This could be a way of perceiving the UK position in EU negotiations. The UK may not have the required cultural skills in negotiation, be clear enough about what it wants or be adequately aligned with other member states to achieve its preferred outcomes (Friedland, 2011).

Intergovernmentalism frequently assumes that the policy preferences of individual states are fixed (Pierson, 2000). This may be true for longer-term and strategic goals, but these may be associated with individual political parties or movements and may change as the context alters. Member states can act together in their own interests, exemplified by member states aligning their actions over the social chapter to overcome the British veto in 1992. Countries can also use 'red-lining' as part of their negotiating position, that is, those elements of any proposed treaty that they will not accept (WRR, 2007). This may produce some concessions and could indicate where negotiation might be most fruitful. However, it may also reduce the flexibility of negotiating positions and allow others to manoeuvre around any member states that employ this method. The UK frequently deploys red-lining as an open and visible statement of its position, which signals independence, but also a lack of willingness to negotiate or join with others. Acting together is still at the heart of intergovernmentalism – it is just one way of achieving it (Burgess, 2009; Wiener and Diez, 2009).

Effects of EU policymaking

1. Europeanisation

Europeanisation is defined and applied in a number of ways (Olsen, 2002), which may weaken its potential use in practice (Kassim, 2004). Like integration, Europeanisation is regarded by some as a policy rather than outcome (Borzel, 2005). The extent to which domestic policies in any member state, whether internal or external, have been influenced by EU membership is usually discussed within the context of Europeanisation, which can occur through a mechanical transposition of EU treaties and specific policies into domestic policy (March and Olsen, 1984; Olsen, 2002). Europeanisation can be viewed from a 'top-down' or 'bottom-up' perspective. From the top down, it occurs through policy transfer in a process between the Commission and member states, although the latter may use policy communities or policy networks in order to learn from the experience of others in implementation. From the bottom up, policies and initiatives are developed through EU-stimulated and -funded programmes that support research, pilot studies, data collection and analysis, and territorial groupings, and then these are adopted through community-wide programmes or practices.

Is Europeanisation an end in itself? Radaelli (2000, p 3) rejects this view, defining Europeanisation as consisting of:

processes of a) construction, b) diffusion and c) institutionalisation of formal and informal roles, procedures, policy paradigms, styles, 'ways of doing things' and shared beliefs and norms which are first defined and consolidated in the EU policy process and then incorporated in the logic of domestic (national and subnational) discourse, political structures and public policies.

Radaelli (2004a) and Goetz and Hix (2001) argue that Europeanisation is a field of inquiry, and can be used to interrogate or discuss its effects in practice. This can be pursued as an empirical approach to Europeanisation that can investigate the ways in which the EU influences the domestic politics and policies of member states. However, it is uncertain whether this debate is confined to the development of each member state towards some European norm of institutions (Risse et al, 2001). Europeanisation could relate to the procedural outcomes of the application of EU treaties, legislation and less formal agreements together with the influence of individual policy approaches set within individual state cultural norms. These may have some transferability between states where there is an appetite for new policy approaches.

There are a number of ways of considering the provenance of the influence of Europeanisation within the institutions and policies of member states. Here, they are grouped into four categories – where Europeanisation is driven by *external* factors, by *internal* factors and whether its consequences are *intended* or *unintended*. Some of these arguments blend into others, and they are discussed in the following.

a. Externally driven Europeanisation

Globalisation is identified as a causal factor of Europeanisation, not least through the delivery of WTO agreements for open competition in public services (Cowles and Risse, 2001). This might be exemplified through the competition processes for utilities that were formally publicly owned, such as roads and rail (Heritier et al, 1996). However, the extent to which services exhibit the same characteristics following a cross-European process may vary and it may be possible to see Europeanisation working at multiple levels.

Where the EU has responsibility for ensuring that member states are compliant with external agreements, the implementation processes are likely to be more formal, and to be set up in such a way that compliance can be measured and verified. Both the Commission and the member states are more likely to adopt a top-down approach to the introduction of these requirements. The formalisation of processes that demonstrate compliance could have a strong Europeanising effect. Within member states, issues that arise in domestic politics as a result of this compliance requirement can be blamed on Europe as part of a political strategy (Radaelli, 2004a). This 'blame' might be for public consumption or as a means of 'explaining' policy, where transposition of EU policies would be less acceptable than 'inventing' new ones (Hood, 2011). In practice, there are few areas where EU policy is not pooled in the domestic policy agenda. As Radaelli states (2004a, p 9), 'Europeanisation often covers slow processes of socialisation of domestic elites into European policy paradigms', and in the UK, the civil service has adopted more of an obscured 'receiver' than transparent 'promoter' stance in this process (Bulmer and Burch, 2009).

b. Internally driven Europeanisation

The pressure to demonstrate compliance may influence styles of policymaking and delivery. These may derive from policy transfer from the Commission or from the member states using the EU as a mechanism to argue that there are specific ways of achieving implementation that will be compliant. This could also occur through policy networks and communities sharing modes of practical delivery. This may not be driven from any objective of Europeanisation, but could depend on the culture of individual member states or that of specific ministries within member states that have adopted this approach (Borzel, 2002; Page, 2010).

As a result, Europeanisation can be varied across states and policy areas. This may further be influenced by the extent to which legislation is set in a prescriptive or framework mode. If there are prescriptive regulatory requirements that member states have agreed that they will meet, then these may provide a greater argument for similarity in delivery. The legal system is one means of promoting Europeanisation (Conant, 2001). However, where compliance can be achieved through framework directives rather than regulations, there may be more flexibility in member state delivery mechanisms.

How far is Europeanisation related to or dependent upon policy networks? These may be regarded as part of a wider approach to Europeanisation and introduce future potential policies. This is particularly the case in the role and development of programme-based projects, where a variety of consortia can bid for funding. This allows the Commission to support an inclusive approach to the development of delivery methods, encourage cross-EU working and then select the project for application that is closest to its original intention (Hachmann, 2011).

Some EU policy priorities will come from pressures and influence from member states or sub-state localities, either individually or in groups. Groups of states with common rural profiles may work together to influence agricultural policy. Places with similar characteristics – for example, islands or peripheries – may work together in order to influence both policies and delivery programmes for localities in these categories. Further, where domestic policies are developed that are not EU-related, they may have been facilitated by EU papers and events (Radaelli, 2000). On the other hand, Borzel (1999, p 574) argues that Europeanisation can weaken the state because it allows territorial and interest groups to 'go round' the state in order to influence the Commission and other member states directly in negotiation and policy development.

In addition to a consideration of Europeanisation of legislation and institutions, is there a Europeanisation of the people, through the creation of a European identity? Risse (2010) examines this issue, and although he rejects the notion that European citizens have converged, he does suggest that people have included being European within their identity. This identity has been fostered through popular culture, such as football tournaments, leisure travel and business engagements, and may have developed over time. Risse argues that this may be underpinned by the cultural elements of 'soft power' (Nye, 2004), including religion and a common European history and heritage, which may be stronger factors of identity in some parts of Europe than others. In geographies where political and national boundaries have frequently been redrawn, EU membership may be seen as a mechanism to confirm defined borders. As Risse points out, these debates also span the spectrum of identity versus interest and people hold multiple identities that are used in different contexts.

c. Europeanisation as an intended consequence

Those who support the integrationist approach will view Europeanisation as a path-dependent process for achieving this end. Not only do member states need to comply with the legal requirements of the treaties they have agreed, integrationists see the methods of delivery as being a key component of developing common institutions. As the EU has grown in size, both in number of states and in competencies, this creates a conundrum. A greater extension of the scale and scope of the EU appears to move closer to an integrationist end. However, the variation of cultures and styles in policy delivery as well as starting points suggests that there could be more of a 'lowest common denominator' approach in an effort to achieve full EU compliance. Where member states have difficulties, dependencies and 'last man standing' behaviours, these can be used to gain more influence or resources.

Europeanisation of policies within member states could lead to homogenised states, but could also lead to transformation within the EU (Borzel, 2005). Europeanisation may occur as a process of institutional adaptation (Radaelli, 2000; Olsen, 2002), and Borzel (2005) suggests that there are a number of components in this adaptation, including coercion, imitation, normative pressure, competitive selection and framing. These need to take into account the starting position (Kassim, 2005) or distance from the agreed outcome and the cultural acceptability of various approaches to achieving common ends. The convergent pathways towards policy adoption also include an explicit assumption that some policy options will be curtailed (Kassim, 2005). It is not possible to exercise autonomy over shared powers unless this is specifically agreed as part of the policy. Where individual member states want to influence the agenda, the fragmented nature of Europe makes this difficult. It is likely to be in informal ways rather than through formal, prepared mechanisms (Bulmer and Burch, 2009; Kuus, 2011a). External policies can be used as a means of achieving domestic objectives and those engaged in policy processes can be silent about their processes to achieve these ends (Bulpitt, 1983).

d. Europeanisation as an unintended consequence

Europeanisation can develop in a number of ways that may be seen as unintended consequences. There are internal pressures to conform or to achieve compliance and this may lead to Europeanisation in some areas. However, this may happen more broadly and over time. As national administrations are drawn into the EU, they can come under more bureaucratic 'adaptive pressure' (Goetz, 2001) and this might be more powerful than pressure on politicians. These changes can be incremental rather than sudden and also suggest that Europeanisation could occur more through administrative rather than political processes (Mair, 2004).

As agreements within the EU form part of any domestic policy agenda, they have become part of national policymaking (Ladrech, 1994). This has grown over time as each new treaty has been developed. Ladrech (2010) found that following the Single European Act 1986 (SEA), Prime Ministers became more interested in EU politics and European policy units started to be established in government ministries. Thus, the widening and deepening of EU responsibilities and subsequent policymaking has provided a series of common agendas that it might be argued have inevitably led to more Europeanisation. Although this might be as the result of agreed actions, some outcomes may be spillover effects and only become apparent over time. These may also carry the EU impact into domestic policy areas in an unintended way.

Europeanisation may occur as member states learn from the implementation of EU policy and use this experience in other areas (Ladrech, 2010). Policies and their delivery might also be copied from one state to another (Bache, 2008). These processes of implementation can also be returned to and influence the Commission (Carbone, 2010a). There are other ways that unintended Europeanisation might occur. Member states might be transformed where changes act in a cumulative way. Further, although countries may use examples from other EU member states, these may be used in different ways or be customised or adapted before implementation.

Another unintended consequence may be the outcome of 'tight–loose' framework directives. The methods of implementation may not be prescribed and variation will be expected, but, in practice, member states may copy from each other. This replication may be a short cut or could be used to demonstrate successful alternative practice to a domestic audience. While not framing these exemplars within a EU context, they allow the government to use a 'best in breed' approach to support policymaking and implementation. The implementation of any EU-agreed policy will be within an existing system and there will be effects and influences of fit and misfit. A misfit between EU and domestic policies will be a focus of change (Bache, 2008). However, there is also the potential for policy convergence.

A further consideration is how outcomes are judged. Applying rigid definitions in each member state could result in literal compliance and different outcomes in practice. Although the EU's influence on each state is frequently assumed to be similar, Borzel (1999) argues that it is differentiated. The domestication of the EU agenda gives the state more powers, as it can control the distribution of resources and outcomes, while the better the fit between EU and domestic policies, the lower the costs of implementation (Borzel, 2002).

2. Institutionalism

Institutionalist theories analyse the ways in which organisations influence and are influenced by policy. It considers the separate roles and influences of agencies, actors and the operating rules and codes that shape relationships and interchanges between them (March and Olsen, 1984; Pollack, 2010). Once decisions are made, they have a role that influences future actions, and they are taken within this context. A temporal process can also be described as path-dependent, where the provenance of any policy is tied to its genealogy.

Institutional theory is concerned with explanation and predictive models about the long-term survival of organisational cultures and their ability to change. Much of the literature is concerned with methods of change that can punctuate and stimulate change, with theorists favouring both sharp shock and incremental models of practice (Baumgartner and Jones, 2002; John and Margetts, 2003). The sharp shock approach may be generated by unexpected or planned events, such as war or elections, where fractures might destabilise institutional continuity. The incrementalist approach, with its added competent of layering (Thelen, 2004), suggests an accretion model, where change is absorbed and internalised through accommodating processes. In these cases, the institution is stronger than the change that is threatening it and survival is seen to be the main objective.

When considering this within an EU and member state context, the pressure for institutional change can come from at least three sources. First, globalised agencies can exert pressure to absorb and implement change either legally or informally. These changes might be applied directly or through the EU as an intermediary interpreter or reinforcer. Second, the pressures for change may derive from agreements made within the EU. Lastly, they may derive from the member states acting in alliances or collaborations of interest in formal arrangements. While the presentation of institutional change, according to institutional theory, will relate to an external appearance of continuity, strength and power of the member state, the reality may be different. Member states may implement policies and initiatives to which they have not agreed but have been governed by the majority or the process.

Institutionalists give primacy to the notion of continuity and this may be a key shaper of policy acceptance (Thelen et al, 1992; Wessels et al, 2003; Thatcher and Coen, 2008; James, 2010b). Carbone (2010b) argues that in treaty formation and change, veto and ratification procedures have been used to achieve institutional ends. On the other hand, Geddes (2004) argues that the path set from the early 1950s has reflected ambivalence and that the EU role as a promoter of institutional change has not become embedded within the consciousness, preferences and understanding of political elites and the public at large.

Institutionalism can operate in other ways. As well as forming policy, governments can create institutions through which control can be maintained through different government scales. Decisions to establish organisations or agencies to make or implement policy are taken by each member state. New formal institutions for the EU are established through treaties and other binding agreements. Organisations that have no specific recognition within EU legal structures can be supported. These may receive EU funding for projects, initiatives and networking activities. These organisations require some legal, corporate and democratic basis before they are recognised to receive EU funding, but they do not have to be part of the administrative and political structures of their member state. Territorial groupings such as the Atlantic Arc or Europe's Islands groups perform this function. They are groupings of territorial interest, which are a type of institution, but they are not required to be similar in all parts of the EU. There is a growth in the role of these institutions, which are developing within the EU substructure, and they may make the EU rather than the member states their main focus. They may also be viewed as being on a path towards greater institutional recognition and a larger role in the future (see Chapter Eight).

Even within institutions, policy dominance in terms of style and issue can also be subject to internal market and political forces. Institutions include informal as well as formal relations between agencies and states. Although institutions can be bureaucratic in nature, this does not mean that they operate blindly. Struggles for dominance are as clear within institutions as between them. On the other hand, the overriding bureaucratic tendency can argue for the status quo (Pierson, 2000) or inertia (Blair, 2010), but even these positions represent political statements rather than unthinking bureaucracy. Supporting the status quo suggests that dominant powers remain in place and that these are maintained through minimal change. This is a means of dealing with potential pressures for power change.

Like economics, institutionalism starts from a premise of equilibrium in the system. Rosamund (2007) argues that the original designers of the EU paid attention to the ways in which the member states and the central institutions would work together. Institutionalism can also be related to neo-functionalist theories, which regard the government as a system that may be regarded as open or closed. Neo-functionalist approaches expect that actions in one part of the system will have implications elsewhere and that there needs to be institutional and political adaptation on a continuous basis. Pollack (2010) argues that neo-functionalist policymaking was a primary driver for EU policy in an earlier period of its formation and development between 1958 and 1963, when the six founder member states and the Commission were aware of the relationships between policies in their efforts to achieve their longer-term goals. The rise of neo-functionalism as an explanatory theory has come to the fore, again suggesting that the EU as a supra-power organisation now has a role in keeping the system. However, Pierson (1996) argues that this credits these institutions with more power than they have. He suggests that although they are responsible for key decisions, their role cannot explain the wider ways in which policies are made and decisions implemented.

Conclusions: what kind of governance machine is the EU?

The factors shaping EU policies have been considered, and included the formal legal powers vested in it through treaties and other agreements. The EU's strategy to achieve 'ever closer union' and how this is driving policymaking has been considered. However, there remains an issue of the EU as a governance machine. Some have argued that it is a form of federation. This is unlike others because it is not a single state. The EU has powers of initiation of policy and legislation within agreed areas covered by treaties. However, the EU does not have the power of initiation over all activities that would be available to a single state (Miller, 2011b; Tommel, 2011). Others have suggested that the EU is part of member state governments, and as an integral component, it has to be factored in to all actions and activities (Lu, 2011). It can be considered as federal because member states pool power in the EU and have power over which powers are given.

This makes member states and the EU hybrid institutions. Their essence is comprised of the intergovernmental and the supranational, which marks out the EU and the member states as *sui generis* (Tommel, 2011). Other global regional organisations that undertake similar functions as the EU in WTO negotiations have different governance architectures and combinations of roles, for example, North American Free Trade Agreement, *Mercado Común del Sur*, Association of South East Asian Nations (Wolinetz, 2011, p 35). The external EU role could be seen as 'regulatory regionalism'. However, membership creates new modes of operating within and between states inside the blocs and these have territorial consequences within states (Hameiri, 2009; Hameiri and Jayasuriya, 2011).

Arguments in favour of a federal model have been advanced by the adoption of the Lisbon Treaty 2009, as it gives the EU powers over the way in which sub-state government works. It is transformative of state constitutions as it changes the legal relationship between scales of government within states through the subsidiarity protocol. The Commission does not have competencies to 'rule' over member states, but does have the power to propose how to implement and enforce their agreements. Thus, the member states hold the power to control the EU.

CHAPTER FIVE

Trade and competition

Introduction

The role of the EU in trade is through the promotion and defence of bilateral agreements with external countries or trading groups and through the negotiation and implementation of treaties with the World Trade Organization (WTO) and its predecessor, the General Agreement on Tariffs and Trade (GATT). This role is central to the EU's core purpose and power (Woolcock, 2010). It makes the EU a global actor of some significance (Bretherton and Vogler, 1999; Rosamund, 2000) and is the role in which the EU stands as an equal to the US (Meunier, 2005). Trade was also its initial purpose. The EU is given its identity through its role in trade negotiations (Damro, 2012), and, beyond this, it gives it global power to influence wider policies in other countries, such as those on governance, social welfare and standards (Smith, 2007). Transfer of responsibility for trade from member states to the EU occurs on accession into membership of the EU (Meunier and Nicolaidis, 2006). The EU provides a strong negotiating group in world discussions, which enables member states to promote their priorities and interests with more weight than they could do singly. This role also provides a central narrative of EU membership for domestic audiences.

Although it has been the implementation of the treaties on trade that have introduced competition into services and the public sector, this should not be confused with EU competition law, which is concerned with the operation of trade within sectors and includes issues such as cartels and monopolies, restrictive practices, and mergers within the Single European Market (SEM) (Eyre and Lodge, 2000; Cini, 2008; Smith, 2007). This is discussed in Chapter Six.

For Britain, trade created the major push for EU membership. As noted in Chapter One, the growth of the European market at the same time as Commonwealth countries were exerting more independence, coupled with the ending of US post-war financial support, all contributed to the moment of membership (Camps, 1964). Although the UK has individual membership of the WTO, the move to increase the agreements between the major trading blocs, either in all member states or bilateral agreements, provides the UK with access to greater markets and more influence, not least as the EU now has the largest market in the world. On the other hand, membership of such a group gives rise to difficulties in both negotiation and delivery. While any individual state may not be able to achieve all of their objectives in negotiation of an agreement, this takes on a different character when these powers are pooled under a single negotiation umbrella, as in the EU. This has been problematic for the UK. Governments of all political parties have consistently clothed EU activity and its accompanying competition role in the 'legend' of domestic political ideology (Holden, 2011).

When developing negotiating positions in its lead WTO role, the EU operates an intergovernmental practice. As agreement of all the member states has to be achieved before the negotiation can be concluded, the Commission has the power of double negotiation, both externally and internally. Externally, it will be using its best endeavours to negotiate the agreed position, although some issues are inevitably more important or achievable than others. However, as has been found over time, attention to detail is important in gaining support from the Council of Ministers (Meunier, 2005). Internally, the negotiation between states can be spread between trade and other negotiations: specific national requirements in trade may be offset against those in other programme areas (Rhinard, 2010). This may support an integration stance.

The role of the EU in leading trade negotiations with the WTO has also been used to lead policy in other areas, including the SEM and the environment (Young, 2004). The EU's ability to trade successfully can be strongly supported by reducing the costs of internal financial and regulatory barriers to trade. More streamlined product requirements can reduce production costs and make the EU more competitive. The adoption of the euro in 2002 is regarded as an essential feature of this policy (Delors, 1989; Bun and Klaassen, 2002).

The application of EU approaches can also streamline and serve to unify approaches across member states. Although this might be seen as an integrative approach that results in Europeanisation, it can also provide a more efficient approach for companies trading across member state boundaries within Europe (McGowan and Seabright, 1995). Further, the Commission has not established a pan-EU approach to the provision of services and regulation, but has adopted a model that supports the development of a regulatory and delivery framework in each member state that meets defined outcomes. These may appear to be similar but will also have the benefit of working within internal business, government and regulatory cultures. Such approaches are also more likely to speed the implementation of legislation and the development of institutions to deliver agreements than otherwise.

Britain retains an ambivalent approach to this EU trade lead. Since 1979, the UK has had a neoliberal stance on trade, but, paradoxically, the privatisation of public services that are defined by the EU as being of *general public interest* (such as utilities) has increasingly been accompanied by more EU and, thus, UK regulatory constructs. The opening of the services sector, including the public sector, to private-sector competition following the GATT agreement in the Uruguay Round (1986–94), has led to a restructuring of the public sector in Britain. As a consequence, this has both allowed the UK economy to develop new markets, but also seen other European providers entering its domestic market. Nuclear energy, waste collection and public transport are all sectors where French suppliers, for example, are strongly represented in the UK. Within the EU, states will attempt to gain any competitive advantage they can through the application of regulatory nuance (Lazer, 2006), either domestically or with other members.

This chapter sets out the EU's role and approach to trade negotiation and the ways in which this has been translated into delivery. The effects of the application of this construct in Britain is then considered, with particular reference to two governance scales – central and local – primarily in an English context. The chapter concludes with a discussion on the ways in which British public policy has been influenced through these experiences.

Conducting trade policy in the EU

The EU's role in the WTO is significant, not only because of its size, but also because it represents the largest market in services (CEC, 2009a). The EU also both leads on non-compliance disputes with other WTO members and defends the EU if others take action against it. The EU has been successful on some issues, such as against the US on steel, but has lost cases on bananas and genetically modified organisms (Dur and Elsig, 2011). Within the WTO, the EU has agreed preferential trading arrangements or 'most favoured nation' status with nine WTO members, many of which have current or past ties with the UK, including Australia, Canada, Hong Kong, Japan, the Republic of Korea, New Zealand, Singapore, Taiwan and the US (Tsoukalis, 2005).

The WTO progresses by 'rounds' of talks that may extend over several years, and when concluded, these are then agreed through a treaty that is implemented by its members. The trade competencies held by the EU means that it is responsible for setting the internal regulatory framework for WTO treaty implementation. In some cases, these agreements may be between all WTO members, and on others, agreements may be concluded between only some members, such as that on government procurement (GPA). Significant areas of EU economic activity are included in WTO agreements, including agriculture and services, with particular attention on public services. The approach taken by the EU is 'rule-based' or regulatory, although this style of negotiation has been less favoured by other members of the WTO since the beginning of the Doha Round in 1995 (Young, 2007; Adlung, 2009).

The role of the EU in trade has been a significant unifying force since the outset (Woolcock, 2010) and also one that has characterised the benefits of membership to governments, businesses and citizens. Since the 1960s, the EU has been able to speak with a single voice in global trade discussions and is a leading player in global economic governance (Dur and Elsig, 2011). Trade has also been a dominant feature of the EU's foreign policy (Dur and Zimmermann, 2007). This position relates not only to its population size of more that 500 million, but also to its market, where the EU has the largest world market (IMF, 2012). On the other hand, what makes it different is that it is a trading union, making international economic policy and enforcing it. It does not have a single currency across the whole of its area, unlike the US or China. As an organisation, it is not a member of the G8 and only has observer status in the International Monetary Fund, while some other EU member states (France, Germany and the UK) can appoint members of the Executive Board. The EU is a member of the WTO alongside individual states.

The EU has had sole competence for trade policy since the Treaty of Rome in 1957 (Woolcock, 2010; Dur and Elsig, 2011). Since then, the extension of trade policy into wider areas of operation has been significant and not always welcomed by member states (Rosamund, 2000). The UK, like all other member states, adopted the *acquis communataire* when it joined; the EU's sole competence for trade was established from the outset but the extension to sectors such as services led to a reconfirmation of this role in the Single European Act 1986 (SEA). Trade policy is set by the Council of Ministers using Qualified Majority Voting (QMV), following proposals from the Commission, which has the right of initiation in this area. Since the Lisbon Treaty 2009, the European Parliament now has a greater role in commercial policy and the consideration of trade issues is now set in the Foreign Affairs Council, which is part of the European Council.

The approach of the EU has been seen as a significant supranationalist model for the management of internal trade markets, and other trading blocs have developed elsewhere in the world, such as in the North America Free Trade Area (NAFTA) and the Association of South East Asian Nations (ASEAN) (Jetschke, 2010; Borzel, 2011). There is a further perceived strength in this model in the way it can conduct trade relationships with other free trade areas. The EU has used its role in global negotiation to liberalise trade and is seen as the main advocate of this stance (Meunier, 2005). At the same time, the EU has not been a single voice in detailed trade negotiations and this has been an irritant to others, as last-minute discussions are required on specific member state issues (Meunier, 2005).

Despite the fundamental nature of the agreement of member states to pool their powers to negotiate trade agreements, there are internal conflicts on the way in which these powers are exercised (Meunier and Nicolaidis, 2006). There has been contestation between the member states and with the Commission, not least where individual member states see a particular approach as being inimical to their own national interests. Despite 50 years of single EU negotiation, the extension of competition from agriculture and manufacturing into services as part of the EU– General Agreement on Trade in Services (GATS) agreement (CEC, 1980) and extended through the GATT Uruguay Round 1986–94 stimulated internal friction and attempts by member states to reduce the role of the EU in negotiation. This round was seen to represent a shift away from traditional trade issues. The EU was founded as a customs union, concerned with borders. The inclusion of services into the ambit of trade competition inevitably focused on practices within states and had to rely on legislation and regulation to achieve compliance (Meunier, 2005). This new approach touched on sensitivities within member states and was to hasten the role of the SEM, which was agreed in the SEA. Both the EU and individual member states signed the agreement that promoted this round, but the transition between GATT and the WTO after the conclusion of the Uruguay Round in 1994 also heightened the debate over sovereignty and the power of initiation.

There is also a tension within the EU between the ideology of the liberalisation that is an inherent part of the global trade agenda and the welfarist and sometimes protectionist culture and character of some of the member states. The EU's role in trade has become synonymous with liberalisation while protecting the domestic political positions of member state governments (Hill and Smith, 2005). As trade agreements are implemented, this may allow governments to place responsibility for liberalisation on the EU or beyond this to the US, where bilateral agreements have been reached (Meunier and

Nicolaidis, 2005). More recently, in the wake of the economic crisis, there has been the reintroduction of the rhetoric and, in some cases, the practices of 'economic patriotism' (Clift and Woll, 2012), where 'homeland' comes before other international agreements. Economic patriotism has to reconcile external agreements while promoting territories and stakeholders (Clift and Woll, 2012) through the use of interventionism or 'state capitalism' (Kaletsky, 2010; Wooldridge, 2012). Rosamund (2012) suggests that it may reach a point where it could be used to open questions of the EU's legitimacy.

The respective roles of member states and the EU have not always been straightforward in trade negotiation. Until the Treaty of Nice 2003, some mixed competencies for aspects of trade between the Commission and member states remained, while the European Council and the Commission are not unified bodies and are characterised by internal competition (Dur and Zimmermann, 2007). Some interpretations of the use of Commission powers have been the subject of internal disputes between the Commission and member states, including those agreements that covered services, foreign direct investment and intellectual property rights (Dur and Elsig, 2011). Although the Commission has pursued these disputes through the European Court of Justice (ECJ), it has not received the support it sought. However, Woolcock (2010) argues that the Commission has built up its competence and institutional memory through its lead negotiation role, which allows it to maintain an advantage over individual member states. The EU's role in trade-related investment policy was made a competence in the Treaty of Lisbon 2009 and is an area that has been under a particular political spotlight in the UK, with some MPs requesting that the Prime Minister opt out of these provisions when implemented (Elphicke and Raab, 2012).

In developing its negotiating position, the EU must take into account the views of all its members through the European Council. Each member state has its own ideological stance on trade (Mandelson, 2011). These positions may also vary between different trade sectors, for example, agriculture and financial services, and may serve to limit the degree of freedom that the Commission has in negotiation, not least where some member states align with the Commission and others align with a different view, as was the case in the negotiation of the WTO Doha Round (Conceicao-Heldt, 2011). Here, the two camps were seen as being either defensive around agriculture and industry or liberalising, which was the Commission's position. Despite some member states having individual membership of the WTO, the Commission increasingly has the greatest access and voice in these discussions (Rhinard, 2010; Poletti, 2011). The dynamics of these positions change each time the EU enlarges. While the interests and views of business and non-governmental organisations (NGOs) are formally included in consideration of policy, the Commission and Council are not obliged to take them into account and their overall influence may be low (Woolcock, 2010).

The EU's responsibility for trade also needs to be considered as a policy vehicle. An intergovernmentalist approach would be the most appropriate one to consider, as some member states have individual membership of the WTO, although the Commission's role in negotiation has expanded over time. A realist view might suggest that the Commission acts as a carrier of messages between individual member states and the trade negotiations, but, in practice, the role of the Commission in representing a single entity to the external world suggests more than this (Pollack, 1997). The Commission can also derive some autonomy from its pivotal relationship in negotiations (Putnam, 1988; Rhinard, 2010). This might promote the integrationist view of the importance of the external trade role for the EU and the ways in which it has been used to develop these powers and wider responsibilities over time. This may be compounded by the way in which trade negotiations have been undertaken by the Commission, which are often seen as opaque and technocratic (Dur and Zimmermann, 2007; Woolcock, 2010).

In the discussions concerning the extension of trade negotiation powers to the EU that accompanied the Uruguay Round discussions (1987–94), the UK was initially in the group of member states that opposed the pooling of more powers, but as the processes continued, the UK saw greater benefits in single negotiations. These benefits were both external, in terms of weight of presence at the negotiating table, and internal, where specific special pleading by member states could reinforce existing trade barriers. On balance, the UK decided that a joint position would be stronger and that this should be through QMV rather than unanimity (Woolcock, 2010). However, following France's lead, there was agreement that certain services, such as those related to health and education, should join those of taxation, where unanimity would be required before action could be taken.

As the EU has no direct implementation role, the Commission, using its initiation powers, has to transpose these trade agreements in a way that will be successful in each member state. Internal positions have to be agreed and can be part of wider negotiations and trade-offs between member states and the Commission (Rhinard, 2010; Woolcock, 2010). The application of trade commitments in each member state depends upon their transposition into legislation that establishes regulatory frameworks. Individual member states may take different views on the implementation of these policies and their methods of demonstrating compliance. The UK's view was that the principle of subsidiarity should apply and that regulating the process of compliance in implementing competition to public services was not appropriate in a deregulatory environment (McGowan and Seabright, 1995).

At the point of introduction of any GATT or WTO treaty provisions, the selection of a specific regulatory framework can have considerable benefits or costs to an individual member state, through ease of adoption and cost of implementation. Some member states take the view that they already have an optimal solution to implementing a trade agreement and promote its application across the whole of the EU (Knill and Leschow, 2001; Knill and Liefferink, 2007). Although much of this influence can emerge at the Council stage, there is also some evidence that first-movers can influence the process at the Commission stage (Heritier et al, 1996; Borzel, 2002). At this point, a process of regulatory competition can ensue (Heritier et al, 1996). Member states can adopt specific strategies to influence the Commission's proposals for regulatory regimes, which can be knowledge-based or through the use of policy communities that may support specific approaches, although they may not always be successful (Haverland and Liefferink, 2012).

In other cases, the existing approach taken by a specific member state can support EU-wide delivery or implementation. The UK's approach on the liberalisation of public-sector markets, particularly for telecommunications, was seen to be helpful to the Commission and there was an alliance between the two (Bulmer et al, 2007). This meant that the language used to develop the policy was English, as were the terms used. However, in the longer term, other member states evolved and modified the UK approach to suit the position of their own industries (Bulmer et al, 2007, p 81).

Introduction of EU legislation on public procurement

The development of the GATS came into force in 1995 and is made up of two parts. The first comprises the framework rules within which the system operates and the second is a national schedule where each state makes specific commitments to provide access to markets to international competitors. From the outset, this schedule has been prepared and maintained by the EU for the member states. On implementing the GATS agreement, services may be defined either by their institutional owner or by their function and it is the responsibility of each state, when implementing the agreement, to determine which approach they take.

Before the discussion on the GATS was commenced in 1987, there was an EU–GATS agreement on public procurement in 1979. This focused on public works, goods and services and was an extension to the previous list of services that added utilities in Directive 80/767 (CEC, 1980). The introduction of this agreement was accompanied by three principles. The first was that each contract with a value over a specified minimum value has to be advertised across the whole of the EU. Second, technical specifications have to be anti-discriminatory so as not to act as a barrier to trade. Third, tendering and award processes have to be based on pre-specified objective criteria (CEC, 1977). It is this EU–GATS agreement that opened UK public-sector works and services to alternative suppliers. This approach was combined with the SEM in 2006.

The adoption of Directive 80/767 set the context for what was to follow in the public sector in the UK. This was amended and extended through Directive 88/295, which required open competition for all public supply contracts. Public bodies were required to publish notices of their intention to purchase so that suppliers could bid for their work. This was extended to works in Directive 89/440 and utilities in Directive 90/351. The extension to services was made as part of the SEM in 1992 through Directive 92/50. These were all later consolidated in 1993 as Directives 93/36, 93/37 and 93/38. These directives were transposed into UK law as regulations rather than through primary legislation.

The effect of these directives was to identify which services were to be exposed to competition and also how this was to be undertaken. They also set limits on the amount of works, supplies or services that could be purchased without going through these legal processes. The style of these directives, that is to say, their focus on procurement rather than the provision of public services, partly masked their role in opening up the market. In the UK, the discussion and agreement to progress to the full liberalisation of trade through the GATS at the Council of Ministers, meeting at Rambouillet in November 1975 was in the period of the Labour government (Crosland, 1976). The trade liberalisation agenda was therefore commenced three years before Thatcher became Prime Minister, and who is generally associated with the initiation of competition policy in the UK.

The influence of this public services procurement liberalisation was considerable. Public services were provided directly and it was not considered as being part of a market or contestable by other providers. Services were not 'purchased' but were provided through directly employed staff. The application of the competition for public services through these EU–GATT agreements as agreed in detail in 1980 and 1993 have had a significant impact on the shape and form of public services in the UK. However, their implementation has been and remains opaque. Further, no connection was made between the EU's role in delivering the agreements and competiton and, at the time, these links were denied by civil servants. The next sections set out in more detail how these agreements were applied in practice in the UK.

Transposition of trade requirements into UK practice and delivery

The UK is conflicted in relation to pooling its trade powers within the EU. The UK has a strong and long-standing trade persona together with recognised skill in negotiation. However, it also has had to acknowledge that it can benefit from being part of a wider grouping that has extensive market power in global discussions and that this advantage is of critical interest to the UK (Price et al, 2000). During the recent past, the UK EU Commissioners have frequently been responsible for trade (Peter Mandelson), external affairs (Chris Patten, Leon Brittan and Christopher Soames) and competition (Leon Brittan, Lord Cockfield and George Thomson).

The EU's role in negotiating trade agreements and advancing the general interests of all member states is rarely discussed in the UK. On taking up the Trade Commissioner's role in Brussels, Peter Mandelson (2011) comments that it was one of the two most important portfolios in the EU as it had powers transferred from member states, and continues to be so (Glennie and Straw, 2012). The role of the SEM in removing trade barriers is also seen to be a major benefit of the EU, although the removal of internal tariffs has promoted similar actions in the WTO (Woolcock, 2010).

The transposition of any EU treaty commitments into policy and legislation in the UK is essentially masked through an ideology 'legend' by the core executive before being communicated to mainstream government departments, agencies and other parts of the public sector. The period of the greatest shift to the opening up of public services and works contracts to competition was agreed by the EU in 1980 and coincided with the Thatcher premiership (1979–90). This provided the core executive with a strong synergy between external commitments and internal political ideology. Despite the Labour government's agreement to full trade liberalisation in 1976, the introduction of these open procurement processes might have proved more difficult if it had been in power for their implementation. The political continuity of the Thatcher ideology was seen as a key feature for the core executive for achieving policy delivery over this period. Different outcomes in the 1983, 1987 and 1992 general elections would have disrupted this delivery process (Rutter et al, 2012a).

The extent to which the EU or domestic choices have a stronger role in implementing legislation is a contested space. Hay and Rosamund (2002) and Young (2012) argue a *de facto* position: that domestic political choice governs implementation as none of the WTO or EU agreements have direct effect or are not implemented in a systematic way in other member states. On the other hand, De Ville (2012) argues a *de jure* position: that the effect of domestic policies and ideologies should be seen as a means of interpreting and shaping the implementation of these requirements. In the UK, the extent and scale of the post-1945 welfare state in direct delivery of public services meant that the effect on public services opened up to competition was greater than in many other member states. The shift has been more structural than transitional, although this may reflect the episodic nature of change management in UK central government. On the other hand, the Thatcherite approach of pursuing the lowest price as a means of tender evaluation has differed from other member states, where criteria-based approaches of tender assessment have allowed for differentiation in provision and more contracts being awarded to local and domestic providers (DETR, 1997). In UK central government, the use of 'price only' contract selection criteria practices persist, although they are generally not used elsewhere.

Despite the assumption that the privatisation of the public sector was a key Thatcher mantra, the reality was different. What characterises these procurement policies in their transposition is that, in retrospect, no one in the UK is quite clear about their provenance. Despite privatisation being seen as a Thatcher policy in 1979, it was not in the Conservative Party's manifesto for that election and there had been no pre-election preparation by ministers or civil servants (Rutter et al, 2012a). Despite the then UK government being ideologically supportive of the introduction of privatisation in the public sector, the application of the processes attracted intervention by the Commission. The UK's approaches were deemed to break 'state aid' rules in the supply of electricity and nuclear power in 1991 during a Conservative government (McGowan and Seabright, 1995).

There are two main policy strands to consider in the implementation of the GATS in the UK. The first was the opening of services. This had a major effect on financial services, the development of Canary Wharf and the 'Big Bang' in 1986 (Majone, 1996; Richardson, 1996). In the EU, this opened more dirigiste systems to neoliberal trading ideologies (Cerney, 1989; Mugge, 2006). The second was the opening up of the public sector. This included works as well as services. These included capital expenditure, such as information technology (IT) and transport, and major service delivery, such as refuse collection and waste management. In the UK, the transposition and delivery of trade policy had an impact on two specific governance scales. In central government, there were two key impacts. First, nationalised utility industries were privatised in the 1980s. Second, the introduction of 'agencification' separated government activities potentially at risk from competition rules into arm's length bodies, although still under the control of their sponsoring departments. At the local scale, services exposed to competition since 1980 have been restructured. These are discussed in more detail in the next section.

Impact of competition on central government

In UK central government, the primary impact of the implementation of trade agreements was on the opening up of the public sector to competition and agencification. The exposure of public services to competition from the private sector, popularly known as privatisation, is regarded as referring initially to the nationalised industries and then to the provision of services within government, such as IT and finance. The approach to competition adopted by the government and civil service resulted in a hybrid system, where the services are funded and run by the private sector but operated through a regulatory framework to make them compatible with EU definitions of services of general public interest.

The second approach considered here is that of agencification, which has had a major impact on the structure and effectiveness of central government. Agencification was primarily undertaken in order to protect the core executive and particularly the civil service from competition by hiving off the parts of the operating departments that might be susceptible to private-sector challenge. These were the services directly delivered to the public and some in the back office. This approach has been successful in protecting the civil service from challenge and change. However, agencification of services has been at the cost of a lack of awareness of direct delivery issues and confusion in the ministerial and public mind about who is in charge. Whenever a service is privatised and placed in an agency, the minister still retains responsibility for what happens and this had led to mixed behaviour patterns and types of response that have at times been problematic for government when things go wrong. Who is responsible and who should be blamed?

1. Competition

Although the introduction of the competiton of nationalised industries was seen to be a central plank of the Thatcher manifesto and programme for government post-1979, it was not a key feature of the election manifesto (Beesley and Laidlaw, 1995; Rutter et al, 2012a) and the approach to opening the market was largely regarded as being 'ad hoc' (Gamble, 2003). Developing an external procurement approach for nationalised industries was a difficult transition to achieve, not least as there was a public affiliation and affection for these companies, which still persists in the use of their pre-privatised popular names today. The competition process needed to deliver ways in which the public could engage in this process through popular capitalism, such as the 'Ask Sid' campaign used in the privatisation of gas (Richardson, 2005).

The introduction of competition into the public sector and services was readily laid at the door of ideology rather than external agreements (Walsh, 1995b; Korac-Kakabdase and Kakabadse, 2002; Bulmer et al, 2007). This was supported through similar examples emerging from other GATT members in other anglophone countries, such as Australia (King and Pitchford, 1998) and New Zealand (Larner and Walters, 2000). These arguments were particularly resonant given their shared roots with the UK in governance practices and cultures.

The methods of opening up public services to competition depended on the starting position in each member state. The UK was at the fully state-owned end of the spectrum. However, the development of more privatised approaches had occurred in the 1950s, with the introduction of commercial television in 1955, and the exploitation of North Sea oil and gas was privatised from the outset (in 1971). The exposure of public services and works to external competition required the preparation of the market and the workforce, who could bid to own and run their services. One of the first services to be privatised by Thatcher was road haulage in 1982, when it was sold to its employees. Another early service to be privatised as part of this agenda and within the EU competition process was telecommunications. The argument given to the public in 1982 to promote competition was the need for external investment in the telephony infrastructure at a time of economic retrenchment (Beesley and Laidlaw, 1995). This argument has continued, with the same argument being given for the privatisation of roads (and the break-up of the Highways Agency) by the Prime Minister in 2012 (Cameron, speech, 19 March 2012).

Like all services that have been privatised as 'services of general public interest', the market is managed by a regulator for example the Office of Telecommunications. The regulator's key roles are to ensure that companies can enter the market, that the cost of investment is contained within the price and not excessive for the investment required, and that companies do not crowd out others in the market (Armstrong and Vickers, 1995). It is also concerned with mergers and acquisitions (M and A), the general structure of the market, and the quality of the service provided. The regulator holds the public interest brief in the provision of these privatised services (Beesley and Laidlaw, 1995).

In some cases, the exposure of UK publicly owned services and utilities to competition anticipated the introduction of the EU legal framework. This was helpful for the UK, as the Commission followed some of the patterns and approaches to competition used in the UK and then rolled these out across the EU. Thus, the UK had first-mover advantage and had fewer adaptation costs in the short term. However, the approach to competition in the UK has largely remained different from the rest of the EU. This has meant the imposition of the regulator as a mechanism to act as a hinge between private-sector practices in comparison with the rest of the EU, where there is investment within a regulated market (Bishop et al, 1995). The presence of the office of a regulator such as OFCOM is a good way of identifying these hybrid public–private services in the UK. The privatisation of British Telecom (BT) occurred following the separation of telephone and postal services through the British Telecommunications Act 1981. This was a key element in the process of preparing BT so that it could compete in the forthcoming competition process while, at the same time, ensuring that any investment was taken out of the public-sector balance sheet with a major loosening of control.

Despite the early EU–GATT agreement (CEC, 1980) and the EU's role in delivery, contemporary commentators and researchers did not include these issues in their consideration of competition. Rather, they identified the primary driver as being efficiency and an expectation that competition in the market would reduce the price of supply to users (Davies and Flanders, 1995). In some areas, such as railways, difficulties in service delivery and major accidents have shifted the organisation between sectors, from public to private and then back to quasi-public. Others, such as British Airways, formed in 1974 following the Civil Aviation Act 1971, retain high levels of long-standing departure slots at Heathrow airport, also formerly nationally owned. In telephony, BT has been privatised but maintains its control over the landline network. In gas and electricity, there were initially multiple providers, when privatised but, over time, this has narrowed through M and A activity and the distinction between the two industries has blurred through combined ownerships. Some public services remain, including the post office, although the process of competition continues.

2. Agencification

The development of agencies by the core executive started with the Central Policy Review Staff (Blackstone and Plowden, 1990; Smith, 1999) and then was led by the Efficiency Unit, established in 1979 specifically for this purpose (Haddon, 2012). This process of reform of the civil service and the management of government was seen as being driven by ideology rather than being stimulated by external agreements (Stewart and Walsh, 1992). The Efficiency Unit undertook 266 'scrutinies' focused on cost-saving (Downey, 1986) and recommended that some of these scrutinised services should be turned into agencies through the Next Steps initiative (Ibbs, 1988; Hogwood, 1995). The first agency was formed in 1988. The services subject to scrutiny included the Passport and Prison services, which later became agencies. In the period between 1988 and 1998, 138 agencies were in existence and over three quarters of all civil servants worked in these agencies (Eden and Hyndman, 1999; Jenkins, 2008).

The Next Steps initiative employed an efficiency narrative for promoting and preparing for change to implement the EU–GATT agreements within the civil service. Like the CPRS, this became a way to introduce externalised or 'privatised' change and specifically became a way of separating policy from delivery, as Thatcher's statement to the Commons in 1988 confirmed. Although sponsoring departments sought to introduce more flexibility in the management of their agencies, including in areas such as recruitment, the Treasury held a more controlling view (Flynn et al, 1990). Although promoted as a mechanism to improve the management of public services and to reduce costs, the provenance of the role of agencies as a model in this process was less clearly set out at the time. There were also suggestions that this approach was based on a Swedish model that had traditionally had a small core executive with services delivered through other means (Fry, 1988b). The agencification of the UK civil service was also considered as a model in other countries in the EU, although it was not seen to have any underlying theory or model to support it (Hogwood, 1994).

As with other reforms, there was no clear exposition as to why agencies were the answer to the question of improving management in government. At the time, a leading civil servant in the Efficiency team stated, almost as an 'act of faith', 'that agencies would be better able to perform the executive functions of government' (Flynn et al, 1988, p 440). The introduction of the Financial Management Initiative (FMI) in 1982 had demonstrated that greater financial control improved productivity and reduced costs (Fry, 2008a). Its purpose had been to improve civil service management, but, again, it achieved a second outcome, which was to account more fully and in financial terms for the business of government. Without some accounting mechanism, it would be more difficult to assess and quantify the potential scale of business to be exposed to competition.

Agencies were seen as a means to shed departmental responsibility, by creating arm's length organisations while continuing to exercise control (Talbot, 2004a). This resulted in confusion. Agencies are quasi-privatised organisations that have a defined client but remain within ministerial responsibility. Defining service and performance outcomes are important features of this approach (Miles and Trott, 2011). The lack of experience of government in managing contracts led to a continuation of the former system. This confusion still remains, as the Home Office and Borders Agency disagreement in late 2011 demonstrated; there was no clear understanding of who was in charge of whom or what.

The introduction of agencification was contentious but it was part of the preparation for competition should it occur (Jenkins, 2008; Jenkins and Gold, 2011). Rather than move parts of the civil service directly into a competitive mode, agencies put departmental delivery into arm's length organisations. This approach enabled any agency to be opened up to competition if this proved to be necessary while maintaining both the core executive and the policy layer within mainstream departments. Some saw the agencies as a 'half-way house' towards competition, but, by 1999, the threat to move the civil service to complete competition was less than initially anticipated (Gains, 2004a). Although agencification was a mechanism to protect the core executive function of policymaking, there was no pressure to lose control of agencies through privatisation if this was not required. Agencies would only be sacrificed to outsourcing if necessary, either due to pressure for competition or poor performance.

What is clear from contemporaneous accounts is that the link to the GATS agreement for services and exposure to competition in the public sector was not discussed by the government, critics or researchers (Willman, 1994). Following the 1992 election, the return of the Major government used 'machinery of government' changes to extend these programmes in what Gains (1999, p 714) describes as a 'window of opportunity'. This also demonstrates the length of time that is taken for this kind of reform to be prepared and implemented. The Rayner Scrutinies during 1979–83 considered a range of services. Once discussions had started on the implementation of GATS, the government could demonstrate that it had a number of potential agencies ready to be privatised, as set out in the *Next Steps report* (Efficiency Unit, 1988). By the time that the extended GATS agreement was concluded in 1993, the scale of central government services to be exposed to competition was less than anticipated. In part, this was because of the scale of privatisation that had occurred or was planned through legislation elsewhere in the public sector, including the utilities and local government.

The introduction of agencies pushed the responsibility for delivery and financial control further down inside the organisation. Without changing the structure and power relations within any organisation the introduction of agency structures may lead to little or no change and the autonomy of agencies has been significantly eroded over time (Walsh, 1995b). Without these changes, the culture of the agency could still respond to the clientelistic relationship with its sponsoring department. Agency budgets are shown within those of their sponsoring government departments and their accounting systems remains the same and not transferred to a private-sector model.

In conclusion, what were the implications and effects of the implementation of agencification within central government? First, the responses were structural and institutional rather than cultural. Agencies created new institutions that remained primarily managed by their sponsoring departments and agencies and practices did not change towards those of the private sector. Finally, there is a potential detachment from responsibility for the agency at times when service delivery is problematic.

Impact of competition on local government

When considering the application of the competition agreements in local government, a key issue for the government was the earlier reforms of local government. In England and Wales in 1974 and in

Scotland in 1975, local authorities were reformed into larger units to promote efficiency in the direct delivery of services. These changes in England and Wales had also been introduced by the Conservatives, who were then faced with implementing the new competition reforms in the early 1980s. However, the switch of party leader from Heath, who introduced the reform in the 1970s, to Thatcher, who implemented the competition reforms made it easier to manage ideologically.

The Conservative government's introduction of competition into local government was promoted as a mechanism to introduce market discipline and efficiency (Walsh, 1995a). This had two components. The first was to expose specific services to the market. The second was to introduce an internal market within local authorities. Costs were externalised between different parts of the organisation, which were regarded as 'purchasers' and encouraged to consider using external providers if the internal, direct service provided was not adequate.

The main thrust of competition policy at the local level was introduced through the implementation of Compulsory Competitive Tendering (CCT) in the Local Government Planning and Land Act 1980 and was initially for construction and maintenance work. The Local Government Act 1988 extended the scope for services to be opened up to competition. The definition of 'works' included cleaning, refuse collection and catering and, in 1989, sports and leisure were added through secondary legislation. Other services were added over time, including housing, legal and property services in 1994 and IT, finance and personnel in 1995. The legal underpinning of competition in local government has been increased through legislation that has shadowed the EU directives on procurement, and these are summarised in Table 5.1.

Opening local authority services to the market commenced with direct labour organisations (DLOs) and catering following the 1980 Act. DLOs were primarily but not exclusively organisations used to build council housing and undertake road maintenance to achieve the post-war reconstruction targets. However, the reduction in funding for these works, exacerbated by the UK financial crisis in 1976 when the UK received a loan from the International Monetary Fund (IMF), meant that these works had reduced. However, in times of higher unemployment, local authorities were frequently unwilling to reduce their labour force. The result was that fewer projects led to rising costs and inefficiencies in DLOs. This fitted the Thatcherite ideology of reducing the local authority role in housing. Although the competitive process was seen to have a slow start, by the early 1990s, most building work was put out to competition.

Table 5.1: European Union legislation on competition and UK implementation

Date	EU	UK
1980	Agreement with GATS on services	Local Government Planning and Land Act
1986	Single European Act	
1988	Directive 88/295 on open procurement	Local Government Act (introduces CCT)
1989	Directive 89/440 on public works	
1992	Directive 92/50 on services	Local Government Act (extended CCT)
1993	Directives 93/36, 93/37, 93/38 on supplies, works and utilities (updating, clarification and consolidation)	
1999		Local Government Act (introduces best value)
2000		Local Government Act – reintroduces local government trading
2004	Directive 2004/18 on consolidation and introduction of framework agreements	
2011		Localism Act passes on fines for non-compliance with EU standards on services to local authorities

Source: Author

The number of services exposed to external competition was expanded through the Local Government Act 1988. It restricted the ability of one local authority to supply goods and services to others. While this had not been a mainstream activity for every local authority, there were established services where one local authority supplied to others or where local authorities had partnerships to share the costs of delivery. These standards included environmental health testing labs, IT services and trading services. Following the introduction of CCT, these joint services and mutual provision had to be disbanded.

CCT legislation concentrated more on introducing competition into 'technical' services, including refuse collection, waste management and grounds maintenance rather than personal services, such as health and education. These were changed in other ways. In social care, this was through the use of private rather than local authority care homes. In education, the process of decoupling schools from local authorities began (Hatcher, 2006; Gorard, 2009).

The approach to competition has also been consistent over time and across political parties. Despite hopes and expectations from local authorities that an incoming Labour government would abolish CCT, in 1997, it initiated the policy of Best Value, where 'compare, compete, challenge and consult' were introduced as guiding principles against which each service had to be measured. The Audit Commission's role was developed to undertake assessments of Best Value processes within local authorities. Competition was thus extended to all local authority services in one step. All local authorities were required to prepare a Best Value performance plan, where each council service had to have an identified time for review. Wilson and Game (2002) suggest that a different approach emerged from the Labour government in their second term that moved away from the Best Value approach to one that developed local service delivery contracts focused on performance, in line with the practices of New Public Management. However, by this time, the introduction of competition for services was well established in local government and there was less need to promote it through specific measures. The culture of local government had changed to one of a mixed economy.

The introduction of competition in local government has had a number of key structuring consequences. There has been a separation between the client and provider roles and the explicit determination of what is to be delivered by whom, when and at what price. This is said by critics to 'dehumanise' services (Clapham, 2002) through the separation of the client from the delivery (Stewart and Walsh, 1992). The proponents of competition argued that direct provision removed any incentive to improve service delivery and efficiency. There is also said to be a bias towards the producer-defined modes of service delivery, rather than the customer, client or user of a service (Varney, 2006).

By 1995, the private sector was successful in winning 17% of work by value (Walsh, 1995a). Initially, as privatised services cost less than existing service provision, these savings also increased as more providers entered the market and competition grew. The primary savings came through the reduction in labour costs (Walsh and Davis, 1993). Over time, further modes and delivery applications of competition have developed. Some services remain primarily delivered by the local authority, such as planning, environmental health and libraries, although there are examples where local authorities have outsourced at least some, if not all, of these services. In housing services, many local authorities have sold their housing stock to another provider. Although they retain responsibilities for homelessness and the preparation of an overarching housing strategy, these are also frequently undertaken by contractors or consultants. In planning, the core services are primarily delivered in-house, but specific expertise on issues such as environmental impact assessments is routinely undertaken externally. Also, the private sector is frequently engaged to provide staff at times of shortage or to undertake specific tasks, such as householder applications or planning appeals.

Critics of contractualisation in public services have suggested that the price of a service will determine the quality that is provided and that indirect employees in some services such as social care may not provide the same quality of service. Critics have also argued that competition drives up costs and prices through the fragmentation of services, difficulties in changing service specifications or where contract periods are long and the costs of failure in services for companies providing them can be considerable. The private sector has continued to press central and local government to create larger packages of works and services to be exposed to competition. As part of this process, central government promoted strategic service partnerships from 2000, which encouraged local authorities to group together to procure services and to tender more than one service for competition, such as all back office services in one local authority or across a number of local authorities (Morphet, 2008). The costs of entry of strategic partnering focused this approach on larger councils, where the cost-saving potential was seen to be at its highest. The government also introduced a framework contract approach through which companies were pre-qualified to be included on a potential list of suppliers, in line with Directive 2004/18, and opened this procurement gateway to local authorities.

However, this was a false dawn for private service providers, not least as many local authorities had already started to reduce the management and delivery costs of their in-house services. The private sector also proposed some contracts based on the volume of work that outsourced services could undertake for other councils or the public sector. In some cases, this has worked with privatised services taking the overflow of housing benefits cases, but these have generally been between local authorities using the same contractor in an internal market. Where contracts have been built on taking in work from elsewhere, some have been successful, but most have underperformed. A number of these shared service contracts have ended in the courts or have been voluntarily terminated.

One of the key issues that arose as a result of the opacity of the underpinning EU legal framework for this process was that local authorities were initially restricted by legislation to select the best tender for work on the basis of price alone (Wilson and Game, 2002). However, the EU had always included an approach that allowed the use of quality criteria to assess tenders for work and the UK eventually had to accede to this approach. This has been used to develop different forms of services and open the pool of potential contractors. When a contract specification or tender uses a criteria-based evaluation, issues such as the company's record in training, its use of local produce and the environmental costs of the business can be taken into account if they are identified as determining factors at the outset.

The Localism Act 2011 has transferred the responsibilities for meeting EU standards of service delivery to local authorities. This is the first time that such a requirement has been made transparent. It lead to requests from local authorities for greater involvement in the EU–UK negotiations of standards and requirements if they are to be responsible for the costs and fines of failing to meet them. This transfer of responsibility is a direct consequence of the application of subsidiarity.

In conclusion, what effect has competition had on local government? First, there was a lack of knowledge and understanding about the provenance of competition policies and the legal requirements for their implementation required as part of the EU–GATS agreements. This was not confined to local authorities, but also to civil servants creating the legal frameworks for delivering these policies. Early experience of implementing CCT in waste and other contracted services indicated a lack of knowledge in the core executive, which was denied in practice. This was not helped by the fiercest period of European sectarianism in government, between 1993 and 1997. In all of this, local government was cast as a victim, unable to control the process. Added to this, some aspects of the transposition of directives meant that processes subsequently had to be revised and the local cost of services increased. A more transparent process may have enabled this to be better managed. The effect of this failure to communicate the underlying drivers of the introduction of competition reinforced an anti-local government perception of the Conservative government. The process was also convenient for a Conservative government that wanted to be seen to be reducing the costs of public services.

Despite the appearance of contracting practices across Organisation for Economic Co-operation and Development (OECD) countries, there was no consideration that these common processes stemmed from the same GATS/WTO impetus. In some countries, such as Italy and the US, the approach taken was negotiation with a sole supplier after selection, whereas in the UK and Sweden, competition was between suppliers once the specification was agreed (Walsh et al, 1995). This restricted the market to a number of larger providers, including those from other EU states, for example, France. Second, it made local authorities consider a wider range of service delivery options that were potentially more efficient and effective over a period of time. It allowed local authorities to make greater costs savings in response to efficiency reviews than other parts of government (Gershon, 2004). According to the Audit Commission, it also made local government the best managed part of the public sector (O'Higgins, 2006). It also enabled the easier adoption of New Public Management and performance-related regimes (Hood, 1991; Walsh et al, 1995; Pollitt and Bouckaert, 2000).

On the other hand, where the legal framework was hidden for most of this period, the costs of some services have risen following outsourcing. Contracts set for long periods (eg 20 years) are more difficult to change when different legal requirements are introduced, such as changes in recycling targets or costs of waste disposal increasing outside contracted financial agreements. A key consideration of the competition agenda was the way in which outsourced local service provision could be democratically accountable. Local politicians assumed that externalising a service would lead to distancing between the council and the provider. It also meant that their role acting as an advocate between their electorate and council services would be reduced. This role could be open to clientelism and queue-jumping practices. The Labour government attempted to eliminate this by a focus on improving service delivery through Best Value and then by emphasising wider community leadership roles for councillors (DETR, 1998).

Another key effect of the introduction of competition into local government has been the fragmentation of the local authority labour force, although this varies between organisations. The use of consultants and temporary, part-time and agency staff in local authorities is now commonplace. In some local authorities, all administrative staff have been moved into externalised back office organisations, which are cited as a means of controlling costs. Also, in the period 1997–2007, when local authorities were particularly the focus of performance management and improvement, there was a strong inclination on the part of some local authorities to privatise failing services to both transfer the risk to reputation and manage staff in new ways to improve performance. The trades unions have also changed their views on this over time. Initially very hostile to change, much of their work was then taken up with the failure of government to introduce the EU directives on employee protection in the Transfer of Public Undertakings (TUPE) to the private sector. More recently, trades unions have accepted that local authorities will want to consider externalisation as an option and this, in turn, has led to restructuring of trades unions in this sector as membership has fallen and delivery organisations have become more complex.

Conclusions

The opening of the public sector to competition has been a formative process for the UK state and these processes continue. In December 2011, the WTO agreed a further development of the General Procurement Agreement (GPA), which manages the framework for competition in public services, and this has yet to be implemented. Second, the role of agencies in central government has been maintained and some are expecting their roles to be extended (Jenkins and Gold, 2011). On the other hand, the accountability of agencies to their users, Parliament, their sponsoring department and ministers remains misunderstood and difficult to achieve in practice (Jenkins, 2008; Rutter et al, 2012a). Inexperience in managing complex procurement issues and the separation of quasi-judicial and political roles remain problematic.

While concentrating on trade and the opening of public services, it is also important to look forward to the next stage of EU-integrated policy on financial services and regulation. One element of this has been the implementation of common financial accounting standards across the EU that are also in line with the US, who lead on the International Accounting Standards Board. However, the level of influence on the process has not been as great as might have been expected and some professional autonomy and independence have remained (Leblond, 2011). This has an important effect in the UK, when the accounting standards for the private and public sectors were united in 2013.

There is no doubt that this and the delivery of agreements to open up public services in works, supplies and services through the GATT agreement had a fundamental influence on shaping British public policy. Political ideology has been allowed to carry the implementation of trade agreements and the restructuring of public services. Thirty years after their implementation, the structure of local government and utilities has been dramatically reformed while the structure of central government has been changed but not exposed to competition in the same way. The utilities have been fully privatised but remain within a strong regulatory framework. The methods that have been chosen are not the same as in other countries and have not been copied. However, the ideological narrative has allowed other EU member states to take a distanced position on neoliberalism and the marketised state, regardless of being required to implement the same agreements (Traghardh, 2012). On the other hand, countries like Sweden and France had a greater proportion of privatised services in some sectors at the start of the process.

Local government now has a mixed economy, with some services being provided by the private sector and others by other public-sector or voluntary agencies. The scale of change has moved away from direct provision of services, even in those local authorities where local employment has always been a primary role. The response to these changes in local government has been varied. Local government has been able to demonstrate that it can reduce service delivery costs through reshaping services to a customer focus. This has encouraged central government to pass on their departmental cuts to local government both in a bid to ensure that their targets are met and to preserve their own critical mass. This has attracted considerable criticism, although customer satisfaction and local government performance are improving (O'Higgins, 2006).

In central government, the split between policy and delivery – departments and agencies – has still not been resolved. Departments are unsure about the role of agencies and have not implemented a client–contractor split within them. The agencies are run as 'arm's length' bodies without longer-term aims and objectives. They are accountable to ministers but primarily report to senior civil servants. When services fail, there are public discussions about who is in charge and how things went wrong. These frequently result in institutional but not cultural restructuring. For the Government Departments acting as 'clients' for these agencies, this has led to a growing gap in their knowledge and understanding of frontline and operational issues whilst the agencies have developed their own priorities and approaches under the radar of Departmental management. Some parts of government have been rotated and repackaged through agencies and other forms of arm's length organisation several times, including English Partnerships, the Homes and Communities Agency and the Tenant's Service Authority. Similar revolves have occurred in employment skills and training programmes through the Manpower Services Commission in the 1970s, to Training and Enterprise Councils in the 1990s to Regional Development Agencies in 1998 and Local Enterprise Partnerships from 2010.

Straw and Glennie (2012) suggest that there will be a third wave of globalisation and competition that takes into account the role of both the BRIC nations and developing countries. Mandelson (2011) argues that this will lead to new models of trade, which Europe will need to consider. As further liberalisation and markets open in new countries, there may be pressure to consolidate suppliers within the EU to provide the scale and mass to compete to deliver public services in India or

China. This might lead the EU into developing new approaches to trade and increase links between the role of trade and the SEM.

CHAPTER SIX

The Single European Market and transport

Introduction

The introduction of the Single European Market (SEM) in 1992 for goods, services, capital and labour through the Single European Act 1986 (SEA) was a significant development in the internal integration and Europeanisation of policy across the EU (Young, 2010). It continues to be a touchstone in the unifying narrative of the EU. It was led by Lord Cockfield, a UK EU Commissioner from 1984 to 1992, and the President of the EU Commission, Jacque Delors (Egan, 2007). Despite being placed in this role by Mrs Thatcher and a neoliberal, Cockfield had numerous disagreements with Thatcher on the Treaty of Rome and its implications for the implementation of the SEM in the period that followed his appointment (Cockfield, 1994). Nevertheless, the role of the UK in establishing the framework of the SEM was fundamental (CEC, 2006a). The proposals to complete the SEM were put forward by Cockfield in a White Paper (CEC, 1985) – a phrase adopted from the UK system of consultations on proposed legislation. Alongside this, there was a report on 'non-Europe' by Cecchini (CEC, 1988), that is, what the costs to trade of continuing without the SEM would be. The White Paper established the requirements for over 300 pieces of legislation and enabled the agenda to be set for the next steps in the development of the EU.

Although the principle of the SEM had been enshrined in the Treaty of Rome 1957, the development and availability of a wider range of commercial and financial services had led to the adoption of different approaches to tariffs in each member state. At the time of the economic crisis of the late 1970s and early 1980s (Sandbrook, 2012), these differential tariffs allowed each member state to operate in a way that supported their own market position. It became clear that while engaging in unified external trade negotiation as part of the General Agreement on Tariffs and Trade (GATT) and the General Agreement on Services (GATS) (see Chapter Six), the need to improve the efficiency of the internal market was equally important. Both the development of the external and the internal market supported the objectives of the integrationists (Armstrong and Bulmer, 1998). Although the EU began as a customs union and enabled the harmonisation of tariffs, it was clear that there were many other obstacles to the movement of goods, services and people. There were varieties of regulation, specifications and quality standards that meant that suppliers had to manage all of these different regulatory systems, creating additional costs. A harmonised regulatory framework was seen to be neoliberal in its position through enhancing the position of business and reducing non-tariff barriers to trade within the market (Egan, 2007; Bache et al, 2011) while undermining the role of member states in determining regulation (Marks et al, 1996; Marks and Wilson, 2000).

The White Paper was written to address the specific barriers to the completion of the SEM – physical, technical and fiscal – and was aimed at creating an area without internal frontiers (Cockfield, 1994). Its progress was relatively smooth, although there were some wider policy areas where inclusion within the SEM was specifically sought, including competition and transport (CEC, 1985), which resulted in legislative proposals.

The objective of free movement of people was set out in the Treaty of Rome but developed slowly and was seen to be of low priority (Huysmans, 2000). It was hampered by the non-transferability of educational qualifications and membership of professional bodies. In order to practice as a dentist, doctor or lawyer, additional competency tests had been set by member states, which acted as barriers to entry in the employment market (Nicolaidis, 1992). If there was to be a harmonised legal, financial and regulatory framework for trading inside the market, this had to be extended to qualifications as part of the free movement of labour. The way chosen to progress this was not through setting up a single system across the EU, but, rather, by using an approach of mutual recognition.

Following the publication of the White Paper and its action programme in 1985, the year 1992 was chosen to give an eight-year time horizon for delivery. Delors had given Cockfield powers over key areas of policy in order to be able to progress the programme and the implementation of the SEM is now seen as one of the major successes in the development of the EU in a global context. It created a new intergovernmental style of organisation while being flexible enough to include new member states.

The implementation of the SEM was not a single event, but a continuing process. However, since 1992, it is said to have lost focus as it became embroiled in delivering a legislative programme to the detriment to the longer-term strategic objectives. A review (CEC, 2006a) focused on deeper integration and explored the potential for improved economic outcomes (Ilzkowitz et al, 2007). SEM integration was identified as slowing down in the context of enlargement and increased globalisation. The review contended that there were numerous new trade barriers that had been inserted by member states in the period since 1992 and, globally, the EU faced new competition from Brazil, Russia, India, China and South Africa (BRICS).

Although the review was undertaken before the economic crisis of 2007/08, the issues that it identified were more universal than focused on the contemporaneous situation. The review proposed a series of areas for further work, including information-sharing on a common platform, which was seen to be a competitive advantage in the US. It also wanted greater links in the relationship between foreign policy and Economic and Monetary Union. Finally, it argued that there should be a policy switch away from the view that SEM completion is a legal activity to one that has an economic focus.

The EU review of the implementation of the SEM was linked to its 20th anniversary in 2012. As in the first implementation of the SEM, an arbitrary date was used as a mechanism to focus a relaunch of policy and implementation programmes. While the 2006 review looked back, a forward look was undertaken in the Monti report (Monti, 2010). Here, the focus returned to the political context for creating the SEM and relocating its provenance in the ideology and objectives of the politicians that supported its creation (CEC, 1985), including Thatcher (1986): 'What we need are strengths that we can only find together ... we must have the full benefit of a single large market' (Monti, 2010, p 2).

In the report, Monti suggests that the SEM has lost its way and is a policy without a strategy, fragmented by different ideologies and cultures in different groups of member states. He recognises that the appetite for integration is not as strong as it was in 1957 or 1987, but confirms that the political objective of Economic and Monetary Union should be progressed. Monti proposed a 'package deal'. This was a more transparent approach than the usual negotiated trade-offs between member states. In considering specific policy areas, Monti focused on those that were contained in the 1985 White Paper annexe (CEC, 1985), with the addition of the digital and green economies. The role of infrastructure is central and is now seen as an investment challenge. The Monti report was incorporated into *Europe 2020* (CEC, 2010a) and used to set the key priorities for the period until 2020.

The EU approach to implementing the Single European Act

The approach within the EU to developing the SEM can be seen through a variety of lenses (Young, 2010). There are those that emphasise the role of supranational actors, particularly in the Commission and the European Court of Justice (ECJ) (Green-Cowles, 1994); while others see this as an intergovernmental initiative proposed and developed by the member states. The SEM can be regarded as a defensive move within a more competitive and globalised world (Sandholtz and Zysman, 1989) and that it was this that brought together governments in creating a single market (Armstrong and Bulmer, 1998). It may also be an example of policy entrepreneurialism by the Commission, which focused on progress to the next stage of European integration using the spillover benefits from the GATS trade round. The Commission was also searching for a means to change the requirements for the method of decision-making inside the EU (Armstrong and Bulmer, 1998), where unanimity between all member states was causing institutional paralysis.

The method of delivery of the SEM was also significant and made use of the methods of punctuated equilibrium in policymaking (Baumgartner and Jones, 2002; John and Margetts, 2003) by harnessing the use of a designated time (Goetz and Mayer-Sahling, 2009) to create an artificial Kuhnian policy switch, although none was specifically needed. The creation of the SEM to function by the end of a particular but arbitrary year – 1992 – gave the opportunity to build a coalition of interests focused on achieving a single market (Cockfield, 1994). Delors was always aware of US governance and economic effectiveness. Delors viewed the economic liberalism of the US to be politically problematic but he was interested in the lack of bureaucracy that enabled businesses to flourish (Grant, 1994). The SEM also introduced other significant changes on the operation of the EU, including the introduction of the use of co-decision with the European Parliament.

On qualifications and the movement of people, the approach to integration was seen as 'negative' rather than positive. The member states had to remove the barriers erected for professionals to practise across the EU based on the qualifications gained in one member state. For the rest of the SEM, the Commission initiated 19 pieces of legislation during 1998–2004, all of which were agreed through the Qualified Majority Voting (QMV) process, that is, none was passed with unanimity (Hayes-Renshaw et al, 2006). The introduction of QMV was a significant aid to faster decision-making, and progress was greater than before. Legislation was passed with the UK being the only vote against. The introduction of QMV and other cooperative measures have been extended over other EU business, and in the Lisbon Treaty 2009, co-decision was named as the 'ordinary legislative procedure' (Jeppesen, 2000; Bache et al, 2011). The use of QMV had other effects. Before this, those seeking to influence decisions could focus on an individual government when unanimity was required. Where QMV was applied, those interests now had to work in policy networks within the Brussels milieu in order to be able to exert a wider influence to express their views (Young, 2010).

The implementation of the SEM is through the transposition of legislation within the member states and although the Commission has responsibility for assessing compliance, it does not have the capacity to do this in practice (Young, 2010). Rather, it relies on certificates of compliance from member states. However, this does not mean that the Commission does not pursue member states when directives are not transposed in an appropriate or timely manner, as cases before the ECJ attest (for examples, see Borzel et al, 2012). By 2003, it was found that the transposition of directives was proceeding at a differential rate in each member state and an implementation deficit target was introduced (Bache et al, 2011). In applying this, it was found that there were persistent offenders, including France, Germany, Greece and Italy, whereas the UK, Denmark, Sweden and Finland were more consistently on target for the transposition of SEM legislation (CEC, 2004).

One of the key elements in introducing the SEM has been the role of the ECJ, which has had to determine disputes through cases brought both by the Commission and the member states. The entrepreneurial role of the Commission in promoting the SEM has suggested an approach of judicial activism (Egan, 2007), and member states have responded to this by taking their own cases to the ECJ. However, in determining local cases on the use of containers for butter and margarine in Belgium and the wheat used in German beer, the ECJ decisions have resulted in fewer powers for the member states and more integrated regulation as a result (Egan, 2007). In the UK, the links between EU policy and the reform of domestic delivery are not made public and there is neither an understanding of the pooled decision-making that underpins these agreements in the SEM, nor their binding nature.

The implementation of the SEM was also aligned with the application of the GATT/GATS agreements on opening up public services and works to competition. This alignment between the introduction of the SEM and public-sector market liberalisation was significant. If these areas were to be open to global competition, then it was important that there was a good opportunity for winning contracts within the EU rather than losing them externally to other countries. Also, the ability to focus on services and the public sector would allow the potential to offer advice and finance for similar ventures within the global market.

However, the role of the SEM in services has been less successful than the opening up of the public sector for services and the supply of goods (Young, 2010), as the selection of suppliers can be associated with cultural and linguistic barriers. In the area of public procurement, despite nine directives being implemented by the end of 1993, it was still likely that contracts would be awarded to domestic suppliers, even where the costs of non-compliance could be more than 34% higher (CEC, 2004; Bache et al, 2011). Some services were omitted from the original provisions of the SEM, although they were included within the GATS/GATT agreements. These were defined as being services of general public interest and included energy, telecommunications, water, health, social care and postal services. These services were generally in public ownership before the implementation of the GATS agreement. However, in the *White Paper on services of general interest* in 2004 (CEC, 2004), joint responsibility between member states and the Commission was proposed. This relied on the fundamental role of these services for the economy, environment, security of supply and social cohesion. The Commission also set out the specific difficulties of these hybrid services, which are needed for the public interest but owned, run and managed by the private sector. Finally, a package of new rules was adopted that identified the ways in which any member state could work with these services and how any aid could be provided (CEC, 2011b).

In considering the role of the SEM in the history of the EU, Armstong and Bulmer (1998) argue that it changed the relationships between the member states, the European Parliament and the Commission. With the move to co-decision and QMV, different relationships and networks were needed. Further, this new governance model created a supranational structure, which is not a state, but is more than an intergovernmental agreement. Despite the UK's position that EU membership was primarily a trade and customs union, it was becoming clear that to survive and prosper within a globalised economy, the need to work together would increase (Rosamund, 2000).

The work of March and Olsen (1984) also suggests that the development of these new working relationships changed not only the institutions, but also their operational cultures. Since the introduction of the SEM, there has been an increase in informal decision-making on economic matters (Puetter, 2012), a switch to framework directives and the Council of Ministers has moved from a concern with legislation to wider policy leadership. Until 1994, directives accounted for 80% of instruments, but since then, the percentage has reduced. A more informal culture may suggest a more intergovernmentalist rather than integrated approach, but it may also be a factor of the growing size of EU membership. This deliberative approach is a means of consensus-building between elites (Puetter, 2012). On the other hand, it may strengthen the hand of the Commission in the way that it frames these discussions (Rhinard, 2010).

Implementation of the Single European Market in the UK

The SEM White Paper (CEC, 1985) set out the barriers to the completion of the SEM. It identified three areas that needed to be tackled in order to achieve completion: physical, technical and fiscal barriers. This was a more conceptual approach than that taken before, when there had been a focus on opening up separate markets in goods, services, people and capital. Setting completion of the SEM within the framework of barriers also enabled the capture of any unforeseen issues. The physical barriers included those controls of the movement of goods and individuals or the free movement of people at borders, including asylum seekers, refugees and visa controls. In the UK, the delivery of the open border legislation was the most difficult. A number of member states signed the Schengen Agreement in 1985. This gave free movement of people within the EU and, by 2004, the UK and Ireland were the only countries with derogations. Since 2011 and the Arab Spring, Schengen is now being reviewed and its operational procedures are likely to be tightened, particularly in the ways in which the rules are interpreted in each member state. However, despite the requirement for a passport or driving licence to enter the UK, there remains a right of entry for EU citizens and this is reflected in the way in which borders are managed.

The technical barriers also included the opening up the process of public procurement, which was part of the GATS agreement. This was significant in the UK and a major determinant in shaping public policy, institutions and markets. The introduction of open public procurement extended the open market to energy, telecommunications, electricity and water by 1992. In the UK, telecommunications were the first privatised service in this group in 1984. Opening the market for electricity supply occurred through the Electricity Act 1989 and the process of breaking up the Central Electricity Generating Board followed in 1990. Gas was privatised from 1986 and water privatisation was introduced in 1989. In Table 6.1, the process of exposing publicly owned companies to competition is shown for the period between 1981 and 1996, covering all the services as set out in the EU White Paper (CEC, 1985).

Table 6.1: UK public offerings of shares

1981	British Aerospace (52%)
	Cable and Wireless (49%)
1982	Amersham International (100%)
	Britoil (51%)
1983	Associated British Ports (52%)
	British Petroleum (7%) (shares also sold in 1977 and 1979)
	Cable and Wireless (22%)
1984	Associated British Ports (48%)
	British Telecom (50.2%)
	Enterprise Oil (100%)
	Jaguar (99%)
1985	British Aerospace (59%)
	Britoil (48%)
	Cable and Wireless (31%)
1986	British Gas (97%)
1987	British Airports Authority (100%)
	British Airways (100%)
	British Petroleum (36.8%)
	Rolls Royce (100%)
1988	British Steel
1989	Water plcs
1990	Electricity distribution plcs
1991	National Power/Powergen (60%)
	Scottish Power/Hydro-electric
1992	British Telecom
1993	Northern Ireland Electricity
1996	Railtrack

Sources: Pre-1987 data from Hyman (1989); post-1987 data from HM Treasury (HMT, 1995).

The next group of technical barriers related to the free movement of labour and the professions, including higher education. The transferability of courses and qualifications led to the modularisation of UK degree programmes to facilitate this and extended to entry qualification. The technical barriers were also proposed to be overcome through the exchange of students for part of their course. The Erasmus programme for exchanges of students and teaching staff between European universities began in 1987.

Although initially about the transferability of professional qualifications between member states for doctors or architects, the free movement of labour has had significant effects on the UK, particularly since enlargement. However, not all migrants to the UK are from the newest EU member states. In 2012, prior to the French national elections, there were 102,470 registered French voters in the UK, which was also part of the new Northern Europe constituency introduced in France in 2010. Further, as there were over 300,000 French citizens living in London in 2012, this made it the sixth largest French city. In London, citizens of each of the member states have created local enclaves with shops and services that suit their national tastes (GLA, 2011).

Further technical barriers were identified in the EU White Paper (CEC, 1985) grouped under the single market for services. The first was financial services (banks, insurance and securities) and capital movement and a second set related to the legal environment for companies, including company law, intellectual property and taxation provisions. The third set related to transport and new technologies, including cabling. The issues concerning services and company operation continue to be a major issue for the UK press and the Conservative Party and were at the heart of the threats to the Prime Minister's position by Conservative backbench MPs that surrounded the exercise of the UK veto in December 2011. The development of transport and other infrastructure was a policy area that was already part of the EU programme, but including it as part of the SEM raised its status, and this will be discussed further later in this chapter.

The last part of the Action Programme related to the removal of fiscal barriers to complete the SEM. Taxation issues caused considerable friction between Cockfield and Thatcher, the latter because she had not appreciated that the Treaty of Rome included harmonisation of Value Added Tax (VAT) (Cockfield, 1994). Any taxation can be used as a means to promote competitive advantage and this was seen to be a key issue in implementation. The gradual abolition of excise duties between member states completed the customs union and the SEM.

In developing the policy that introduced the SEM, Cockfield discovered the extent to which knowledge of the EU, its legislation and the agreements that the UK had made on joining were poorly understood by the political establishment in Britain. In considering the response of UK politicians to the SEM proposals, he states that:

> it reflects so clearly what since has regrettably been my diagnosis of politicians in our own country to the Community: they recall little of its history, know nothing of its philosophy; and even more striking is the virtually complete absence of hard factual knowledge. Perhaps the most trenchant criticism of all is that they were and remain unaware of these deficiencies. (Cockfield, 1994, p 38)

Buller (2000) suggests that the SEA was both the zenith of the UK's influence in the 1980s and the origin of its decline. It was seen as a triumph for Mrs Thatcher, but her subsequent realisation of the extent of the SEA's influence, based on her inadequate knowledge of the detail of both what was included in the UK's agreements on membership and their implications for the working within a single system, caused difficulties (Cockfield, 1994). Her subsequent obduracy in fulfilling the UK's obligations in the SEM led to her downfall (Allen, 2005).

As her successor, Major also had political difficulty with the detail of the delivery of the SEM, particularly on the social agenda, which included employment law (Taylor, 1994). This included the transposition of the Acquired Rights Directive in 1993, which was an important element of the competition agenda. This 1977 directive transferred the employment rights of employees when a public service was privatised. To the government, this undermined the potential for efficiencies and the attractiveness of the public sector to the private sector. This practice of ignoring the requirements of employment directives continued into other areas, including working time and protection for young workers. This set of issues was inherited by Major and while the policies had been set out in the White Paper (CEC, 1985), both politicians and officials seemed to regard these as a 'pick and mix' set of options rather than binding agreements.

During the UK Presidency in 1992, Major was more engaged and influential in developing other aspects of the SEM and used this to lead the shaping of the EU as it appears today. This included the creation of mechanisms for enlargement, which meant the reformulation of the structural funds programme that Britain had helped to introduce at the time of its own membership. It also further developed the implementation of the principle of subsidiarity, which has had an important role in reshaping the British constitution subsequently (Paterson, 1994; see also Chapter Eight).

As part of this process, Major also supported the development of the Trans-European Networks (TENs) as an essential feature of the SEM to improve internal competitiveness. The TENs included transport, energy and telecommunications and have been formative in EU and UK policy since. Transport and energy policy are both fully pooled within the EU and included within GATS agreements. They are particularly related to both competition policy and principles for territorial cohesion in the Lisbon Treaty 2009. Energy and transport are also hybrid, as they are privatised within the UK, but defined as services of general public interest in the EU. As a response to this, the UK has developed a regulatory framework to bridge these arrangements. The role of TEN-T for transport in the UK has also been significant in creating investment priorities through the agreed routes and other key transport hubs, which have had implications for localities.

The summit at the end of the UK Presidency in Edinburgh in 1992, chaired by Major, promoted a raft of changes that are still used as a basis for decision-making. The first was the expansion of the EU into the former European Free Trade Area countries and then further extension to newly independent Eastern European states. This moved towards the goals of the Treaty of Rome but was also beneficial in the opening up of a new educated market for consumer goods and offering a skilled labour force on lower wage rates, potentially making the EU more competitive. On the other hand, there were also concerns about infrastructure costs and support to agriculture and industry in the candidate states. Where member states were in receipt of structural funds to support lagging economies, such as Spain, Italy, Portugal and Ireland, enlargement would change their relative positions, including the UK in relation to Scotland, Wales and Northern Ireland.

The Major proposals guaranteed existing recipients of structural funds one last 'good' four-year settlement. Major also introduced the European Investment Fund for infrastructure, created by the European Investment Bank, which could finance the missing links in transport, energy and telecommunications. This was seen to be an important new financial instrument. It was the first in this area and leveraged private-sector investment (Banister et al, 2000). TEN-T projects were also identified, including three projects in the UK. The first was for high-speed train links for London–Paris–Brussels–Amsterdam–Cologne via the Channel Tunnel, which was commenced in 1988 and opened in 1994. The Amsterdam service commenced in 2012 and the Cologne service is expected by 2014. The second project was the implementation of high-speed rail on the West Coast Main Line railway. This was completed in 2008 and now complies with the EU's definition of high-speed rail. The third project was the improvement of the road corridor between Northern Ireland and the Benelux countries and has been fulfilled by the upgrading of the A14. All three TEN-T projects for the UK included in this first programme have been implemented.

Since 1992, the implementation of the SEM has been through legislation within specific sectors, including financial services, which have become an increasingly important feature of the structure of the UK economy since the Big Bang in 1988. The UK's increasing dependency on financial services may have led to economic patriotism, where there is overt compliance with the legal framework provided by the EU but the promotion of the distinctiveness of the national culture and receptiveness can create non-tariff benefits (Clift and Woll, 2012; Morgan, 2011). The EU White Paper (CEC, 2005) set out how the SEM would operate for financial services, including methods of supervisory control. These changes were proposed before the economic crisis but have been strengthened since and supported by a 'road map' for implementation through the SEM (CEC, 2009a). The measure to change the financial supervisory arrangements across the EU reached political agreement in 2010 (CEC, 2010e) and is now being implemented.

In the UK, this has led to the implementation of major changes to the Financial Services Authority (FSA) and the Bank of England. The FSA was formed from the former Securities and Investment Board in 1997 and its role was further developed through the Financial Services and Markets Act 2000. After the general election in 2010, it was announced that the FSA would be abolished and replaced by the Financial Conduct Authority and the Prudential Regulatory Authority. It is also proposed that the Bank of England be managed by a supervisory board and the Monetary Policy Committee be replaced by a Financial Policy Committee. All these changes are set out in the Financial Services Bill 2011 (Edmonds, 2012) and form part of a new macro-prudential policy.

The UK government has also commenced the implementation of other measures set out in the SEM review. A 'procurement pledge' that opens up all government purchasing from 2012 (BIS, 2012) has been made. Specific proposals on the reform of infrastructure financing have been a key focus in Pre-Budget Reports in 2010 and 2011, including: the introduction of National Infrastructure Plans (NIPs) 1 and 2 (HMT, 2010, 2011); the introduction of National Infrastructure Planning Policies; the establishment of Infrastructure UK by the Treasury; the creation of an infrastructure pipeline (HMT, 2012); and the tabling of a Growth and Infrastructure Bill 2012. As is clear from the jointly agreed statement between the Commission and the UK government, infrastructure provision has been identified as one of the UK's key weaknesses in achieving the Europe 2020 targets (CEC, 2012d).

The UK government still promotes EU-generated legislation as domestic policy. Another example from Monti is the development of cross-border infrastructure projects, such as that proposed for energy pipelines from Iceland as part of a European energy supergrid (Carrington, 2012). This follows a 'soft policy' initiative of a memorandum of understanding through which the North Sea Countries Offshore Grid Initiative (CEC, 2010b) was established. This has been mentioned in prime ministerial speeches (Cameron, 2011), but not that the North Sea Grid forms part of a Europe-wide supergrid proposed in the Monti report (CEC, 2011e).

A further example of where the UK is implementing a SEM review proposal is the agreement to introduce smart metering across member states, which is described as the UK government's vision on the Department of Energy and Climate Change website (DECC, 2012). Another example is the proposal to complete the implementation of the Services Directive, which was agreed in 2006 (CEC, 2006a) and had to be transposed by 2009. The Services Directive clearly aligned the achievement of the completion of the SEM with the economic agenda of competitiveness through establishing the potential for pan-EU providers, and was always regarded as a more politicised agenda (Loder, 2011). This is particularly pertinent in the UK as the directive includes the opening of the market for health care services to competition and also covers rights of access to social care under article 23 (Dilnott, 2011). The Services Directive specifically excludes public health. This demonstrates the context for UK health service reforms set out in the Health and Social Care Act 2012 and the transfer of public health responsibilities to local government from 2013.

What has been clear in both the initial transposition of the SEA and this more recent Services Directive into UK policy and law is that they are examples where a European link is made but there is no specific reference made to the EU's role. These are pooled sovereignty areas and a more open consideration of the issues and policy intent might be expected. As Cockfield (1994, p 141) reflected on the UK's reception of the SEM: 'the information given to Parliament on European affairs was at best incomplete and at times exiguous to the point of being thought misleading'. One issue that emerges from this approach to transposing policy and legislation into the UK is its lack of integration. The implementation of the Monti review is seen as an integrated process, but the roll-out in the UK is not only submerged, but also fragmented. Given that the SEM is one of the key EU areas that politicians and the press regard as being in the UK's interests, this approach remains strangely occluded.

Influence of the Single European Market in the UK: the case of transport policy

The EU's policy on transport has been focused on competition, cohesion and sustainability (Duhr et al, 2010). Transport has been part of the EU's common agenda since the Treaty of Rome and the first outline of a Common Transport Policy was published in 1958. This was developed from the SEM and then through the integrated environmental agenda (see Chapter Seven) to the publication of *Sustainable mobility* (CEC, 1992), which focused on opening up the transport market. The TENs were introduced through the Treaty on European Union in 1993. This was followed by a further White Paper published in 2001, which was focused on developing more sustainable transport as part of the EU's integrated environmental policy. This integration was particularly for rail and short sea routes for freight and air transport. A review of the implementation of this White Paper was conducted in 2006 (CEC, 2006c) and set out proposals that draw transport into territorial cohesion policies through multi-level governance 'contracts'. The joint approaches to transport as both a key element of the SEM and as a means of promoting territorial cohesion has continued though the Monti report (Monti, 2010) and the review of TEN-T (CEC, 2010c). In this, the integration of and linkages between the EU transport spines and local transport systems have been emphasised.

Up to 1992, major transport projects had been funded through EU regional policy, which focused on lagging regions. Infrastructure investment was regarded as a rebalancing policy rather than a mainstream economic investment tool. The implementation of the SEM had always been on the premise that it would be 'blind' to lagging regions and economies and, in 1988, it was agreed that structural funds would be used to manage these issues (Cockfield, 1994). However, shortly after this, the potential for enlargement emerged following the fall of the Berlin Wall. Thus, a difficult deal on structural funds had to be renegotiated. A tapered approach to phase out the selective approach to structural funds and replace this with policy that covered all territories through the principle of territorial cohesion was proposed by Major in 1992.

Until this point, much of the transport expenditure had been spent in connecting the four countries with the highest priority for cohesion funds – Spain, Portugal, Greece and Ireland – to the heart of the EU. Enlargement brought in new member states with poorer infrastructures and a greater economic need. A TEN that would support the intra-EU economy and define the key access routes across the EU's territory was proposed (Balchin et al, 1999). This also enabled Delors's notion that, like the US, the EU would benefit from a single and integrated network of communications and utilities. It also helped to overcome disagreements between the UK's free market and the state-led model in France and Germany (Duhr et al, 2010).

The TENs were introduced through the White Paper on *Growth, competitiveness and employment* (Delors, 1994), which set out the way forward for the EU following the implementation of the SEM and included several dimensions that had formative roles. First, TENs created key corridors along which transport (TEN-T) and other utilities would be focused and improved. Second, the role of public transport was increased, rather than investment policies being based solely on roads. This had been a major issue in countries receiving structural funds and although a consideration for accession states, a priority for roads would not meet the EU's integrated environmental policy so that access to employment and local distribution were sustainable and efficient. Third, public transport services have been opened to the private sector.

The EU continues to set its transport policy in the language of completing the SEM and the need to ensure that both the west and east of Europe have comparable transport systems (CEC, 2011e). A more coherent approach to transport planning between and within states with a key focus on the improved efficiency of existing infrastructure is being proposed. The EU is moving towards the creation of a single European transport area with common technologies and pricing structures. A key focus is also on changing behaviour and all cities are to have urban mobility plans, urban mobility audits and a scoreboard that will link this to regional development and cohesion funds. It is possible to see the links between this and policies for city regions (see Chapter Eight). Following Major's lead in 1992, the UK's role in delivering transport policy continued through the appointment of a UK Commissioner for transport, Neil Kinnock, in 1995.

How has the EU shaped the UK's transport policies?

The EU's influence on the shape of UK transport policy has occurred in several ways, including defining strategic routes for investment, the switch to public transport and sustainability in urban areas, and the application of open procurement methods to the transport industry, which are discussed later. These influences have also had unintended consequences for those areas that have not been priorities for investment, including some east–west routes. It should also be noted that the majority of EU states regard transport as part of public policy whereas governments in the UK have regarded it as a market-based service (Stevens, 2004; Monti, 2010).

1. Routes and corridors – the strategic approach

The SEM's objective for a single infrastructure within the EU has identified and reinforced specific movement corridors, which have attracted funding and development (Duhr et al, 2010), and has been reinforced through the creation of a pan-European rail network (Villiers, 2012). These routes have been privileged over others and have reinforced not only rail networks, but also coach travel and other transport connections to these spines. Within the UK, the designation of the TEN-T routes has not been one where there has been much discussion of the options and alternatives. There was an acceptance of the routes adopted in 1993 and subsequently implemented. Before this and in anticipation, the *Roads for prosperity* White Paper (DfT, 1989) took up the more politically aligned elements of SEM transport policy and translated it to the UK through a major road-building programme (Glaister et al, 2006), and both EU and UK resources can be used in their improvement. However, for parts of the country that are not on TEN-T routes, the lack of investment has been significant. Places that have suffered through not being identified have been the centre of the country, such as Nottingham, Derby and Sheffield, and the east–west lines, such as those between the west of England and Cardiff, Edinburgh and Glasgow, Manchester to Leeds, and Newcastle to Carlisle.

The EU has developed rail policy through directives that have focused on the role and interoperability of the networks across the whole of the EU. The high-speed network (HS) was developed from 1990 onwards and the directive on interoperability for the HS network came into effect in 2002. One of the key influences on the structure of the UK railway was the directive which indicated that separate accounts should be kept for the track and the rail services, but this did not imply that they should be broken up into different organisations (Butcher, 2012). However, the Conservative government decided to implement this separation through the creation of Railtrack in 1994 and operating companies through its competition processes. No other EU member state took this approach. Following the Hatfield rail disaster in 2000, Railtrack was taken over by Network Rail, a hybrid company that is not for profit and has the structure of a trust or charity in that any profits have to be invested back into railway infrastructure. Individual rail routes are operated as tendered franchises by train-operating companies.

The SEM review in 2006 included transport policy and, in preparation, the UK government commissioned a review of transport and the economy by Eddington (2006). This was focused primarily on the way in which UK business was connected and competitive in its access to transport in comparison with other European countries. The review did not refer to the EU's role in transport policy or transport's role in the SEM. The Eddington review focused on the economic consequences of a lack of transport investment and suggested a more centralist approach to national infrastructure projects. This was both for their passage through the planning system and their funding. The Eddington review did not propose any specific projects for investment.

The government responded to the Eddington review by establishing the Infrastructure Planning Commission in the Planning Act 2008. This Commission was to operate independently, as Eddington suggested, receiving its policy advice from Parliament, making decisions within a year and being independent of ministers. This independence was to be short-lived and, in 2012, it was combined with the Planning Inspectorate and brought within the ambit of the Department of Communities and Local Government, although National Planning Policy for infrastructure is still made by Parliament. However, unlike the system before 2008, planning policy for different types of infrastructure is proposed and owned by different government departments. This ensures project ownership but may lead to competition for resources and fragmentation in delivery.

In 2011, EU transport policy was reviewed (CEC, 2011e) as part of the Monti process, which has recommended an EU core transport network by 2030. The funding for core routes will be partly from a special fund created by the European Investment Bank of 31.7 billion euros until 2020, out of an estimated cost of 250 billion euros for the whole investment. This fund can contribute 20% of the costs and up to 50% for the studies. Where routes cross borders, the contribution can increase to 40% of the cost. Member states and the private sector are also expected to contribute. Unlike the previous approach, the

TEN-T network for 2030 is accompanied by feeder routes so that this strategic policy relates to the principle of territorial cohesion. In terms of the additional projects in the new programme, the UK has an interest in 27 sub-projects and these are shown in Table 6.2. More priority has been given to the Motorways of the Sea, which includes improvements for the intermodal corridors between the UK and Spain and improvements at Tilbury. In addition to the project linking Ireland and the UK to the Benelux countries, a further project that considers the UK's and Ireland's links to mainland Europe has been added. In this programme, there are more information technology (IT) and system-based projects for the whole of Europe, including for railways, airspace and roads.

The UK government published the *National Infrastructure Plan* (HMT, 2010) as a mechanism for drawing this approach together. It was focused on infrastructure types such as broadband, but the only reference to EU policy and legislation was environmental law, despite broadband being a key feature of the Monti proposals for the next stage of the SEM. In the indicative map of the UK's committed proposals, none of the TEN-T projects appear to be included. The main focus was on investment processes. In the *National Infrastructure Plan 2* (HMT, 2011), the key issue discussed was on the UK's performance in different infrastructure sectors relative to other countries in the EU and a focus on funding infrastructure, which, again, is a main feature of the Monti review. In addition to the influence on the mode and location of transport projects, there has also been a role for the European Investment Bank in supporting UK transport infrastructure (www.eib.org). Over time, the UK's approach has become more programmatic, with longer-term horizons and more major projects being adopted that extend beyond usual electoral timescales, seeking cross-party political support and operating in a depoliticised environment where possible.

2. Sustainable mobility – local transport systems

The development of the TEN-T programme has been criticised for its failure to interconnect with local transport systems based around functional economic areas (FEAs) and cities. The economic role of transport within FEAs and their links to national and international spine routes is now seen to be significant, as well as their internal connectivity (Clayton et al, 2011). The transport policies for sub-state spaces have also been seen as part of the integrated approach to environment policy and where most impact might be achieved in reducing spillovers, such as air quality effects and emissions. These links are made explicit in the

2011 EU White Paper on transport (CEC, 2011d), which embraces the twin objectives of competition and efficiency.

Table 6.2: UK TEN-T projects to 2020

No	EU project
1	Rail interoperability
2	NW Scotland freight management corridor
3	Intermodal corridor for rail and sea freight, Tilbury to Bilbao
4	Motorways of the Sea
5	Motorways of the Sea – training and university collaboration
6	North Sea onshore power network – DFDS (Hull)
7	Road/rail freight improvements between Ireland, the UK and the Benelux countries; improvements of freight rail links at Cambridge and Nuneaton
8	Port Salford – canal/road/rail global interchange as part of mainland improvements between Ireland, the UK and Europe– four studies
9	Improvements to the port of Felixstowe as part of mainland improvements between Ireland, the UK and Europe and Ireland, improvements between the UK and the Benelux countries
10	Review of functional airspace across the UK and Ireland
11	Improve A8 road in Northern Ireland as part of improvements between Ireland, the UK and the Benelux countries
12	Improve A6 corridor in Northern Ireland
13	Improve links between Felixstowe and the West Midlands for freight by rail and road, including the A14 corridor for mainland improvements between Ireland, the UK and Europe
14	Improve congestion on A14 through better management of improvements between Ireland, the UK and the Benelux countries
15	Dredging for deep water container terminal and logistics centre Thurrock in Thames Gateway
16	Harmonising rail freight corridors
17	Easyway travel for freight and individuals using IT
18	Aircraft datalink systems
19	Improving the rail link between Derry and Ballymena
20	Improving the implementation of large infrastructure projects and develop an infrastructure project assessment tool
21	Manchester airport third rail platform
22	Improvements to A14, M6 and A1 roads to reduce bottlenecks as part of improvements between Ireland, the UK and the Benelux countries
23	European Rail Traffic Management System
24	Easyway travel information exchange for freight and individuals using IT
25	Single European Sky
26	Trans European Satellite navigation system
27	European rail traffic management system

Source: CEC TEN-T Executive Agency (2011) (http://tentea.ec.europa.eu/en/ten-t_projects/ten-t_ projects_by_country/united_kingdom.htm).

1989 introduced a paradigm shift for local transport policy thinking in the UK, when the government moved from a 'predict and provide' model to one that was more sustainable and integrated, focusing on demand management (Goodwin, 1999; Vigar, 2001). A differential approach emerged to the management of strategic routes by government agencies and urban transport, which is provided by a multiplicity of public and private agencies and organisations. This fragmentation had been exacerbated through the marketisation of bus services and train operations and the pro-Thatcherite policies for car ownership and use (Goodwin, 1999).

The transport White Paper *Sustainable mobility* (CEC, 1992) set the context and direction for successive transport policy developments at the local level. The UK government shifted as transport and environmental policy started to have an increasingly important role in the delivery of the SEM and wider EU integration objectives (Steer, 1995; Banister et al, 2000) and *This Common Inheritance* (DoE, 1990) was published. This were followed by fiscal measures such as increasing petrol fuel duty (Glaister et al, 2006), which were part of the *Fifth environmental action programme* (CEC, 1993) to improve sustainability (Morphet, 1993). It also included legislative measures that would affect local transport, including air quality and proposed fiscal measures such as road user charging. When congestion charging was introduced in London in 2003, the link was made between with air quality outcomes but not linked to any EU-agreed objectives. Similarly, the consultation on the proposed introduction of charging for heavy goods vehicles is couched in the language of competition and the case for charging is made on the basis that the UK is now one of the few European countries not to have a charging system. It then discusses its implementation within the EU legal framework rather than mentioning that it is an agreed EU policy (DfT, 2012b).

The election of the Labour government in 1997 brought a more integrated approach to transport policy through planning, operations and networks. This combined local, strategic, economic and environmental objectives (DETR, 1998) through the bundling of transport, environment and local government functions in one government department, reflected the integrated approach. It also developed more experimental approaches to integration in cities through the transfer of transport powers to the Mayor of London from 2000. This approach has subsequently been used as a model for other conurbations in England (DfT, 2012a; HMG, 2012). However, it has also been criticised as a 'cocktail' of initiatives without any overarching narrative on the provenance of this mix of policies, for example, in the 1998 White Paper (Mackie, 1998, p 401).

The scale of these changes in the introduction of sustainable transport policies and the political context of the UK needs to be considered. Thatcherism ideologically espoused neoliberal individualism, which was epitomised by car ownership and use. The siege of petrol delivery drivers in 1999 under Blair, and threats to take similar action under Cameron in 2012, were major issues for the electorate and business. The cultural link between place of work, residence and public transport was broken in the 1980s and the readjustment to more sustainable modes has been related to higher petrol prices and the rise of two-partner working families, which have greater benefits from shorter and more accessible journey distances (Graham, 2000).

The EU Green Paper *Towards a new culture for urban mobility* (CEC, 2007) and its associated programme (CEC, 2009c) has continued to shape UK transport policy, with its focus on intra-urban transport integration. This approach informed the *Sub-national review of economic development and regeneration* for England (HMT, 2007) and has shifted subsequent policy to focus on cities and FEAs (DfT, 2012a). The development of transport policy based on more efficient use of space, demand management (including the use of road pricing) and more efficient vehicles are all now part of the approach, and were included in the EU's next transport White Paper *Roadmap to a single European transport area* (CEC, 2011e). Particular attention is paid to the distribution of land uses. In urban areas, mobility audits and plans are proposed to be set within a European scoreboard so that urban areas can be compared.

It is possible to see the development of the application of EU transport policy in the UK, although, since 1999, delivery varies in each nation as transport is a devolved policy area. England (HMG, 2011b), Wales (Welsh Assembly Government, 2012) and Scotland (Scottish Government, 2012) have all published new approaches to city policy and in Northern Ireland this has been included within the revised Regional Plan (DRD, 2012). In England, this approach has been further devolved to Local Enterprise Partnerships from 2014 (DfT, 2012a) and has been associated with the promotion of more strategic local planning processes set out in the National Planning Policy Framework (DCLG, 2012). In practical terms, this will devolve the process and powers for determining which transport projects are most likely to be useful in meeting local objectives and the funding to deliver them.

In England, the exemplar FEA is Manchester, where multi-local authority and agency working is at its most developed. Here, the *Greater*

Manchester growth plan (MEAP, 2012) has identified the role of transport as a key factor in the FEA's economy and one of the four pillars for success. There is a particular link between intra- and inter-urban transport modes, including further connections to Manchester airport. As noted earlier, the Manchester airport railway station improvement is one of the UK's TEN-T projects to 2020. As part of the *Greater Manchester growth plan*, an infrastructure plan is being prepared that will both identify where policy and project implementation is required and how this will be funded.

In Scotland, the cities policy has been set out jointly by the Scottish government and the five cities in the new Scottish Cities Alliance. This is also focused on the links between infrastructure investment and economic growth. Earlier measures in the Planning (Scotland) Act 2006 mean that these cities have already begun their wider strategic planning processes (Tayplan, 2012). In Scotland, the impact of this transport policy will be specifically benchmarked. In Wales, the development of the policy includes the clear relationship between cities and the economy; in Northern Ireland, the new regional plan sets the transport policies for the urban areas of Belfast and Derry explicitly (DRD, 2012).

These four policy statements on transport in urban areas within the UK, prepared and issued by each of the nations, were published within a narrow time frame of three months and, apart from England, three were in the same month, that is, March 2012. Post-devolution, such a common approach would seem to be unlikely and although there could be some discussion about potential policy networking between governments, the focus, timing and approach of each of the four initiatives suggest a response to the Monti report (Monti, 2010) and transport policy White Paper (CEC, 2011e).

The Centre for Cities, a think tank set up to promote policy in this area and headed by a former senior civil servant, nudges policy in the direction set by the EU context and requirements, but the links are not overt. It is also responsible for a UK cities benchmarking project that will support the benchmarking processes required as part of the EU's cities policies (Centre for Cities, 2012) and is promoting further intra-city transport organisation and delivery (Clayton et al, 2011). Similarly, the Institute for Public Policy Research (IPPR), another think tank, is particularly focusing on cities policy and delivery in Northern England through the promotion of transport and infrastructure as the third pillar of their approach to economic growth (IPPR, 2012).

3. Privatisation, competition and delivery

The British approach to the liberalisation of the transport system has been one that has been used elsewhere in the EU and is generally seen as the prevailing mode of operation and delivery (Glaister et al, 2006; Duhr et al, 2010). The exception has been for rail services, where the separation between the owners of the track and the train-operating companies is unique to the UK. The role of the GATS and the subsequent WTO General Procurement Agreement has shaped the processes, while the identification of transport as a service of general public interest (CEC, 2004) has meant that any privatisation is within a regulated market.

The introduction of open procurement in transport has operated differently in each mode in the UK. In air transport, although BOAC and BEA were state-owned airlines in the UK, there have also always been private operators and similarly with airports. In other sectors, such as rail, the nationalisation of the system in 1947 meant that competition would be more challenging in the UK. For bus operations, there was a mixed economy, with larger cities running their own passenger transport services but privatised services elsewhere.

The introduction of open procurement through deregulation in the UK commenced in 1980 with coach travel, and then freight (1982), buses (1984), airlines (1984), airports (1985), docks (1989) and ports (1991) followed. The reform of air traffic control (1996) has been associated with later policies on integration of the service across the EU as part of the TEN-T programme to 2030. At the local level, bus provision was opened from 1988, while London Underground was made a separate entity in 1985. Both these show interesting features of the implementation of privatised transport services. Transport for London bus services are run by different companies but all buses and staff are required to have a common livery, pricing structure and interoperability. This is unlike the application of similar processes in other cities, such as Manchester, where bus services are identified by their service provider livery and do not have interoperable tickets or pricing structures. In London, the point of competition is at the service level, whereas in other cities, it is at the bus stop.

As part of the approach to achieving the EU's urban transport policies, services are becoming more integrated and this will change some of the competition models (DfT, 2012a). Hitherto, there have been some negative policy consequences for services that have arisen from the competition modes that have been applied to different transport sectors. Separate approaches have made integration difficult without mechanisms to incentivise interoperable service arrangements. Neither the government nor the railway companies have been focused on the most popular routes and how to improve their capacity (see, eg, Leunig, 2012). Transport has also been a sector where there has been considerable government restructuring following the introduction of competition. Although there has been regulator activity in the energy and telecommunications markets, they have not been restructured by the regulator, but, rather, by the market, where mergers and acquisitions have concentrated providers. In transport, the services have been restructured as they have failed to cope with major accidents, changing public policy, increased labour participation rates, sustainable urban policies and externalised environmental costs.

Conclusions

The development of the SEM has had a considerable shaping effect on UK public policy. Although the initial impulse to develop and implement the SEM came from the UK, its development and application has been less welcome in practice. The role of the SEM in generating more integrated approaches to environment policy and the first wave of subsidiarity has had considerable effects for the UK. Following Thatcher's first enthusiasm, the SEM was then taken forward by her successor, John Major, who promoted further integration through transport and territorial initiatives as well as through a second round of subsidiarity. The implementation of the EU's external trade agreements have partly been delivered through the SEM, through the regulation of the private sector, including employment rights. Although the UK initially refused to sign the Social Chapter, this was reversed in 1997. In some sectors, such as financial services, the SEM has been developed in the wake of innovation in the market and, despite objections from the UK, seems likely to continue. The SEM is the foundation of the EU and it continues to develop with it.

The UK's routes, urban transport systems and transport operators have all been shaped by the UK's pooling of policy within the EU and transport's central role within the SEM. However, as transport is now a devolved policy area in the UK, delivery may vary between the UK's nations and FEAs at sub-state level. The absence of a national strategy or plan for the UK and England requires new ways of developing an integrated delivery programme at the national level, which may be assisted by EU compliance deadlines and frameworks. Transport policy is significant in EU terms, not least as it is the key method of efficient distribution within and between markets. As a policy area, it is a fundamental support in the SEM and may gain in importance as global competition increases.

While the SEM is a key element in the delivery of public services, there has been a failure in the UK to integrate the range of EU policy and legislative programmes into common narratives and organisational arrangements. This can be exemplified through the delivery of transport policy. While the SEM is now focusing on integrated urban transport systems as a key driver to support economic growth, in the UK, the dispersal of these policy leads stretch across at least six government departments – the Treasury, and the Departments for Transport, Communities and Local Government, Business, Industry and Skills, Environment, Food and rural affairs and Energy and Climate Change. This suggests that coordination and delivery will be difficult in practice. The lead role on cities was placed with the Deputy Prime Minister in the Cabinet Office, with support from a minister in the DCLG in 2011. The 2012 cabinet reshuffle moved the DCLG minister to the Treasury while he retained his responsibility for cities, creating a policy duality in the core executive. All the other government departments also retained their roles. The solution proposed to this continued fragmentation in central government is to pass the responsibility for coordination of transport services to the cities and other FEAs in England through the creation of Local Transport Bodies (DfT, 2012b). The delivery of this aspect of the SEM may now have passed into an implementation mode, which is of less interest to the UK core executive than negotiating the fundamentals of policy.

Environment and sustainability

Introduction

The role of the EU in environmental policy is critical to its powers and identity. Environmental effects are not contained within administrative borders. Regulatory standards can impose costs on business and their absence can transfer costs to communities and taxpayers. It is a policy arena where the stimulus for joint action has come from external agreements similar to trade (see Chapter Five). The environment has been used in conjunction with internal policy objectives to promote the single market (see Chapter Seven), as a mechanism to further develop the role of the EU (see Chapter Four) and to implement the principle of subsidiarity (see Chapter Eight). In the EU, the environment was the first policy area to develop and operate an integrative approach across all sectors and it was also early in the use multi-annual action programmes to set out legislative intentions. All of these issues have had an impact on British public policy, and, in some cases, the EU's environment policy has had wider effects on other areas.

Environmental policy has been important in providing experience for the UK on the way in which the EU operates. This includes the consequences of underestimating the likely scale of outcomes (Knill and Liefferink, 2007) through an episodic and narrow focus on negotiation (O'Riordan and Rowbotham, 1996). Environment policy has also been important at the local level in the UK (Morphet, 1998). Prior to the EU taking forward the environment as a leading policy in 1987, it was considered to be local and operational in the UK, delivered through discretionary procedures by local authorities and government inspectorates (Haigh, 1996; Jordan, 2008). The environment was not regarded as a critical policy area by the government or civil service or one that needed central leadership or attention (O'Riordan and Rowbotham, 1996; Jordan, 2001; Bulmer and Burch, 2009). Since the 1980s, environment policy has moved from this position to an issue at the heart of trade, economic, foreign and international policies as well as a key electoral issue in some parts of the UK. The UK's environmental policies are now derived from pooling its sovereignty on these issues within the EU (Miller, 2010). The development of the international role of environmental policy for the EU, negotiated by the Commission, has been critical to achieving the objectives in the Treaty of Rome 1957. It has also been used as a mechanism to widen the EU's role from trade into other substantive policy areas.

The agreement to pool member states' responsibilities for environmental regulation was included in the Treaty of Rome 1957, with the first actions taken by the EU in 1959 (McCormick, 2001). As part of the Danish entry negotiations in 1972, this role was extended. Before this, the Nordic Council, comprising Denmark, Finland, Iceland, Norway and Sweden, had already developed a common position on environmental standards that were higher than those in other parts of the world (Jordan et al, 2003). The Stockholm Conference on the Human Environment in 1972 was a direct antecedent of the UN Brundtland Commission's report *Our common future* (Brundtland, 1987), which supported the UN Earth Summit in Rio in 1992. The development of the first European Environmental Action Programme (EAP) was influenced primarily by policy communities leading up to the Stockholm Conference (Meyer, 2011).

In negotiating membership of the EU, Scandinavian countries were concerned that they would be required to lower their environmental standards. There were mixed motives and interests in this. Denmark had few natural energy resources and wanted to ensure resource-efficient technologies were supported as part of defending their economic security against fluctuating oil prices. In comparison, Norway, rich in gas and oil, was concerned about the loss of control over these resources and eventually voted not to join the EU, although it became part of the European Economic Area (EEA). (The EEA takes all the EU's legislation but does not participate in its formulation.) Sweden and Finland joined the EU in 1995, while Iceland, a member of the EEA, is a candidate for EU membership.

The pressure to introduce environmental issues into the trade agenda of the EU also came after the Stockholm Conference. Up to this point, few environmental actions had been taken (Leontitsis, 2011), although member states increased its own regulations. This change was also stimulated by the US National Environmental Policy Act 1969 and the establishment of the US Environment Protection Agency in 1970. The EU was concerned about this emerging action as increased environmental standards could make it difficult for European exporters and could potentially be used as non-tariff barriers to trade (Knill and Liefferink, 2007; Swann, 2010). This competitive pressure from the US led to an import of policy ideas into the EU on environmental matters from elsewhere in the world (Meyer, 2011) – an example of policy mobility.

After 1972, the professional recognition of practitioners who were responsible for applying these standards (Nicolaïdis, 1992) emerged as an issue. Some professions, such as environmental health officers and engineers, quickly grasped the implications of the pooling of powers in the EU and engaged directly during the development of policy and legislation rather than only applying it once agreed (Morphet, 1998). They extended professional policy communities within and between member states to develop their role and influence (Morphet and Hams, 1994; Evans and Theobald, 2003).

EU environment policy has continued to expand as trade regulation has become more internationalised (Macrory and Hession, 1996), and intertwined (Knill and Liefferink, 2007). The Commission has taken over the negotiating position on the environment from individual member states (see Chapter Five) and the pooling of policy is now viewed as being comprehensive (CEC, 2012a).

Environmental planning and its relationship to health and the countryside were well established as a domestic policy when the UK joined the EU in 1972. Planning policy had been through a recent review, resulting in new legislation in 1968 focusing on maintaining and conserving quality environments and buildings (Nadin and Cullingworth, 2006). The UK was less advanced in environmental regulation on heavy industry, such as steel-making and the use of fossil fuels. The discovery of North Sea gas and oil also promised an energy bonanza, which had costs associated with its extraction and use, but which could give the UK an energy advantage. There was little interest in regulating activities that had environmental costs and consequences. The UK core executive was less engaged in this process and used arm's length organisations, such as the Institute for European Environmental Policy (IEEP) and the Green Alliance, as a means of attempting to exercise influence in Europe. In the period since 1987, environmental policy has grown in scale and importance while administrative and technical roles have developed more rapidly than political leadership (Jordan, 2001, 2004).

Development of EU environmental competencies and programmes

The EU's role in environment policy developed through the negotiation of international trade agreements. From this, it is argued, the Commission has used the development of its international role to advance integration through the *elasticisation* of policy areas, using the environment, with its borderless issues. This has been achieved through the Single European Act 1986 (SEA) and the SEM in 1992 (Hooghe et al, 1996; Cini, 2008; Lenschow, 2010). The parallel preparations for the UN Earth Summit in Rio and the SEM in 1992 also allowed for the development of a more significant environmental agenda. This was then used to promote integration within and between the EU's policy areas, including regional policy, transport, trade, environmental quality and waste.

The development of the EU's role in environmental policy and legislation has been significant. It is the first policy area that has grown in importance in parallel with the development of the EU. The Treaty of Rome 1957 contained commitments to 'ever closer union' between member states for existing areas of policy, including home affairs and transport. The development of an EU-wide approach was expected to take time, as there were existing interests to reconcile. For the environment, the member states did not have existing policies and legislation to be considered so that an EU approach to the environment and sustainability could be developed in a new policy space. The environment has emerged as a leading EU policy area and one where policies may be considered to be more Europeanised from the outset rather than over time.

1. Policy development

As in other pooled policy areas, the Commission has the power of policy initiation but has no role in direct implementation, which is the responsibility of the member states. The Commission is responsible for monitoring compliance and is supported by the European Environment Agency in this role. The Commission has the power to bring a case to the European Court of Justice (ECJ) against any member state if it considers that the transposition and implementation of legislation does not meet the legal requirements. It has also been supported and reinforced by member states with high environmental standards (Leontitsis, 2011).

Influences on the policy agenda are derived from internal and external pressures. External pressures include responses to environmental disasters, for example, in Torrey Canyon in 1967 and Seveso in 1976, and changes in regulatory regimes in third-party countries, where the EU might have trade links. Pressures are also derived from international law and treaties that oblige adherence to environmental standards and practices, such as the UN agreement on climate change in Kyoto in

2005. Internal pressures for action came from the Treaty of Rome and the commitment to develop each such policy area further as part of the development of the EU (McCormick, 2001).

The EU environmental policy agenda can be considered through their periodisation (Jessop, 2004; Goetz and Mayer-Sahling, 2009) as environmental policies have occurred in distinct phases (Lenschow, 2010). The first was 1957–87, when environmental policy was established. The approach of the Commission was one of 'rational bureaucracy', that is, to avoid damage or harm to the environment (Meyer, 2011). The potential for individual member states to introduce their own regulation on environmental issues suggested a move towards a common approach at the Paris Summit in 1972, when it was agreed that the Commission would draw up the first EAP for the period 1973–76, followed by the second for 1977–81 and the third for 1982–1986. These action programmes did not have a legal basis but were used to set out EU-wide approaches, including the precautionary or preventive principle and also that the 'polluter pays'. Operating without any specific powers meant that the EU acted within 'catch-all' legislation, which allowed for action to be taken where there were no specific powers but where action was needed. Unanimity in the Council was required before any matter was allowed to proceed (Leontitsis, 2011).

The SEA created a separate legal basis for environmental protection as an EU competence. This was located in two differing legal constructs. The first was one where member states could use environmental regulation at the base level agreed by the EU, and this needed unanimity. However, a second approach incorporated the effects of the environment into the SEM and, in this case, it required only Qualified Majority Voting (QMV) for any action to be agreed. This approach reduced the ability of any member state to block environmental legislation through self-interest. The EU used the SEM provisions for the environment more frequently in an attempt to bypass unanimity (Leontitsis, 2011), although it was challenged by member states (Burchall and Lightfoot, 2002). At the outset, these two policy adoption methods operated together. This caused complications in practice and contestation between the Commission and the member states.

The fourth EAP ran from 1987 to 1992 and widened the scope of the environmental programme, although there was a concentration on agricultural reforms and environmental hazards. As it prepared for the implementation of the SEA, the environment agenda was already widening beyond what had gone before (Nathan, 1987). This phase was concerned with tackling the effects of differential regulation as barriers to trade within the SEM when the SEA was implemented in 1992.

The Maastricht Treaty on the European Union 1993 (TEU) extended both the 'visibility' of the role of the environment (Leontitsis, 2011) and the application of QMV to almost all environmental policy, although unanimity was required for town and country planning and energy.

Towards sustainability (CEC 1993), the fifth EAP (1993–2000), mirrored the approach developed at the Rio UN Earth Summit. It was a more coherent approach and acted as a means of integrating environmental policy into others at source. The fifth EAP included new instruments such as taxes and introduced shared responsibility. 'All in all, the Fifth EAP continued the trend towards more sophisticated environmental governance at the EU level' (Leontitsis, 2011, p 452). It was significant because it was the first developed under the aegis of the SEA and the integrated focus meant a fuller, wider and deeper EAP than had been prepared before. In addition, the proposed legislation could now be agreed through QMV rather than unanimity procedures, so progress in implementation could be quicker.

The fifth EAP contained 15 implementation tables comprised of objectives, actions and targets. These included action on the core environmental concerns of air quality, waste, acidification, water quality and quantity, nuclear energy, and biodiversity. However, they also stretched into quality of life, noise in urban areas and risk management, and across other sectors into agriculture, energy, transport and tourism. They also included horizontal or integrating measures, such as improving data quality, spatial and sectoral planning, and fiscal measures. The last table was concerned with training, skills and professional standards as well as funding. Each of these individual actions had an indentified lead and a time frame for delivery within the EAP. This extended the role of the EAP in new ways.

This subsequent phase of the development of EU environmental policymaking strengthened the role of the EU in environmental policy (Miller, 2012). The Amsterdam Treaty in 1997 included the principle of sustainable development and mainstreaming environmental policy through integration into the other policy areas of the EU (Shaw et al, 2000). The co-decision process became the norm, with an increased role for the European Parliament. Unanimity has been kept for more controversial areas. It also developed the application of the principle of subsidiarity, which influenced the character and style of the sixth EAP. The *European governance White Paper* (CEC, 2001) proposed softer framework directives, which could be implemented by member states in ways that were culturally more aligned to existing approaches. It also proposed the use of 'soft law' measures, including guidelines, declarations and opinions, the Open Method of Coordination (OMC), and the use of pilot projects. This approach was seen to be experimental as not all of the issues that were expected to arise had prepared solutions (Eberlein and Kerwer, 2004).

The development of EU environmental policy coordination through the lattice of vertical and horizontal measures (Lenschow, 2010, p 308) to create an integrated approach introduced in the fifth EAP was the basis of the development of the sixth EAP. This prioritised the integrated approach and stretched across the whole of the EU through the application of Environmental Policy Integration (EPI) (Jordan and Lenschow, 2000). However, over time, there has been conflict with economic challenges and internal differences between Directorates General on approaches to take, for example, that on car emissions in 2008 (Lenschow, 2010).

The sixth EAP (for 2002–12) (CEC, 2001) lasted longer than the previous programmes. It had four thematic areas: climate change; nature and biodiversity; environment and health; and natural resources and waste. No targets or actions were set for these themes, which were then expected to be developed through seven strategies: air; pesticides; waste prevention and recycling; natural resources; soil; marine environment; and urban environment. These became both a framework for action and a governance mechanism for delivery. As with earlier EAPs, this was seen as part of a continuous process. It was also the first EAP to be adopted by co-decision between the Council and the Parliament and was regarded as more legitimate for that reason (CEC, 2011d). The sixth EAP has been implemented through framework directives. These bring together directives in specific areas, such as water treatment and waste, and make them more inclusive by filling in the policy context in which they are expected to operate. These seek the delivery of wider-ranging goals (Lenschow, 2010). However, the report on progress in delivering the sixth EAP indicates that this approach has not been fully successful (Armstrong, 2002; Schout and Jordan, 2005). First, the sixth EAP and main funding cycles within the EU were not in the same time frames. Second, despite progress in policy measures, there has been a shortfall in member state implementation. The framework construction of the sixth EAP has been seen to be its weakness. In the evaluation of its progress, it is seen to be too strategically ambitious and unlikely to be fulfilled (Von Homeyer and Withana, 2011). However, it is also interesting to note that this evaluation was undertaken by three independent bodies, one of whom was the IEEP, an organisation that has been consistent in this view about the role of EAPs from the outset (Haigh, 1987, 1996; Wilkinson, 1997).

The development of the seventh EAP (for 2012–20) has returned to a more detailed approach. It has strengthened its alliance with the overarching economic programme set out in *Europe 2020* (CEC, 2010a). The seventh EAP is focused on approaches to 'filling in' significant policy gaps. The commitment to integration with other policies remains together with strengthening the policy coherence of these relationships, including with agriculture, fisheries and cohesion policies (economic, social and territorial) (CEC, 2012a, 2012b). Health and well-being are expected to be expanded as public health has been confirmed as a public sector role in the Lisbon Treaty 2009. The development of the EAPs into urban policies is also further extended. Although not explicit in the seventh EAP, the insertion of the territorial cohesion protocol in the Lisbon Treaty 2009 could develop the role of EPI into a more systematic evaluative approach if they are used together.

The EU is frequently characterised as becoming more centralised on environmental policy and the attitude to the seventh EAP suggests that it will be returning to this approach. On some estimates, the EU policy lead on the environment could now cover up to 100% of member states' environmental policies (Jordan, 2001; Miller, 2010; CEC, 2012a). Has this resulted in environmental policies that are becoming more Europeanised or similar? Liefferink and Jordan (2005) have shown that a process of convergence has meant that different member states have had to take on new modes of delivery that differ from their institutional norms. However, the transposition of directives does not require the same policy instruments to be used to achieve the same ends, creating a *tight–loose* approach to implementation and compliance.

In the period since 2000, the softer approach to the application of environmental powers can also be seen in the Council of Ministers. Here, there are few votes, so although there is QMV on the environment, there has been no significant issue where this has been used. The UK has been concerned about the loss of sovereignty (Shaw et al, 2000). This has also been the view of other countries, including the Netherlands, which has always taken a leading role in environmental policy but has been found to be failing to appropriately implement an environment directive (Evers et al, 2009). This has sent a ripple of concern and anger through the Dutch environmental establishment and a questioning of the role and expense of implementing environmental priorities within a difficult economic environment.

Reception of the EU environmental agenda in the UK

The EU has been enthusiastic about environment policy and has extended its scope beyond that envisaged by the UK (Bradbeer, 2001). The UK initially expressed a lack of interest in the environment (during 1973–83), then adopted a defensive position (during 1983–92) and, from 1992, moved to slow convergence (Lowe and Ward, 1998):

> The European Community's environmental policy is effectively embodied in the items of Community legislation which then have to be implemented in the Member States … community policy cannot therefore be regarded as some abstract concept existing on its own and separate from national policies. (Haigh, 1987, p 1)

As Haigh (1996, p 155, author's emphasis) points out, national sovereignty is indivisible but it can be *ceded* to the EU in order to achieve more than could be within a single state. The use of this argument and term provides a clear view of the perception of the UK as giving away power rather than pooling it and, as such, it encapsulates much of the approach towards the EU in the UK. The environment is also the policy area where the principle of subsidiarity was first adopted in the SEA, and it has since been extended to all other policy areas, completing this process in the Lisbon Treaty 2009. This principle has had a wider influence on the governance scales and institutional structures in the UK (see Chapter Eight).

Before formal entry to the EU, the UK promoted a debate on the countryside from 1962 onwards. This was seen as part of a wider growth in interest in the natural and physical environment that led to the European Year of Conservation in 1970 (Eden, 2003; Meyer, 2011). However, UK entry negotiations in 1972 were more concerned with trade and regional development issues. The assumption was that the UK's internationally recognised public health tradition, delivered through housing, planning and environmental health regulation, would set the standards for the rest of the EU (Sharp, 1998; Jordan, 2008). This meant that any EU concerns would either see the UK in the lead or not troubled by any environmental regulation. The UK also regarded environmental regulation as a local government matter dealt with through negotiation between the regulators and the regulated at specific locations. One immediate response to the pooling of environmental regulation on joining the EU was to establish a Department of the

Environment in 1970, a renaming of the Ministry of Housing and Local Government, which suggested the expected scope, scale and range of environmental regulation within the EU and its likely effects in the UK.

From the outset, the UK saw the environment as being an *international* issue or one that could be pursued domestically in local authorities rather than as being of concern at the EU scale. Thus, the UK did not engage with the EU on environmental issues and, as a result, had less influence than those member states that became more involved. Instead, the UK attempted to influence environment policy when it seemed to be in the way of its own interests and from the margins. In 1978, when the House of Lords considered the issue of UK sovereignty, including the role of environmental policy, no witnesses could supply information about how much EU legislation had been implemented or its effects (Jordan, 2008).

The integrating role of the environment in EU policy in the development of the SEA was understood by the UK core executive too late in the negotiations to influence the outcomes (Haigh, 1987, 1996). The UK also took the view that it had been misled about the integrating role and breadth of policy likely to develop from the SEA. As the UK assumed that its own existing policy framework would be adequate, it was both unprepared for and unengaged in the negotiation process. It was also diverted by the government's focus on the establishment of the SEM. Following this and some environment infringement cases, the UK changed its strategy from resistance to engagement in the late 1980s. This proved to be a more effective approach in influencing different regulatory paradigms between the UK's cost-oriented approach and Germany's 'best available technology' approach (Duhr et al, 2010).

Initially, the UK's approach to the EU's intentions for environmental policy might be characterised as distracted complacency or even denial. EU environmental policy is delivered through *regulatory regimes* based on quantifiable and universal standards. Before 1972, '"the British approach" was predominantly reactive rather than anticipatory, tactical rather than strategic, pragmatic rather than ambitious and case by case rather than uniform' (Jordan, 2008, p 233). The UK did not appear to have any long-term policy objectives, and breaches of the system were rarely prosecuted, but, rather, dealt with by negotiation and agreement that were not in the public domain (Bradbeer, 2001).

A major EU principle in environmental policy is based on the sources of pollution rather than their effects. This requires a more centralised approach to regulatory regimes (Haigh, 1987; Jordan, 2008). The response to this in UK central government was agencification. This centralised the function but then immediately took an arm's length approach to its management and delivery, creating a centrally controlled and locally operated system and resulting in UK policy development being cut adrift from delivery (Boden, 1998 et al; Gains, 2004b). Regulatory agencies could take on operational responsibility, reduce civil service headcounts and not hamper central approaches to domestic policymaking (Moynihan, 2006; Talbot, 2004b).

When delivery required the transposition of legislation, the UK implemented EU law through administrative circulars rather than secondary legislation. This brought problems with the ECJ. The UK central government culture of change is episodic and it is difficult for any government department to get more than two pieces of legislation through each year. When there are major programmes of EU legislation to transpose into UK law, this requires new and innovative approaches (Bradbeer, 2001). The UK's non-engagement with emerging EU environmental policy became acute when there were successive UK failures to comply or to implement legislation set out in EU directives and regulations, including that for Integrated Pollution Control. This has continued and, in 2007, the UK had an initial Commission warning for failure to comply with environmental directives. The UK has also failed to comply with other directives, including those for air quality and bathing water. Further, the UK was taken to the ECJ for its failure to transpose the directive on environmental impact assessment correctly in 2006 and this had to be redesigned through the issue of new regulations in 2008. The UK has not engaged with domestic partners, encouraging them to go to the EU direct and lobby there. This left the UK in a more restricted position than anticipated (Bulmer and Burch, 2009) and resulted in the increase of the scope of EU legislation – which was the opposite of what the UK intended (Jordan, 2008).

This underestimation of the extent and role of EU environmental legislation in the UK is said to be due to the silo nature of government departments and the inability to negotiate within the EU on other than pre-agreed positions (Fairbrass and Jordan, 2001). One of the key determinants of this approach is the attitude of the UK civil service (Bulmer and Burch, 2009). This can be illustrated through discussions on issues of climate change that required an integrated approach. At least four government departments needed to be involved (the Treasury and the Departments for Trade, Transport and the Environment) and the UK's negotiating position was never seen to be coherent. O'Riordan and Rowbotham (1996) identified the reasons for this. First, there is a pecking order between departments so that the Treasury's views on any taxation measures would be considered first. There were also power struggles between departments as the environment appeared to be increasing in importance from its previous low status. This in turn upset the relatively stable policy communities in government that could inhibit as well as promote change (Steimo et al, 1993; O'Riordan and Jager, 1996; O'Riordan and Jordan, 1996). Finally, senior civil servants are generalists and take advice from specialists, who are also more likely to be involved in delivery. However, requests for advice can be narrowly cast and result in advice set within the terms in which it has been requested, rather than answering the wider questions (Hill, 2006).

While the UK participates in treaty development and EAPs are negotiated by the core executive in all member states, discussion on specific legislation and implementation is left to specialist civil servants, who are at lower grades and are rarely able to surface issues to ministers. Those engaged in delivery see the process as being one that is technical rather than policy-driven, with less focus on integration. The wider implications of legislation on trade or places are not likely to be taken into account. These specialist negotiating groups meet regularly, so operational officials have their own working arrangements and a group mentality can develop, which leads them to act autonomously, form a working bond and develop agendas (Keohane and Nye, 1989). In this case, the Commission, ministers or home departments are seen as the barriers to proposed regulations or legislation. Hayes-Renshaw et al (2006) suggest that over 70% of all EU decisions are taken in technocratic working groups; politicians do not participate in these day-to-day negotiations (Peterson, 2009).

In the UK, specialist environmental policy communities operate (Weale, 1992; Jordan, A., 1998; Jordan et al, 2003; Stone, 2008) in specific areas, for example, industrial pollution (Smith, 2000), and different territories, for example, Scotland (Bomberg, 1994; Keating et al, 2009). These are likely to develop relationships with EU-wide policy communities and interest groups to manage the agenda (Mazey and Richardson, 2000). Domestic Parliaments undertake lower levels of scrutiny and political ownership, which suggests that member states are caught in a procedural trap (Liefferink and Jordan, 2005). In some cases, this represents forced learning or policy transfer. In others, it may lead to depoliticisation (Burnham, 2001; Flinders and Buller, 2006).

When the integrated environment policy was negotiated, the UK's focus was on the development of the SEA, with its emphasis on trade (Cockfield, 1994) and concern to negotiate a rebate (Thatcher, 1995). It did not recognise the SEM's relationship with other policy areas, including the environment. This late understanding left less time to prepare for implementation and it was finally captured as part of the raft of legislation that was enacted in the Environmental Protection

Act 1990. Delivery was through new agencies, and an increase in a regulatory regime that went against the liberal ideology of the Conservative government in order to provide a more acceptable political narrative to deliver this policy, it was coupled with the implementation of the agreements on trade and opening up the local public sector to private-sector competition, which also had to be introduced during the same time period (see Chapter Five). This created an opportunity to focus the public debate on more efficient local authorities and limit private-sector concerns about the cost of more environmental legislation through the opportunities made available by opening up the local government market.

It was also regarded as a means to reduce the power of public-sector unions, who were actively engaged in front-line delivery services, such as refuse collection (Morphet, 2008). The introduction of explicit procurement processes for directly provided internal services was focused on local rather than central government. This also became a method to carry the required changes in environmental policy without overt policy explanations. The EU requirements were submerged into the heated and disputed debates about exposing local public services to the competition.

The first areas of work that were required to be subject to competition in the UK were waste collection and disposal, highway and transport works, and grounds maintenance, which were all subject to changes introduced by EU environmental legislation. The application of Compulsory Competitive Tendering (CCT) for these services in local government meant that the specification of service would immediately be within agreed EU regimes. This was a single move that enabled the UK to demonstrate compliance with two strands of EU policy simultaneously. It also transferred the pressure to achieve the percentage value of public services open to competition from central government to local government and the utilities. These changes in delivery also set the context for establishing the Environment Agency to deliver central government's role in 1996. However, as an organisation, it has not been exposed to competition in the same way as local government.

In the period that followed the introduction of CCT, local authorities developed mixed economies. Larger local authorities and private-sector providers developed an approach to contracting that would allow additional work to be undertaken for other local authorities and the income to be pooled, thus reducing the cost of the host contract. Elsewhere, groups of local authorities have joined together. Environmental services have become a major area of business for the private sector and waste collection has become the fourth-largest area of local government expenditure at £7 billion per annum (LGA, 2010).

Alongside the major contracting approaches developed as part of the competition regime, voluntary and community-sector organisations have also become service providers. This has been a long-standing area of community involvement, with credits being given to groups (Sharp and Luckin, 2006) for recycling, composting (Slater et al, 2010) and furniture (Curran and Williams, 2010). This practice has been incorporated into the Coalition government's Big Society initiative from 2010, with further rewards being offered. However, it is also aligned with achieving more community acceptance of local waste disposal facilities (DEFRA, 2011), which have consistently been problematic (Clifford, 2006).

The links between environmental policy in the EU and the thread of increasing subsidiarity has also been an important issue for the UK. At the Edinburgh Council in 1992, chaired by the then Prime Minister, John Major, it was agreed that framework directives were preferable to other kinds of legislation as they gave member states more freedom in delivery. The Commission would lead on subsidiarity and there would be earlier consultation. This would allow member states longer preparation time and citizen engagement could be increased (Jeppesen, 2000). In a perceived loosening, environmental standards were changed to minimum requirements that could be increased by member states if they wished.

The introduction of subsidiarity as part of environmental policy had much wider implications for the UK in practice. Under the UK's unwritten constitution, sub-national government, including local government, has no general powers of competence, unlike local authorities in the rest of Europe. All actions by UK local authorities have to be shown to be within their existing legislative powers on a case-by-case basis. Further, Thatcher's legislation had tightened the financial control on local authorities and did nothing to suggest that the centralising role would not be increased. In the 1990s, the role of the environment, and particularly Local Agenda 21, was one of the few freedoms that local authorities had to express their local priorities and to deliver them to their communities (Morphet and Hams, 1994; Morphet, 1998).

From 1992 onwards, the EU decided that the potential for problems in the environmental policy area was high and efforts were made to construct directives in ways that were more culturally in tune with UK methods. More attention was paid to processes than specific environmental outcomes. Following this, the UK became more of a receiver (Bulmer and Burch, 2009) of policy, concerned with its implementation, although still lagging in some key areas. The UK is now in a period of minimisation, attempting to reduce the impact of legislation, arguing for an environmental interpretation of subsidiarity and being equivocal over support for environmental objectives in the context of economic uncertainty. Bradbeer (2001) argues that within the context of more subsidiarity, there could be a loosening of environmental compliance within the UK.

This raises issues of why member states decide to pool their powers in policy areas such as the environment if they wish to retain control over their own affairs. Golub (1996) argues that this is due to politicians using the EU to promote policies that could not be achieved within a domestic policy agenda, although once an element of sovereign power is pooled, it is hard to take back (Miller, 2011b). Another factor may be the amount of time that the EU legislative processes take from their first discussions of treaty inclusion to delivery. This can take over 10 years and cover one or two electoral cycles (Jordan, 2003). This could account for the sense of depoliticisation on the one hand, and the increase in the administrative role in law-making on the other (Burnham, 2001; Buller and Flinders, 2005; Flinders and Buller, 2006). Overall, it can be argued that although membership of the EU led to some major changes in the way policy development occurs in the UK, these changes have been largely absorbed and internalised so that domesticated responses have appeared to be the norm (Jordan, 2008). There was a short period when Blair, as Prime Minister, took a different, more proactive, view behind the scenes, despite maintaining a narrative of missed opportunities for the Euro-sceptic press (Stephens, 2001; Daddow, 2007). This resulted in the adoption of some of the 'soft law' measures and OMC, but did not change the culture of UK negotiation and implementation of EU policy.

The UK has attempted some of its own approaches to leading environmental policy delivery. One example is the introduction of the Strategic Environmental Assessment (EA) Directive. The UK took a role in the development of this directive because its objective was to reduce the impact of its proactive integrated approach (Fairbrass and Jordan, 2004). Rather than take an integrated approach at source, in 1998, the UK developed the Cardiff process, through which it was decided that each sector should bring forward specific strategies for incorporating environmental priorities (Jordan and Lenschow, 2000). This started with transport, agriculture and energy. When promoting the Cardiff process, the familiar New Labour approach of targets was introduced together with a suite of indicators for use in benchmarking.

However, this process soon faltered and despite a UK research project that supported its maintenance (Fergusson et al, 2001), it did not survive a Commission review (Leontitsis, 2011), which recommended inclusion in the EU's Sustainable Development Strategy adopted in Gothenburg in 2001 (Shout and Jordan, 2005).

The Cardiff process was thus replaced by the implementation of EPI. The application of EPI across member states has been varied (Jordan and Lenschow, 2010), with integrated and fractured approaches leaving the tension between the economy and the environment unresolved (Leontitsis, 2011). The UK is seen as centrally coordinated in its negotiation and policymaking (Russell and Jordan, 2009), which is assumed to be helpful in the implementation of EU legislation, but Jordan and Lenschow (2000) also indicate that such an approach needs strong political leadership to manage specific policy initiatives.

In the Blair government, integration was promoted initially through the appointment of a green minister in every government and an ethical foreign policy (Cook, 1997). The creation of the Department of the DETR in 1997 was a potentially major step in demonstrating this integration between environment, transport and the regions in England. However, this approach did not last and, in 2001, environment and transport responsibilities were removed from this 'super-department'. A new Department for Environment and Rural Affairs (DEFRA) was created and the former Department of Transport was reinstated. Instead, EPI was implemented through sustainability indicators. Individual elements of the sixth EAP were pursued, such as the creation of the Department of Energy and Climate Change in 2008 to lead energy policy. The Coalition government's programme (HMG, 2010) promised the greenest government, but the transition between the sixth and seventh EAPs may have delayed the implementation of associated policies and legislation. The seventh EAP has returned to a legislative and controlled approach to delivering environment policy and represents a move away from the looser approach that the British government prefers.

How has the UK fared in comparison with other member states?

How have environmental policy and legislation influenced domestic practices in other member states? When EU policies and legislation require changes in institutional arrangements within government, there will be a tendency to undertake this within the orthodoxy of prevailing organisational cultures (Bulmer and Burch, 2009). Knill and Lenschow

(2001) reviewed the reception and adoption of four specific pieces of EU environmental legislation on drinking water, environmental information, environmental audit and environmental impact assessment (EIA) in the UK and Germany. In looking at the implementation of these four policies, they found that there was a key role for actors in the system and their relationship to the changes was significant. Where the proposed changes were similar to existing practices or processes within the state, these could be easily adapted and adopted.

In the UK, the Environmental Audit Regulation was closely aligned to the British Standard 7750 and procedures for examination and verification were already known by professionals and organisations. The UK implemented standards on environmental information beyond the scope of the requirements in comparison with Germany, where this was resisted. Knill and Lenschow (2001) argue that this was based on the primary focus of the civil servants required to implement the directive. In the German system, civil servants hold their first duty to the state and not to the people. This made them resistant to the idea of sharing information.

On the EIA Directive, both the UK and Germany actively opposed the implementation and have failed to adopt it fully. The UK was taken to the ECJ on this issue and lost in 2006. It has subsequently had to issue new regulations in 2008. In Germany, there was resistance to the integrated approach to assessment compared with prevailing systems of separate evaluation. In the UK, resistance was general rather than specific. Knill and Lenschow (2001) argue that the EIA Directive was closely akin to existing practices and did not take much effort to adopt. However, they suggest that the time during which the EIA Directive was being developed was a period when there was a close focus on deregulation and improving the image of the UK as being the 'dirty man of Europe', which this did not seem to specifically address. Knill and Lenschow argue that this directive was too dull to excite any interest and it was also clear that there was an assumption that it would catch very few cases per year – the Department of the Environment library expected approximately 12 cases per year when it was first implemented in 1990. Even in this first application, the UK transposition omitted certain categories and had to be revised in the Planning and Compensation Act 1991. Thus, there was an assumption that existing practices would be adequate and that EIA was for exceptional circumstances. It was an example of *distracted denial* in the UK.

The UK has been regarded as a laggard in the development and implementation of EU environmental policy in comparison with other northern EU member states (Heritier et al, 1996; Sbragia, 2012; Leontitsis, 2011). However, there have been periods when the UK has had a more positive approach to developing EU policy and implementation that have been successful. In the 1990s, the UK was able to influence the regulatory model used to demonstrate compliance to one that more closely represented its own method of measurement. This has created difficulties for other countries, including Germany (Jordan, 2001).

Implications of pooling the UK's environmental policy in the EU

The development and application of EU environmental legislation suggests that there could be a number of policy agenda-setting and delivery lessons for the UK in developing its approach. However, as noted earlier, it is uncertain how many of these have been internalised into policymaking processes. Rather, the UK takes a passive–aggressive stance towards EU environmental policy development.

However, in considering the experience of the environment as an EU-pooled policy area, a number of key implications can now be identified. First, EAPs are intentions to deliver, not aspirational programmes. The legislation and initiatives within the programme were EU commitments and it was the Commission's responsibility to initiate policy and legislation to implement the fifth EAP. Once this policy and legislation had been agreed by member states, it was the UK government's responsibility to implement it, which, despite of a lack of legal obligation on the UK, has been achieved.

Second, the UK's attempts to influence EU policymaking in this area, as in others, have not been sustained. The environment is an area where there are strong and developed policy communities, both from within the member states' governments' policy specialists and voluntary and third-sector organisations (Webster, 1998). The Cardiff process was an attempt to influence the scale of integration envisaged as part of the EU and member state decision-making processes. This did not succeed and the replacement version of EPI has also been problematic. In putting forward the seventh EAP, the Commission has been able to propose a return to specific legislative proposals. The UK still maintains its reluctance to support this approach and continues to develop new ways of challenging environmental legislation as it comes forward.

A third lesson that the UK has yet to internalise is that failure to implement or comply with environmental legislation will lead to legal action against it by the EU. These legal infractions demonstrate that the UK's record in implementing EU legislation is not as perfect as is commonly thought. In 2008, the UK had 31 environmental infringements and was fifth after Italy, Spain, Ireland and France, whilst, in 2009, it had 25 and was again fifth after Spain, Ireland, the Czech Republic and France (CEC, 2012c). In terms of active cases being pursued by the Commission on environmental infringements, the UK was joint fifth in the number of cases being pursued in 2009 (CEC, 2012c).

Conclusions

The approach of EU EAPs has been programmatic, providing a bridge between treaty agreements on strategic shared competencies and the details of legislation for implementation. This has provided an opportunity for member states to consider how to prepare or influence detailed policy development and delivery. The programmatic approach also allows for the monitoring of delivery of direct policies and integration. This programmatic approach was based on the Dutch model (Tews et al, 2003) and has extended in scope. The UK government regarded this style of programme to be aspirational rather than a formulated work programme and failure to accept this led to the core executive being underprepared for implementation. The UK made a number of misinterpretations of EU environmental policy in the negotiation of the SEA, which have had longer-lasting effects.

After 1992, the EU developed a more holistic and integrated approach to sustainability. This was difficult for UK central government as it required working across government departments, but at the local level, it was grasped enthusiastically by local authorities. By the early 1990s, they had taken the view, in a Thatcherite context, that they had minimal influence on any local delivery. Local Agenda 21, arising from the 1992 Earth Summit and supported through the Local Government Training Board, was seen as a means through which local leadership and expression could be developed (Morphet, 1998; Morphet et al, 1994). The demise of Thatcher in 1990 allowed a change in approach at the local level and the then Secretary of State, John Gummer, together with Michael Heseltine in the Board of Trade, allowed for a more developed local approach.

Since then, the role of local government in delivering EU policies through their operational services, such as waste collection and disposal, has become more overt. This has been further developed through the transposition of EU environmental fines regimes direct to local authorities in the Localism Act 2011. This signals a more open approach to recognising the EU's relationship to English domestic practice. On the other hand, this more transparent response may lead to greater calls for engagement in negotiation, not least where the financial consequences of the legislation are passed.

What have been the effects of the EU on British public policy on the environment after 50 years of engagement? There are some arguments to suggest that the UK has learned to be more *communitaire* in its approach to negotiation on environmental matters (Jordan, 2004). Although central coordination of EU issues within government has increased (Kassim, 2004, 2005), this has been within prevailing cultures and structures (Sharp, 1998; Hallsworth, 2011). Bulmer and Burch (2009) argue that EU negotiations have been incorporated into the UK central government's approach to policymaking and that this absorption is now complete. The prevailing UK policy style at the beginning of this period is very similar to that currently used by separated policy streams and responsibilities, late delivery, and a focus on pragmatism in application where this is possible.

The environment policy area is now more widespread but is not integrated despite attempts to provide national policy delivery through Sustainable Development Strategies (in 1994, 1999 and 2005). The operational departments have split and divided responsibilities – planning is in the Department for Communities and Local Government (DCLG), while marine spatial planning is in DEFRA. Local energy production is also a planning matter for the DCLG, while energy and climate change is in Department of Energy and Climate Change and energy market regulation is associated with the Department of Business and Industry. The Department for Transport has responsibility for sustainable transport while the Treasury has responsibility for infrastructure planning, and national infrastructure planning policy statements are developed by different government departments and approved by Parliament. There is no department that has the leadership role for pulling together sustainable policies and the attempts to achieve this through the role of the Deputy Prime Minister have been thwarted by the larger, more powerful, departments.

At the local level, the application of EU environmental legislation remains problematic. In 2011, the UK government was referred to the ECJ by the Commission for the high costs of challenging environmental project decisions, which is prohibiting individuals and communities from objecting (Reynolds, 2011). These cases receive little or no publicity, while the UK likes to maintain its position of being seen as a good implementer of EU legislation. Finally, the government's decision to pass the costs of the failure to deliver EU-agreed environmental standards to local authorities in the Localism Act 2011 could have longer-term effects on future UK negotiations on environmental standards in the EU – a possible unintended consequence?

CHAPTER EIGHT

Territory and subsidiarity

Introduction

As the EU has developed from the Treaty of Rome in 1957, it has expanded its interest from sectors to spaces. EU policies for industry, transport and the environment has increasingly been set within their territorial context. The development of the role of territory and place within the EU's interest was accelerated by the UK's accession in 1972. The UK's main driver for joining the EU was trade and access to markets, together with a concern for the economically lagging regions (Glasson and Marshall, 2007). The UK had to demonstrate that the EU would be able to continue financial support or locational steering to these areas.

The introduction of this territorial dimension, delivered through regional policies and structural funds, immediately became a mechanism to promote wider EU policies. This allowed direct relationships between sub-state governments and the Commission while developing relationships between places and promoting enlargement. Vertical and horizontal integration between and within places started to emerge. The Single European Act 1986 (SEA) promoted the principle of subsidiarity based on the borderless spillover effects of environmental issues and costs for trade, but also became a means through which Multi-Level Governance (MLG) policies could be developed.

The role of the EU's regional and structural policies were further developed in the 1990s and increasingly widened in their scope through the development of pan-EU mega-regions (CEC, 2004) and the European Spatial Development Perspective (CEC, 1999; Duhr et al, 2010; Faludi, 2010). The shift away from a selective to an integrated territorial approach was also a UK initiative, proposed by Major at the Edinburgh Council in 1992. This has subsequently developed into a policy that is as much concerned with intra-regional disparities as inter-regional differences. During the 1990s, subsidiarity increased its role. In 2009, the principle of subsidiarity was completed in the Lisbon Treaty and related to a new structuring principle of territorial cohesion. All of these developments have had significant implications for the UK, including devolution in Scotland, Wales and London, the development and dissolution of quasi-democratic regional structures in England, a general power of competence for local government, and new parish powers. The role of the EU in shaping sub-state governance, institutions and policies in the UK will be discussed in this chapter.

EU policies as spatial instruments

The introduction of a formal selective regional policy into the EU commenced with British membership in 1972 and was a shift away from existing edge to edge practices in the founder member states. Devolution developed in France (in 1969), Italy (in 1970) and later in Spain (in 1978). The response from the EU was to begin to develop policy for a 'Europe of the regions' (Harvie, 1994; Murphy, 2011).

While negotiating its membership of the EU in 1972, sub-state governance structures were also being reviewed in the UK. The London Government Act 1963 created the London Boroughs and was followed by a review of English local authority scales and functions by the Redcliffe-Maud Commission (Redcliffe-Maud, 1969), implemented in 1974. One of the members of the Commission, Derek Senior, published a minority report which proposed that sub-state governance should focus on autonomous city regions (Senior, 1969). Senior's recommendations were not adopted and the resulting structure gave cities single-tier government but not the autonomy Senior suggested. There were also proposals for change in local government in Scotland following a Royal Commission (Wheatley, 1969). The case for devolution in Scotland was advanced and a referendum was held on the issue in 1979. However, democratic regions were never proposed as part of this sub-state structure in the UK, although administrative regions, established in the 1930s, continued.

The introduction of regional policy in the EU established the European Regional Development Fund (ERDF) in 1972. The purpose of the ERDF is to improve the performance of lagging regions, bringing them closer to the EU average for income and other economic and social indicators. The scale of the budget for structural funds grew to one third of the EU budget and it is arguable that the regional structural funds were the only openly redistributive funding measure in the EU (Allen, 2010). In 1986, the SEA introduced the principle of cohesion. This was a significant shift. Cohesion allowed the application of the territorial policy to the economic agenda of the EU as a whole and introduced changes in the application of EU funds. Projects were required to link together in programmes and partnership delivery was also introduced. The creation of the Cohesion Fund introduced the

INTERREG programme in 1989, which could be used by all localities, not just those eligible for ERDF. Funds were not only focused on lagging regions, but also on cross-border areas, cities or rural areas that had common characteristics. The objective of this development was to build solidarity within the EU's territory.

While the main focus on regionalism within the EU has primarily been on the application of structural funds, regional policy has been developing in parallel. As part of the enlargement of the EU from 2004 onwards, aspirant member states have been required to establish regional sub-state structures and institutions with political autonomy. In this, the EU has been a significant promoter of decentralised decision-making (Bourne, 2007). Regions are seen to be an important scale in the enlargement process for three reasons: economic, cultural and political. The economic geography of regions has always been a focus for EU growth policies and the basic governance unit for policy delivery. The cultural reasons are related to using regions as mechanisms to legitimately contain differences within a state (Henderson, 2010a). Regions can be used to retain central state power while recognising difference, for example, in the UK or Spain. The political drivers of regions suggest that they improve democratic engagement and create 'institutional completeness' (Breton, 1964, quoted in Henderson, 2010a) and may serve to increase trust. However, individuals who support provincial governments may have less trust in national ones (Henderson, 2010b). This could be a key driver for EU integration policies. The political reason has been the development of sub-state government as part of state-building and to develop capacity at this level.

The EU's regional policy has been focused on delivery, as regional and sub-state governments are frequently the main implementers of EU policies. Governments consider this to be threatening to their position as they lose their ability to influence and control sub-state governance agendas (Marks, 1992), although the effects will differ in each member state (Borzel, 2001). On the other hand, Allen (2010) argues that the bargain between the EU and the member states on funds and their application creates greater control than generally recognised. Allen suggests that EU regional funds act as local political 'spending money' that enables the EU to both fulfil its objectives of a sub-state contract and promote an EU agenda of combined geographies. However, it could also be used by member state governments to buy off their localities with notional freedoms and funding. Where policies are delivered through regulations, this reduces governments' ability to localise their delivery.

The expanding role of EU policy and spending programmes has led to the establishment of regional offices in Brussels. They lobby for their place-based interests and advise home regions about proposed EU activities. These offices can have differential impacts relating to the size and importance of their member state. This may privilege larger member states or those that have had EU membership longest (Murphy, 2011). At the same time, the information which is gleaned from the staff in these offices can also be used to lobby and influence member states (Kettunen and Kull, 2009). They can also be used as a mechanism by member states to test out different approaches or obtain information useful in state-level negotiations. In some cases, the offices from different member states join forces to create alliances to promote specific outcomes and initiatives or to undertake indirect lobbying for each other.

The EU's Cohesion policy and Fund has done much to support the practical application of MLG (Bache, 2008). When the EU requires partnerships for integrated cohesion projects, it has the effect of deconstructing the EU into territorial spaces, which can be reassembled for different purposes, including across borders. This is a significant factor in the promotion of MLG. In the UK, there is no tier of regional government and only one land border, unlike many of the other member states. Since 1999, the UK has devolved responsibilities in Scotland, Wales and Northern Ireland for the interpretation and delivery of EU legislation in areas such as agriculture, transport and environmental issues. However, although representatives of the nations can be involved in EU negotiations, they can only represent the UK position. Devolution delivers after policy and legislation is agreed centrally. Is this MLG or a separation between policy and delivery?

Multi-Level Governance: theory, outcome or policy?

Regional policies in the EU have developed internally and have had institutional responses in member states. These policies for place and sub-state government have extended into the principles of MLG. MLG is an essential feature of the EU and has been developing as a stronger component of the legal and operational framework since 1972, although it is not the only governance structure or scale where it is exhibited (Peters and Pierre, 2009). MLG has multiple conceptual personalities, including as a theory (Marks and Hooghe, 2004), a normative theory (Bache and Flinders, 2004b) or an amalgam of theories (George, 2004). It can be seen as a site of interdisciplinary intertextuality (Bache and Flinders, 2004a; Welch and Kennedy-Pipe, 2004) or an analytical tool

(George, 2004). It is also considered as a model or paradigm (Jordan, 1999), a description (Jordan, 2001) or *sui generis* that is unable to be classified (Hix, 1998; Bache and Flinders, 2004a, 2004b). It is rarely considered as a policy – that is, an intended consequence of EU strategy, legislation and delivery to deliver a theory, model or paradigm to achieve specific ends – although that appears to be its role in practice.

1. Multi-Level Governance as sui generis

Before discussing the different ways in which MLG can be viewed, it is important to consider whether MLG in the EU can be categorised at all. Hix (1998) argues that the EU is without categorisation because its intergovernmental structure includes relationships with states and organisations that are not hierarchical. Bache and Flinders (2004a, 2004b) argue that the EU is *sui generis* as it is neither a country that can be seen as having domestic political characteristics nor an international organisation. Thus, MLG within and between European states differs from a federal structure, such as the US, or an international organisation that is bound by individual state treaties, such as the World Trade Organization (WTO), or the influence of membership, such as Organisation for Economic Co-operation and Development (OECD). However, the discussion here identifies the ways in which MLG can be considered. Rather than being without categorisation, the evolving policy impulse of MLG in the EU has a specific culture, style and purpose and is being implemented across the largest world market. In other ways, this latticed approach to horizontal and vertical governance integration may be the only way that the EU can maintain its strength and its accountability structures.

2. Multi-Level Governance as theory

The discussions about theories of MLG are frequently set in the context of the relationship between national governments and the international organisations of which they are members (Cairney, 2012). This is an intergovernmentalist approach and considers, for example, the relationships between membership of the WTO as an individual state and through the EU, where negotiations are undertaken on behalf of all member states. One focus of the discussion about the role of MLG as a theory is on the issues and tensions that are generated in its application. George (2004) discusses these in the context of the 'spillovers' from the European project. MLG can be viewed as a problematic point of disconnection in the work of the EU, where member states can make formal and informal alliances to provide an extra layer of 'transactional' networking, interpretation and influence on policy development and delivery (Sandholtz and Zysman, 1989; Peters and Pierre, 2004). These relationships can be further extended where particular scales of government are dissatisfied with central government (Gamble, 2004).

A second focus of MLG theory is on its functional role. Much of the debate on MLG has developed into a discussion on centralisation versus fragmentation in spheres of authority (Rosenau, 2004). MLG can perform roles in engaging different tiers of government in common agendas, potentially as a means of creating a democratic mandate against or within which wider governance approaches to models can be set. Conversely, Peters and Pierre (2004) argue that MLG is a combination of networks and hierarchies that operate both formally and informally simultaneously but exclude formal decision-making processes of government or intergovernmental processes. The main concern remains about transparency of influence in these processes as policy and legislation is formed but these issues remain the same at all levels of democratically accountable government and not only an issue for the EU.

3. Multi-Level Governance as an analytical framework

MLG can also be an analytical framework within which decision-making and inter-scalar government relations can be examined (Marks, 1992, 1993), through a consideration of the quality of the exchange, negotiation and coordination (Pierre and Stoker, 2000). MLG recognises that policy and legislation has a 'territorial reach' (Marks and Hooghe, 2004, p 16) that is represented through democratically accountable bodies, for example, Parliaments and other governance bodies set up for particular purposes. Marks and Hooghe (2004) developed this approach into two types of MLG, where Type 1 is formal, which in its most pure form is federal government, and Type II is formal but flexible, and can include a range of actors other than those directly elected. This approach to framework was developed in response to the Single European Market's (SEM's) role in changing the nature of European decision-making. Marks and Hooghe (2004) state that the implementation of the SEM confirmed a path towards greater integration, which is based on cooperation rather than unification into a single state (Faludi, 2011).

In this analytical framework, Marks and Hooghe (2004) recognise that policymaking extends beyond the member states and their pooled sovereignty. The SEM introduced 'influencers' in policy development beyond governments. Others, such as Kitzinger (1973), have argued that these influencing forces have been there from the outset, although the introduction of the SEM did more to codify their role, whether through the European Economic and Social Committee or the Committee of the Regions (CoR). Much of Marks and Hooghe's concern has been whether the EU is a Type I or a Type II example of MLG. However, the EU represents characteristics of both types in that it is a formal arrangement bound by treaties, which are the highest form of international agreement, while, like any governmental organisation, the structure, agencies and technologies used to achieve the agreed objectives can be more flexible. Both formal governance arrangements, including pooled sovereignty, and informal methods of delivery are subject to influence (Jordan, 1990, 2003).

4. Multi-Level Governance as an outcome

When considering MLG as an outcome, Marks (1992, 1993) relates this to the EU's organisational structure and role. The key question here is whether the EU's multi-scalar policy gives rise to MLG as an intended or unintended consequence (Peters and Pierre, 2009). If MLG is an unintended consequence, then there may be cultures, methods or communication within the EU that foster this outcome. These could include policy communities and mobilities, which develop as member states consider the ways in which they are intending to implement specific policies or legislation (Marks and Hooghe, 2004; Kuus, 2011a, 2011b, 2011c).

If MLG is an intended outcome, then it could be viewed as a soft power mechanism (Nye, 2004) promoted by the Commission to develop and deepen its relationships with sub-state governments as a 'softly, softly' approach towards integration. The positioning of professionals and politicians working together is a mechanism for self-determined methods of multi-scalar working. These approaches can be identified through experimentation funded through the EU's cross-governance projects to promote policy development and learning. These create a more positive relationship between sub-state governance and the EU while also enabling the development of multiple policy solutions through projects. In this way, a Commission-preferred solution can be selected from multi-scalar exemplars, thus creating solution 'ownership' from sub-state levels.

5. Multi-Level Governance as a model

MLG can also be considered as a model or paradigm (Jordan, 1999, 2001), both within the EU and within individual states, with particular reference to regional government (Pierre and Stoker, 2000). The EU's role is derived from pooling member state powers on specific issues. There is an assumption of a state model that vertically aligns institutions within a hierarchy of power. MLG suggests less formal models or arrangements where there are flexible and voluntaristic arrangements between organisations that have different roles and influence upon the state. It represents the shift from government to governance.

6. Multi-Level Governance as a policy

However, in terms of the EU, it may be more fruitful to consider MLG as a policy – that is, an intended purpose. Within this, MLG does not have any model of the allocation of responsibilities between scales of government (Pierre and Stoker, 2000). As Hix (1998) indicates, it may be a mistake to see policymaking in the EU in the same way as that undertaken in individual states. The intergovernmental structures and indirect delivery role of the EU means that there is as much focus on its delivery apparatus as on its substantive policies. If the policies cannot be interpreted and delivered by member states, this is problematic, not least as the Commission has to use legal remedies for non-compliance. If the policy cannot be delivered, this compliance route might be undermined if applied across all member states. At the same time, the furtherance of the principles of the Treaty of Rome for 'ever closer union' similarly applies to the policy agenda as well as the delivery programme. This promotes MLG as an objective outcome within the EU, and uses its potential to engage and harness policy and expenditure to common ends.

Pursuing MLG as a policy mechanism can have at least three objectives. The first is efficiency. Scales of the state promote different ends or means to achieve outcomes. The resulting competition and the associated administrative costs between scales of government are wasteful and dilute the achievement of what may be common ends. A study by the Audit Commission (2004) and the *Total place* initiative (LGA, 2010) have exemplified this within England. Second, working across boundaries both horizontally and vertically can help the EU to become more competitive in a global market. The EU has the largest market, yet, despite common trade frameworks, still has diseconomies in comparison with others, for example, the US. The third role of

MLG is to generate unity of purpose and cohesion within the EU by engaging people and governments at all scales. The EU has been criticised for being distant from communities, with a democratic deficit. The Commission is aware that this is undermining its legitimacy (Barroso, 2012). Governments may also prefer to demonstrate distance from the EU while engaging more directly behind the scenes (Daddow and Gaskarth, 2011).

Promoting MLG as a policy strengthens both horizontal and vertical integration within the EU and can be seen through the lenses of culture, efficiency and affectivity. These policies have expanded over time and can be considered as integration 'lite', that is, not designed to deliver a fully integrated or federal Europe within the short or medium term. Nevertheless, much of the EU's work programme is concerned with some degree of horizontal and vertical integration.

The cultural underpinning of horizontal integration stems from the approach to territory in both France and Germany (Marsh and Rhodes, 1992; Harvie, 1994; Booth, 2009) prior to membership of the UK into the EU, after which a more selective approach was taken. It has been generated through projects that privilege activities that are across country borders, such as Trans-European Transport Network projects, where higher levels of funding are provided. In regional development, INTERREG projects are designed to support joint working across member states, although these localities may not always be coterminous. It is supported by the European Observation Network, a research programme that engages localities in policymaking (CEC, 2010d). There are also initiatives such as the PEACE programme on the island of Ireland. Lastly, there are projects that encourage groupings of places or those with similar interests, such as cities and peripheral rural areas. Horizontal integration was recognised through the establishment of the CoR in 1994 and has developed into an integral part of the soft measures of EU policymaking. The CoR is a weak organisation with few powers (Bourne, 2007), but the opinions of the CoR are taken seriously. These horizontal integration measures improve knowledge and share problem-solving across the EU's territory.

The efficiency argument for MLG as policy is that EU competiveness can be improved by removing the barriers identified in the SEM's inception (CEC, 1985; Monti, 2010). These are identified as both the intended and unintended consequences of building the largest global internal market. There are also unintended consequences of the use of cultural norms and costs of entry to markets that do not promote competition.

The third objective of integration is that of affectivity – emotion – making people feel more positive about Europe and their role in it. This primarily works through horizontal integration. The affectivity argument for MLG in the EU is based on the development of the EU as a place and a symbol. Delors adopted a flag and an anthem when President of the Commission. Since then, there has been much effort by the Commission to ensure that these symbols of collective governance are used and recognised. All projects funded by the EU, together with the bodies distributing these funds, are requested to display the EU flag.

Through the use of funds in localities, the EU can appear in the role of a benevolent grandparent, one step removed from the often-difficult relationship between sub-state and central governments (Krahmann, 2003). The Commission has been able to develop relationships with sub-state government institutions that are eager to access funding and support for their territories. This is particularly so in the UK, where there have been arguments about central Government withholding or underspending EU funds that have been made available or allocated to localities. As in all grandparent relationships, states feel aggrieved because they have to maintain relations with sub-state governments in a variety of roles and not only provide additional funding for occasional projects.

As well as horizontal integration, there have also been proposals to improve vertical integration between the EU and layers of government within states. This anchors policies to places and attempts to remove the costs of competition between scales of government (Barca, 2009). It is based on the interlinking EU policies of subsidiarity and territorial cohesion, which are discussed in more detail later. It can also be set within wider international benchmarking by the OECD. This approach has been influenced by Krugman's (1991) new economic geography and places a high value on the effectiveness of integrated multi-scalar governance models and strong leadership to deliver social, economic and environmental outcomes (Charbit, 2011). It is also mirrored in a similar initiative of the World Bank for developing countries (Brigham, 2011).

Within the EU, this approach to territorial assemblages has developed further. The potential for adopting and recognising legal structures for sub-state localities across borders through European Groupings of Territorial Cooperation (EGTCs) was recognised (Layard and Holder, 2010; Holder and Layard, 2011) and introduced through a regulation. Their objective is to 'facilitate and promote cross-border, transnational and interregional cooperation between its members' (CEC, 2006b, Article 1). An EGTC is made up of localities in at least two member states, regional authorities, local authorities and/ or bodies governed by public law. Within the bounds of its remit, an EGTC acts on behalf of its members. EGTCs thus enjoy the status accorded to legal entities by national law. An EGTC may be entrusted with implementing programmes co-financed by the EU or any other cross-border cooperation project.

These cross-state cooperative governance models have been developed in the EU through, for example, the Black Sea and Danube Councils. These new governance forms create partnerships and common working across their areas, but also have place-based contracts across government scales at local levels within their areas. Although the UK has yet to join in the formation of any formal EGTC, the creation of the British Irish Council (BIC) as part of the Belfast Agreement in 1998 was modelled on the Baltic Sea Council. The BIC comprises the four nations of the UK, Ireland and the States of Jersey, Guernsey and the Isle of Man, and senior politicians from all states meet regularly. The BIC has been based in Jersey and had no dedicated secretariat. It developed a series of working groups on intra-BIC cooperation and policy-sharing. They include a variety of topics, such as energy, transport, drug abuse and spatial planning. In 2012, the BIC established in new permanent headquarters in Edinburgh, seconded staff and began to actively review its programme of activities (Clifford and Morphet, 2012).

Another device that has promoted cross-boundary working is polycentricity, which is located in the principles of economic geography. This has encouraged working between multiple centres in functional (urban) economic areas to enhance the effectiveness and efficiency of urban agglomerations (Turok and Bailey, 2004). The theory is based on the notions of complementarity and accessibility to promote employment access for those currently excluded or marginalised in the labour market (Centre for Cities, 2012). Polycentricity first emerged as an approach to services allocation and functional spatial relationships in the European Spatial Development Perspective (CEC, 1999) and works particularly in Germany and across land borders, for example, on the island of Ireland. Like MLG, polycentricity has been seen as normative rather than evidence based, and promoted across the whole of the EU regardless of the differential success rates in its application (Davoudi and Strange, 2008, Faludi, 2010). The concept has also been used in peripheral regions, such as the Atlantic Arc, where cities and large towns have complementary services and assets (Groth et al, 2011).

As a policy objective in the EU, MLG is subject to little critical inquiry. It can be seen in the context of a retreat from an integrated state to one where the location of competencies is important (Bickerton,

2011). Conversely, MLG may strengthen the centre of the EU and member states rather than sub-state government given the institutional 'grip' and is apparent in each member state and 'controls' power relations and access between the central state and the EU (Peters and Pierre, 2004). Sub-state governance is still viewed as a hierarchical institutional form rather than as a contract between equals (Allen, 2012).

MLG is also present outside institutional settings, operating policy and practice networks for places and scales. In this role, it is regarded as an integrating tool and as a means of improving efficient and effective practice through exchanges of ideas and the convergence of cultural practices. However, this overlooks the parallel institutional changes. As noted earlier, critics of MLG have elided governance and government and have suggested that the state is 'hollowed out' or reduced as a consequence, leaving a conceptual confusion as to where responsibility lies. However, MLG can also be seen as a transformation of government, strengthening new relationships by informal and formal overlapping (Geddes, 2004; Murphy, 2011). These have been emerging since the introduction of the subsidiarity principle in the SEA in 1986.

The role of subsidiarity

Subsidiarity was first introduced in the SEA and then subsequently developed through the Treaty of the European Union 1992 (TEU). This followed a discussion proposed by Denmark at the Birmingham Council during the UK's Presidency of the EU in 1992 that a 'decision must be taken as closely as possible to the citizen. Greater unity can be achieved without excessive centralization. It is for each member state to decide how its powers should be exercised domestically' (CEC, 1992a Annex 1 para 1.8).

It can also be interpreted as a rule, where a policy should be assigned to the level of governance that can discharge it most efficiently (Scott, 2001). Within the UK, this debate on subsidiarity was directed towards 'traditional' EU debates on limiting the powers of the EU (Duff, 1993; Paterson, 1994), rather than on its wider implications. Major introduced it as a mechanism to reduce the 'centralising trend' (Parliamentary debate, 20/21 May 1992).

The implications of subsidiarity for the UK were considered (DETR, 1999). Duff (1993) predicted that the development of subsidiarity would be greater devolution in the EU. Duff also wondered how much longer the UK could hold out as a centralist state despite both the Prime Minister and Foreign Minister stating that subsidiarity had nothing to do with devolution (Foreign Affairs Committee 1991-2HC 223-II).

As with other EU issues, the implications of the application of the principle were discussed and understood by the House of Commons Foreign Affairs Committee, but they chose to assume that it related to relationships between the state and the EU, rather than the state devolving to nations and localities (Drewry and Giddings, 2004). The adoption and application has been significant. As a treaty protocol, it has shaped governance scales and relationships within member states, not least within the UK. The principle of subsidiarity is that of equality between tiers of government, shifting this from a long-standing hierarchical relationship. This is shown in Figures 8.1 and 8.2. In the UK, the application of subsidiarity has changed the relationship between Parliament and the EU, promoted devolution, and a general power of competence for local government and an increase in the powers and role of parish councils. The UK Parliament's relationship with the EU has been difficult (Giddings and Drewry, 2004) and when subsidiarity was considered by the House of Commons, it concluded that this would not make much difference to the current system (HoC, 2008). However, through the Lisbon Treaty, subsidiarity has extended to the role of member state Parliaments, forming a virtual third chamber within the EU (Cooper, 2012).

There are some weaknesses in the application of subsidiarity, not least who will enforce it. Lawyers have taken the view that it would be a difficult concept to operate as they saw it as non-judicable (Bainbridge and Teasdale, 1995). Further, in the application of subsidiarity, there has to be sufficient fluidity to allow competencies to be reassigned between different levels. Scott (2001) argues that as sub-state governments have no role within the EU other than through their own government, subsidiarity has little effective purchase. Scott further argues that subsidiarity reinforces the nation state while creating the conditions for sub-national governments to campaign for independence. This might be the case, but it is also important to consider the application of the principle of territorial cohesion (CEC, 2009b), where all scales, including the EU, act together in support of localities and territories. The application of subsidiarity is an essential constituent of MLG. As Millar and Scott (1993, p 94) point out, subsidiarity is not only a devolving policy, but also one that:

> implies that responsibility is shared between tiers of government and that each tier is responsible for those functions that it is best able to discharge. This means that the various tiers must be in continual contact through clearly defined institutional arrangements.

Figure 8.1: Multi-level Governance: traditional model

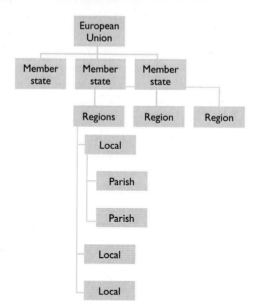

By focusing on MLG without considering the underpinning principle of subsidiarity, it is possible to overlook its transformational role. This leads to an undervaluation of MLG, defining it as the result of political flex between layers of the vertical state (March and Olsen, 1984; Peters and Pierre, 2004). In applying subsidiarity, local state governance levels are equalised or privileged so that their voice counts in a way that has the same or similar weight to that of the central state. This creates horizontal and vertical agreements between equals who together need to determine how each will contribute. This approach harnesses the centre to the local in governance relations.

In applying subsidiarity, the EU has promoted this alignment through multi-scalar contracts around place so that integrated programmes are prepared and delivered in ways that meet common ends (Barca, 2009). Multi-scalar contracts are proposed that lock together the different governance scales of the state in common objectives agreed between equals. The delivery of each of the components is then undertaken at the appropriate scale. The development of this approach in the UK has been proposed by the Political and Constitutional Reform Select Committee in the House of Commons, which has issued an illustrative proposed code for central and local government (HoC, 2012).

Figure 8.2: Multi-level Governance policy diagram

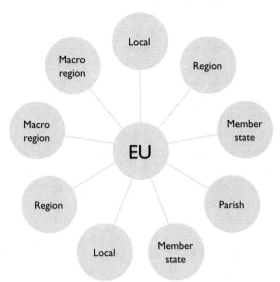

Territorial cohesion

The completion of the subsidiarity protocol in the Lisbon Treaty 2009 has been accompanied by a new principle of territorial cohesion. This is the third lens through which EU policies will be examined and added to existing principles of economic and social cohesion. The definition of territorial cohesion is not explicit (Mirwaldt et al, 2009), although its key objectives are further European integration through policy spheres, including sectors, as they relate to places (CEC, 2009b). This application of territorial cohesion to sectoral policy is an integrating measure and as significant as that applied to the environment through the SEA. The Commission's *Green Paper on territorial cohesion* (CEC, 2008a) suggests that the subsidiarity protocol will be used to encourage the internal integration of policies and to develop the benefits of territorial difference within the EU. The Commission states that it sees territorial cohesion as a direct development from the application of structural fund policies, but a move away from the regional scale as the principal level of consideration. In addition, territorial cohesion is suitable to all parts of the EU's space, not just those that are lagging behind EU averages (CEC, 2011f). The primary focus in territorial cohesion policy is economic growth and resilience, particularly in areas that are congested or sparsely populated. The policy is also linked to those for transport and the environment and is concerned to promote ways in which localities can have access to services and energy supplies.

The application of territorial cohesion policies is focused on two scales. First, the policies and programmes of the EU need to be considered and assessed through a territorial lens. Like environment policy, this covers all sectoral areas within the EU's competencies for both infrastructure investment and softer programmes in areas such as skills development. It also includes strategic policies, such as those for research, competition and maritime areas. Territorial cohesion will also apply within and between member states where activities that are within EU competencies are delivered. As part of this approach, the EU has adopted a *Territorial agenda 2020* (CEC, 2011f) alongside its economic agenda, *Europe 2020* (CEC, 2010a).

One of the key issues of such a wide-ranging and potentially influential policy is its application in practice. Here, the Commission has identified some specific instruments (CEC, 2008b). These are primarily focused on governance, which is defined as a permanent and cooperative process. All EU and, by implication, member state policies will be 'territorialised' and Territorial Impact Assessments (TIAs) are to be used to evaluate policies, programmes and projects from a territorial perspective (CEC, 2010c) prior to decisions being made (Bohme et al, 2011). These assessments should be against the summative criteria of territorial efficiency, territorial quality and territorial identity (Camagni, 2010), such as those identified by the OECD (Charbit, 2011).

How has subsidiarity shaped and influenced British public policies?

Subsidiarity has always been challenging in the UK, which is characterised as a centralised state. However, since the wide range of constitutional reforms introduced since 1997, it could be argued that this is less the case. These reforms have included human rights, the legal and court system, the House of Lords, and the House of Commons (Peele, 2000). It has seen the introduction and continuation of the process of devolution in Scotland and Wales and a new devolution settlement in Northern Ireland (in 2007). Within England and Wales, local authorities have been given a general power of competence that now gives them the legal personality of organisations and individuals (in the Localism Act 2011). The regional tier that had been reconstructed and occupied by the centre from 1993 has been abolished and replaced by self-determining functional economic areas (FEAs) and parishes, while neighbourhoods have been given more powers and rights.

However, critics argue that the UK core executive still controls resources (Pugalis, 2010), powers and information. Although there are more opportunities for localities to self-manage, there is still some way to go in changing the culture of the centre. This, they argue, requires institutional reform rather than constitutional reform (Pierre and Stoker, 2000). The Coalition government has promised that services will be run by a variety of providers, including communities, through its Open Government initiative (HMG, 2011a, 2012), but there is little evidence that this will create a significant shift in power relations or methods of resource distribution.

From 1997, the Labour government responded to the EU subsidiarity protocol. The preceding Major government had been at war over Europe and with a new government, it was possible for the civil service to use the machinery of government to develop approaches and programmes that underpinned a change in government style, objectives and policy (Hix, 2000). As Hazell (1999a) noted in 1997, the incoming government introduced 12 constitutional bills. Although this was announced as a major reform in the constitutional settlement before the Labour Party came into power, once elected, these constitutional changes were managed separately and not seen as a single programme of reform of the UK constitution. However, 15 years later, it can be argued that that is what was achieved.

1. English regional policy

Since its inception in the 1930s, regional policy in the UK has been directed towards localities with poorer performing economies (Glasson and Marshall, 2007). Only in the period since 2007 could it be argued that integrated economic and planning strategies have emerged. Before this, successive waves of policies, including new towns, selective assistance and regional economic planning councils, relied on trickle-down theory. Regional policy has always been a central function of the state and this continued when the UK joined the EU, with ERDF and other cohesion programmes administered centrally (Hazell, 1999a). Competition between regions has also been used as a reason why the central state has needed a role, despite the evidence from the rest of Europe that local political leadership and a strong sense of territorial identity have been central to economic success. One of the key sites of this contestation between central and local government has been on the use of these EU structural funds in the UK. The Treasury has been concerned to ensure that the EU does not give more funding to areas than would otherwise be due to them through domestic funding mechanisms. This is the principle of 'additionality'. EU funding cannot substitute for member state funding. A second issue has been where the Treasury has refused to release EU funds.

The introduction of subsidiarity in 1986, and enhanced in 1992, created some difficultly for the centralised state. Still locked into post-Thatcherite centralist conventions, it was difficult to make any changes in the structure of the state and sub-state powers. The opportunity of the general election in 1992 to effect 'machinery of government' changes in policy was also not available as the Conservatives remained in office. Europe was the focus of most contestation within the government in the 1992–97 period. As a response, the civil service proposed a raft of reforms that inserted a centrally run regional scale of government but without any directly elected accountability. Following fact-finding missions to France, the establishment of Government Offices of the Regions (GOs) were promoted as the main link between the local and central states, and introduced in 1993. Even in their establishment, they reflected the continued separation and rivalry within government departments as each vied to ensure that their mandarins were appointed to the new Regional Director posts.

Over time, these GOs were expanded to include wider representation of government departments, although, within each GO, civil servants were still tied to their 'home' departments. Civil servants in the GOs were described as being 'co-located' rather than a single team. These staff had their first allegiance to their home department, and not to the Regional Director. GOs were expected to be the 'go to' organisation for local authorities and other organisations when seeking government advice and support (Bulmer et al, 2002). In practice, GOs varied in their quality, and where the head of the GO was delivering a home department's mainstream agenda, for example, receipt of structural funds or transport, they had greater influence in their region on this issue. GOs also became the main location for the delivery of the government's planning agenda and were used by the central departments, including the Treasury, to promote house-building to unwilling local authorities. The GOs also took over the responsibility for allocating EU funds, establishing programme committees in order to provide some semblance of governance. However, these arrangements did not meet EU criteria for the democratic management of EU funds.

Local authority leaders and chief executives quickly recognised that all the key decisions were still taken in the centre and although it was important to have good relationships with GOs, it was also necessary to retain working relationships with policy leads in central departments. From the outset, GOs were underpowered, not least because, within England, ministers hold functional rather than territorial responsibilities.

There were some successive attempts to designate ministers for regions but these started in a fanfare of activity and seldom lasted. From 2007, a minister sitting for a West Midlands constituency was appointed as the convenor of the regional ministers and was seen to have some success in championing the role of regions. The transformation of GOs into offices for specifically appointed regional ministers was considered as a policy option in 2009 (Hope and Leslie, 2009), but was overtaken by the abolition of regional institutions by the Coalition government in 2010.

For those who supported the insertion of a regional tier of government in England, the introduction of GOs was seen to be a move in the right direction. GOs were supported by the establishment of Regional Development Agencies (RDAs), as non-departmental government bodies, to undertake a delivery role in 1998. GOs worked closely with RDAs, which were comprised of former officials from central government departments and their agencies. These officials had been morphing their roles and priorities between agencies in the employment, competition and skills agendas since 1972. The language and communication between GOs and RDAs was in the same dialect in comparison with either organisation's conversations with local authorities, and this separation remained until their abolition in 2010. Some larger local authorities, such as county councils, managed to obtain unofficial agreements with their RDAs on priorities in funding packages or projects, bypassing smaller local authorities, but this worked only when RDAs' roles were threatened with reduction or unwelcome change.

Although GOs were established to manage funding and powers available to sub-state levels, particularly local authorities, they were democratically accountable to local government. Bulmer et al (2002) argue that their establishment supported more systematic approaches to regionalism in England through more programmatic approaches, developing consciousness and operational arrangements between regional interests. At their best, GOs could help to organise interests within a region and act as a conduit for expressing views to the centre. They could ensure that ministers visited the right projects and negotiated the funds that were divided between regions. On the other hand, GO staff retained their conflicted loyalties within the organisation. GOs also gave ministers and officials at the centre an opportunity to demonstrate that they were listening to the local level.

The adoption of the protocol on subsidiarity in 2009 meant that these existing regional arrangements would no longer serve. The election of the Coalition government in 2010 meant that the machinery of government could be used to implement the necessary post-Lisbon changes within the new ideological wrapper. Abolition of all regional structures – GOs, RDAs and Regional Assemblies and Regional Plans – was commenced in 2010. They were replaced by local authorities as the democratically accountable units, which could join together in clusters and groups, particularly within Local Nature Partnerships (LNPs) or Local Enterprise Partnerships (LEPs). Local funding powers were reformed through the general power of competence (in the Localism Act 2011).

Carter (2002) considers that the UK adapted to changes in EU subsidiarity policy rather than being transformed by them (Murphy, 2011). However, there seem to be differences in responding to EU policy for strategic or constitutional issues and resources at the operational level, where civil servants might have more day-to-day influence. At the strategic level, the application of EU policy in the UK led to devolution, which has meant a major structural reform in the way that the country is governed, but there has been no change in the constitution and the UK remains a unitary state for external purposes (Happold, 2000).

The introduction of devolution created the impetus for growth policies in Cardiff and Edinburgh. In England, a strategy emerged to develop a major growth pole outside the South-East in Manchester. Following the bomb that destroyed part of Manchester's city centre in 1996, the delivery of the Commonwealth Games in 2002, the move of the BBC to Salford in 2012 and the introduction of integrated governance and the repatriation of taxation to Manchester have all been part of a consistent but unacknowledged growth pole policy. This was supported by TEN-T investment in the West Coast Main Line completed in 2008 and the proposed investment in the route of High Speed Train 2.

Multi-scalar contracts were introduced in 2003. Initially, Public Service Agreements in England were contracts between central government and individual local authorities (Morphet, 2008). These were developed into Local Area Agreements (LAAs), where public-sector partners in each local authority area and central government agreed targets chosen from a menu of national indicators and also used in Scotland through Single Outcome Agreements. This approach was developed into Total Place budgets (LGA, 2010) as a mechanism to pool central and local objectives and budgets for places and people. LAAs were suspended by the Coalition government in 2010, but single central and local Community Budgets have continued. In Manchester, central and local government officials have been located in the same teams and budgets have been pooled and aligned. Local government has criticised the slow progress on joint-working and devolved budgets, but they suggest the delivery of vertically integrated policies.

This multi-scalar approach continues at sub-regional or FEA level. In 2006, in addition to the EGTC, the EU also launched a new approach to the application of social, economic and territorial cohesion in cities (Hahn, 2011). This included the development of city-wide Integrated Territorial Investment (ITI) programmes for FEAs. This approach has started to emerge in the UK. In 2007, following a policy review (HMG, 2007), Multi Area Agreements were introduced across FEAs. These were soft governance mechanisms confined to the largest cities as a 'cities' policy. Following the general election of 2010, the Coalition government introduced Local Enterprise Partnerships (LEPs), which were open to all areas, self-determined in their boundaries, but had no specific legal powers. LEPs now cover the whole of England's territory and 99% of local authorities belong to them. LEPs are mechanisms for vertical and horizontal integration (Morphet, 2011) and are developing programmatic structures in response to devolved funding for specific programmes, such as transport, skills and EU programmes. The government has launched an additional cities programme, which is focused on governance and is a better fit with OECD models of cities as generators of growth through strong leadership. In England, there have been criticisms of LEPs, particularly that they have no defined powers and the areas chosen were determined by political rather than economic factors (Pugalis, 2010). There have also been criticisms about the business-led approach of LEPs and their lack of democratic accountability, although leading LEPs like Greater Manchester are forming legally binding joint committees between the LEP local authorities to insert this layer of leadership and accountability.

However, despite this, LEPs have created a sub-state mechanism for achieving horizontal and vertical integration, which is also mirrored elsewhere in the UK. Cities policies have been announced in Scotland (Scottish Government, 2012), Wales (Welsh Government, 2012) and Northern Ireland (DRD, 2012) and all have common features of horizontal and vertical engagement. The operation of these policies within FEAs requires joint-working and they are focused specifically on economic growth and employment. The provision of transport, skills and housing is seen as part of the requirements for growth and this scale of horizontal and vertical integration is primarily based on infrastructure investment and is outward-focused. They are in direct comparison with the multi-scalar Community Budgeting approaches, which are primarily focused on generating efficiencies through removing organisational duplication and overheads. However, despite their different approaches, both are focused on an increase in place-based integration, which is likely to increase to meet the emerging practices of subsidiarity as set out in the Heseltine Review (2012).

2. Devolution

Devolution is the result of both internal and external pressures. Across the UK, nations that make up the union have wanted devolved powers and this culminated in 1979 with a referendum on devolution in Scotland. This was not successful but it led to increasing practices of policy separation. The external pressure to promote devolution came following the adoption of subsidiarity from 1986 onwards (Paterson, 1994) and was developed through the Scottish Constitutional Convention in 1989.

The implementation of devolution in Scotland, Wales and London was a central feature of the Labour manifesto before the general election in 1997. This 'rectified' past Thatcherite ideological reconstructions, such as the abolition of the Greater London Council. This was accompanied by the Peace Process in Northern Ireland, which was agreed in 1998, and also a new position for local government when the government signed the charter of self-government in 1997 and introduced the general power of well-being in the Local Government Act 2000. In Scotland and Wales, devolution started as a continuing process in 1999.

The position in London was different. Before it was abolished in 1985, the GLC had significant powers over London's public services. These have been increasingly restored and extended to the Mayor since 1999. London was the first UK city to have a directly elected mayor with responsibilities transferred from the GO for London, such as those for regeneration. The Mayor also has responsibility for the Metropolitan Police, which had formerly been directly run by the Home Secretary. The Mayor may now be the second most powerful politician in the UK based on London's population size, its influence, the reach of powers and the size of budget.

One of the key issues following devolution was the relationship with the EU. Hepburn and McLoughlin (2011) argue that Europe has been a mechanism through which nationalism has been advanced in Scotland and Ireland, specifically through relationships with the Commission. Before devolution, the UK government had detailed consultation on EU policy issues with Scotland, Northern Ireland and Wales (Bulmer et al, 2002; Bulmer and Burch, 2008). This has remained and it is the delivery of EU policies that has been the core of the devolution settlement. It is estimated that this comprised 80% of devolved responsibilities (Bulmer et al, 2002). This could be attributed to the core executive's view that delivery was less important than policy and therefore devolved without any loss of power or responsibility. There was also a need to demonstrate that subsidiarity compliance had been achieved (Hood, 2011).

The devolved nations became responsible for the interpretation and delivery of the UK's pooled policy in areas such as transport, agriculture, energy, rural affairs, planning, housing and regeneration, but not for direct EU negotiation. New formal arrangements were established through Concordats (Scott, 2001). However, much of the effort seems to have been directed at maintaining the status quo, as Bulmer et al (2002, p 39) state:

> it is evident that those responsible for drafting the EU concordat (both within Whitehall and the territorial administrations) began from the premise that the prevailing administrative arrangements for handling EU business in the UK operated extremely well ... the challenge facing officials was to ensure that any changes to the UK's European policy procedures did not weaken a tried and proven policy.

The UK nations retain a separate presence in Brussels to gather information, provide input into national discussions and promote soft lobbying (Bulmer et al, 2002; Murphy, 2011). The Commission is also influenced by local issues and case studies when considering policies and legislation. There is little evidence that any of the nations have 'any influence over how UK Ministers conduct themselves in the EU' (Wright, 2004, p 236) or that this position is necessarily different from other member states (Thielemann, 2000).

Devolution has also caused problems for government departments based in London. As there is no separation of English policy, they have to take a position representing both England and the UK. In these cases, issues are moderated by the UK Permanent Representation to the EU (Bulmer et al, 2002, pp 122–6). There have also been occasions where changes in EU policy have required a more centralised approach to delivery, such as that of strategic infrastructure for transport and energy (CEC, 2006c). Here, the UK needed to ensure compliance on policies that had been devolved, so government used the non-devolved issue of security as a means of wrapping UK policy (Wicks, 2009). The Infrastructure Act 2012 applies to all parts of the UK without any link to the devolution settlement.

Proposals to hold a referendum on ending Scotland's relationship with the UK, to become an independent state, have raised issues of the position of both Scotland and the UK in relation to EU membership. There could be a number of possible options (Thorp and Thompson, 2011): Scotland and the remainder of the UK stay in; both come out; both remain in membership but on a different basis; or the remainder of the UK stays in membership while Scotland reapplies (Happold, 2000). Mackay (2011) argues that progressing independence suggests that a federal structure could emerge for the UK alongside the other territories of the Isle of Man and the states of Guernsey and Jersey.

3. Local government

Since 1986, it has taken several steps before local government has achieved a general power of competence. The consideration of local authority size and function coincided with the UK's entry to the EU, when larger local authorities were created across England in 1974. Following the emergence of subsidiarity, there needed to be some reconsideration of central government's position on local government. Successive Conservative governments since 1979 had reduced the role of local government and councillors and this may have been engineered to ensure the ease of implementation of subsequent changes. Although rebuilding local government is generally credited with the incoming Labour government in 1997, there were already signs that change was underway. This was in three main areas: institutional, philosophical and popular. Institutional change was implemented through the creation of more unitary local authorities in England and the creation of complete unitary local government in Wales and Scotland in 1996. Second, a discussion about the role of local government in the future started. Foster and Plowden (1996) suggested that the state was being 'hollowed out' and that too much centralisation was actually counter to the efficient and effective running of the country. They argued that services managed within and by communities, such as the police, were likely to be more effective.

Yet, within local government, leaders were distracted from the application of subsidiarity through rounds of local government reorganisation at the local level, which were seen to be 'self-determined', that is, the product of bottom-up proposals, an example of the 'divide and rule' principle at work. While local authorities were located in warfare with each other, particularly between county and district councils, there was not likely to be any attention paid to the application of subsidiarity. At the same time, the local authority associations were encouraged to engage with the EU through their membership of the new CoRs established in 1994, where elected local government leaders representing UK localities sat alongside directly elected regional politicians from other parts of Europe. This was a disparity, but there was a sense of promise for future recognition (Bongers and Chatfield, 1993; Morphet, 1994).

There was also little public confidence in local government and there remained concerns about ethics and corruption (Foster and Plowden, 1996; Morphet, 2008). These had to be overcome before local government could achieve an independent standing, as required under subsidiarity. Another issue to be confronted was that of seeming inefficiency, although the introduction of open procurement and potential outsourcing also had begun to change this view. Local government had turned inward after sustained attack since 1979 and had to be shown to be fit to take more powers and independence. The process of change started in 1997, through improving local authority performance and public confidence (Hood, 1998). Local authorities have implemented customer-focused working, including personalisation of services and managed detailed policy changes for schools, welfare and public health (Morphet, 2008).

The constitutional settlement for local government through a general power of competence given to local authorities in the Localism Act 2011 means that they are no longer 'creatures of statute', that is, having a specific legal power for every action (Sear, 2012). The provenance of this change is located in subsidiarity. Despite differences in political ideology, the principle of localism was a common feature in the policies of the Labour government that introduced it in 2003 and the Coalition government that implemented it in 2011. The passage of the Localism Bill was fraught with numerous changes for planning and neighbourhoods. Yet, the most important features of the Bill, the changes to local government powers, were rarely discussed apart from at the Bill's press launch (Hope, 2010). By diverting attention towards other parts of the Bill, the constitutional position of local authorities in England was changed. As Hazell (2006) has commented, in all the constitutional changes, local government in England has been among the most privileged. Yet, old cultures die hard, as ministers continue to intervene in local issues such as the frequency of refuse collection (Pickles, 2012).

Conclusions

The application of spatial and territory-based policies and programmes within the principle of subsidiarity has had a major effect on the British constitution and the nature of government since 1986. First, the UK is now four nations, where delivery responsibilities of the state are devolved, with the exception of security and financial policy. The devolution settlement means that the four nations of the UK are responsible for the UK's compliance with EU legislation in devolved policy areas. However, the Government is less transparent on negotiating positions for new policies, programmes and legislation. The position of England remains anomalous in this situation. Government ministers confuse the UK with England, and this distinction is either misunderstood or ignored as inconvenient by a large part of the core executive. Those in the Cabinet Office looking into the future will be taking long-term EU commitments into account, but this is a small element of the core executive, which remains oblivious to this distinction (Hallsworth, 2011). This issue surfaces occasionally. Jenkins (2011), for example, has recently made a case for an English Parliament, while Lodge et al (2012) have argued that there is a growing popular case for separate governance for England. Rather, as occurred in the 1990s, the central state has diverted attention from this issue by devolving the powers of the English state to local authorities.

Although it is possible to see the territorial ambitions for Scotland, Wales and Northern Ireland, it is difficult to state any equivalent territorial objectives for England. There is no spatial or economic plan that sets out these objectives, as there are in the other nations of the UK. This suggests an unwillingness to confront the issue of England and appears related to any potential loss of power for the core executive. Indeed, as Hazell (1999b) anticipated, Bulmer and Burch (2009) found and Hallsworth (2011) projected, this is not an issue on the agenda of the English civil service.

Although the UK gives the appearance of growing national difference and independence since 1997, it is difficult to see this extending beyond the national determination of delivery methods for centrally negotiated EU/UK policies and legislation. The nations have no individual recognition within the EU, unlike sub-state government in Germany. Similarly, in local government and FEAs, more power over priorities, resources and delivery has been devolved, but these remain within agreed frameworks. Perhaps this is as far as devolution can go given that the UK is bound by the agreements made for pooled EU competencies. However, there may be further pressure for a joint approach to negotiating UK policy positions and a wider involvement by sub-state government in these processes. If the current centralised approach continues, will the UK meet the subsidiarity protocol test that it has agreed in the Lisbon Treaty 2009?

CHAPTER NINE

How does Europe shape British public policy?

Introduction

British public policy has been shaped by Europe in a number of ways. In this chapter, these shaping influences are considered using the issues, processes and outcomes that have been discussed in the rest of this book. In particular, they are considered through their role in the policy process, persistence in delivery and overarching principles such as subsidiarity. It will also consider those priorities where Europe has been the agent of change but not its source, such as opening the public sector to competition. Third, there will be a discussion of how these policy priorities have shaped outcomes, particularly in restructuring the state and its institutions, such as agencies, local government and devolution. It will consider the impact on political culture, the trend towards depoliticisation and lack of strategic expression that characterises the UK and England, although not the other nations of the UK. There will also be a discussion of the unintended consequences of this legacy and the habituated culture of engagement.

The opaque nature of the relationship that is discussed in Chapter One has persisted for 50 years since the UK's negotiation for entry into the EU and then through its subsequent membership. However, the externalised performance of this role has served to mask a number of different approaches and relationships between the UK and the EU. Although these have been cast as primarily antagonistic and subordinate throughout the whole period, different Prime Ministers have nuanced the external tone and internal conduct of these relationships. The majority of Prime Ministers have had specific objectives in relation to the EU and these have been their main focus as they have pursued membership (Macmillan, Heath and Wilson), the renegotiation of terms (Thatcher) or policy redirection (Thatcher, Major and Blair). These Prime Ministers have let other issues ride, both in the EU and in the application of EU legislation in the domestic context, while pursuing their main objectives.

Where Prime Ministers have focused on issues, they have been largely successful. Thatcher renegotiated the agreement for the UK's financial contribution at Fontainebleau and saw the introduction of the Single European Market (SEM) in 1986. Major introduced methods of funding that would lay the foundations for enlargement and further economic growth in the Maastricht Treaty 1992. Blair introduced benchmarking through the Open Method of Coordination (OMC) and extended the role of subsidiarity through the Amsterdam 1999 and Lisbon Treaties (agreed in 2007 and ratified in 2009), but Margaret Thatcher was the last Prime Minister to make a publicly positive case for the EU through the creation of the SEM. The influence of these agreements on the EU and on the UK has been long-standing – whether through the single market (Thatcher), subsidiarity (Thatcher, Major and Blair) or wider territorial policy (Major and Blair). Some Prime Ministers have had a laissez-faire or defensive stance towards Europe in policy development (Callaghan, Brown and Cameron), but have still been active in delivery. Callaghan implemented the post-EU membership legislative transposition in the UK, while Brown and Cameron implemented subsidiarity through sub-state restructuring and the delivery of the SEM for financial services.

In reflecting on the provenance and genealogy of UK membership, a number of key influencers and shapers can be identified, and these remain as important today as in 1972. Despite the overarching focus on the economy and trade, the UK's membership of the EU is driven by practical politics and a defensive position. This tension between the magnetic pull of the US and the economic interests in the EU has been at the centre of the 'heart versus head' position that has prevailed since the 1960s. The UK has placed importance on influencing key political and economic allies from within the EU. Although examples of successful European states outside the EU are frequently cited by those who wish the UK to leave (Miller, 2011b), these states are either part of the European Economic Area (Norway, Lichtenstein and Iceland), where they have agreed to take all the EU's legislation without having a role in discussing it and pay a financial contribution, or are candidates for membership (Montenegro, Macedonia, Turkey, Serbia and Iceland). Switzerland is another example of a state outside membership, but it has over 100 bilateral agreements with the EU and both contributes funds to the EU for social and economic cohesion projects and receives payments for the use of its roads and tunnels (Thorp, 2011). Alternative arrangements with the Commonwealth still exist and could be further enhanced, but Commonwealth nations are increasingly more independent. The US has always been in favour of the UK's membership of the EU and, at times, US policy has favoured a federal Europe.

Since 1957, the EU's objectives have been maintained and have progressively been achieved. The main objective has always been political union to establish global economic strength and internal stability. This objective has meant that individual member states have agreed that pooling powers is likely to be more effective than maintaining policy sovereignty. Long-standing EU member states have always held the same ambivalent attitude towards the UK as the UK has held to Europe and while there have been numerous attempts to develop more integrated working, the two cultures have remained. While states joining the EU have adopted its approach and operational norms, the UK has remained apart. Even where there is growing Euro-scepticism in a number of countries, including Finland and the Netherlands, these countries have still remained within the majority.

After 40 years of membership, the UK remains a distanced member of the EU, reinforced by Cameron's veto pledge in 2013. Yet, the UK continues to engage in implementing EU agreements made through treaties and subsequent legislation. Bulmer and Burch (2009) describe this as the UK's 'reception' stance and found that the UK has appeared assiduous in implementing these 'received' policies while standing some way off from owning them. However, as shown in Chapter Seven, the UK has also failed to implement environmental legislation and has been subsequently challenged on this. On the other hand, Bulmer and Burch (2009) state that the UK has been very poor in its projection of policy within the EU, frequently failing to achieve influence and adoption in developing strategic policy agendas, despite a proactive if covert stance by the UK under New Labour (Holden, 2011). The UK's overall positive record on EU policy implementation has been achieved without much political ownership, and in some more politically contentious areas, this has been undertaken opaquely to achieve influence but not upset the domestic Euro-sceptic press (Nugent and Phinnemore, 2010). Although there has always been a perceived mismatch between European and UK government structures and practices, this may now be less so following the implementation of subsidiarity through devolution (Schnapper, 2011).

There are major elements of active British public policy in the last 40 years that have at least some EU provenance, including localism, devolution, local government reform, employment, competition, environment, energy, transport and rural and urban policy. Yet, few policy debates in these arenas have considered the role of decisions and commitments made by the UK in the EU and how these agreements have shaped policies and outcomes. Formal EU decisions, expressed as directives and regulations, can be tracked through their process of adoption and implementation (Miller, 2010). This is less the case for the major treaties and their implications – whether these are made by the EU, including Maastricht, Amsterdam and Lisbon, or the EU's role in implementing treaty agreements made in other fora, such as with the World Trade Organization (WTO). Neither type is generally discussed or understood in the UK, unlike other member states. Although Parliamentary scrutiny of proposed EU policy and legislation has increased through the creation of a specialist committee, these issues are rarely included in daily debates and select committees (Baines, 2004; Wright, 2004). It is also important to recognise that post-devolution, diverging arrangements for both scrutiny and implementation of EU agreements are now apparent in the Parliament and Assemblies of Scotland, Wales and Northern Ireland. This blindness to policy development and discussion may increasingly be an English position.

Policy influence is not only exerted through specific agreements or legislation, but also through the policy spaces created within policy communities and networks where ideas and knowledge are shared. Policy ideas are taken from communities that have salience and are seen to be 'respected'. Yet, there is little transparency or accountability of these processes. UK policymaking is characterised as being independent and wholly within the UK's remit. Neither politicians nor civil servants admit that policy is pooled with all other EU member states (Bulmer and Burch, 2009; Hallsworth, 2011) and much of this is hidden in plain sight. Since devolution, UK positions on EU policies have been shared through an agreement, and implementation has been interpreted by nations on devolved matters (Schnapper, 2011). UK civil servants have responsibility for delivery in England, UK policy compliance and coordinating the UK position on future policy.

Although the UK may have a good record in implementing EU policies (Bulmer and Burch, 2009), there are also costs involved in this late acknowledgement of EU provenance. The scale of the distance between the UK central policy communities and implementation means that frequently no preparation for delivery has been made and costs are subsequently incurred. There are examples here in the implementation of waste, water and air quality directives. This failure to acknowledge the relationship between UK and EU policy reinforces separation and difference. Further, it does not encourage the engagement of experienced policy communities, leaving it to specific EU specialists within government departments and professional and trade groups to undertake policy and legislative negotiations.

Policy shaping in practice

The implementation of EU policy within the UK is led primarily by those who do not participate in negotiation, and the wider policy community is left with preformed policies and an underlying lack of understanding as to why they cannot influence delivery parameters. If those implementing the policy are not involved, this reduces the capacity and capability of the negotiation process. Although the UK is a full member of an organisation into which it has pooled its own powers for specific policy areas, it continues to act as if it is the EU that hands down law and policy without any UK participation in their development or adoption. Although in part this might be assumed to be an outward stance to meet the populist press (Nugent and Phinnemore, 2010) and Parliamentary concerns about loss of sovereignty in legislation, there is evidence that the strategy, style and substance of influence is less effective than other member states (Borzel, 2002; Bulmer and Burch, 2009; Carbone, 2010b). How does policy shaping occur in practice?

1. The policy process

In considering the ways in which Europe shapes the UK policy process, a number of issues need to be considered, including agenda-setting, policy style and more mechanical strategies such as 'gold-plating'. These components coexist and are frequently used together. However, one overriding consideration in this discussion is the influence of the EU through its 'absence', which creates an aporia in the overt policy process in the UK. EU-derived policies have yet to reach the status of being 'the elephant in the room' in UK policy practice.

a. Setting the agenda

The EU also has a strategic influence on the shape of future policy through agenda-setting (Kingdon, 2003), policy framing (Cairney, 2012) and the power of initiation (Princen and Rhinard, 2006; Rhinard, 2010). The EU has increasingly used fixed-term programmes to deliver its wider objectives (Hooghe, 2001). This approach includes five-year policy agendas and commitments, such as set out in *Europe 2020* (CEC, 2010a; HMT, 2010), legislative programmes (CEC, 1993), funding (CEC, 2007) and treaty developments. When EU policies are implemented, member states' domestic politics, cultures and institutions all have an influence on their application Carbone, 2010a; McCourt, 2011; Goetz and Mayer-Sahling, 2009).

The British civil service is independent of the political cycles of Parliaments and governments. This differs from practices in other EU states and the US, where senior officials change as different parties take power following elections or reformed coalitions. This can lead to differences in understanding. Although there are special advisers to ministers in the UK who are political appointees, there is an inherent tension between them and career civil servants. This was heightened during the period 1997–2010, since when there have been attempts by the civil service to recapture the space (Rutter et al, 2011). A manual that sets out the operating arrangements between the civil service and the government was produced for the first time in 2011 (O'Donnell, 2011a).

b. A programmatic approach: flows and episodes

The focus on longer-term objectives and work programmes to translate treaties into delivery has been largely overlooked in the UK context. The culture of the UK core executive embodies an episodic approach to policymaking and legislation, which contrasts with the flow model of policymaking and delivery within the EU and other member states. The UK has no recognisable long-term strategy for the future of the UK (Jenkin, 2012). Scotland, Wales and Northern Ireland each have their own strategic objectives that are bounded by their ideology of difference and their relationship with Westminster. England has no identifiable strategic or national objectives that are distinct.

The EU policy model has influenced and shaped the development of both strategic policies and the programmatic style of government in the UK. The introduction of Comprehensive Spending Reviews (CSRs) in 1997, running for five to seven years (two years of preparation, three years of delivery, two years of wind-down), with their emphasis on Public Service Agreements (PSAs) or contracts for government departments, have been a key feature of programming legislation and expenditure (Morphet, 2008). Although PSAs have been eschewed by the Coalition government since 2010, they have been replaced with a single plan for the period 2010–15 delivered through Departmental Business Plans, which are updated on a six-monthly basis (HMG, 2010). The introduction of the CSR process and the Pre-Budget Report each November has had the effect of moving the public-sector budget to a calendar-year cycle in line with EU programmes and practices while keeping the private sector financial year from April to April with the Budget speech made in March each year.

c. Persistence in delivery

The development and delivery of EU policy in the UK is primarily focused on the transposition of legislation and its subsequent implementation through domestic institutions (Zubek, 2011). The core executive may be excluded from the detailed discussions on this process, which is undertaken by operational civil servants (Dimitrakopoulos, 2001). The UK has a reasonable record of successful transposition and delivery of legislation, although it has been weak in some areas, such as the environment. However, the UK's most persistent and possibly most successful domestic policies have primarily been those with a strategic EU provenance (see Table 1.1 in Chapter One). Examples here include subsidiarity, exposing public services to competition and transport priorities. Each of these has been implemented in the UK through legislation and programmes and their essence has taken root in national policymaking discourse. They have been persistent in the face of political differences and across general elections.

d. Style of operation

At the heart of the UK's public relationship with the EU is a lack of transparency and openness. This has become a habituated trait, reaching a point when it almost cannot be breached. This may have been influenced by the culture of the Cold War in the post-war period, when UK membership of the EU was negotiated (Sanders, 1990; Hennessy, 2003) and it has continued. This public stance is also replicated within Whitehall, where EU issues are managed and minimised by being kept 'under the radar' or 'off the agenda' (Hood, 2011).

This culture of opacity has two main promoters. The first is politicians, who do not want to reveal the extent to which policy is made within the EU, where their roles are pooled with other member states. Rather than ministers having a leading role in creating policy, as set out in their electoral manifestos, much of their agenda is set by EU agreements, made by their predecessors, sometimes a decade before. Politicians have become more concerned with setting these commitments within political ideologies that can then create appropriate carriers for delivery. However, politicians have an equally important role in negotiating current policy and its development into legislation and future programmes. This process of long-term negotiation is distant and one with little current accountability. Politicians are not prepared for this before government; it is an insider's unspoken shared experience. Most policies are bargains between political elites in member states and are seen to be 'delinked' from democratic accountability (Scott et al, 1994). This retrospective delivery has contributed to a lack of political ownership and to a growth in depoliticisation for ministers, where disengagement and the inability to push personal policies can seem difficult and distant (Burnham, 2001; Buller and Flinders, 2005). It has made power in government appear illusory.

The second promoter of the culture of opacity is the civil service, where conduct of negotiation on EU treaties has been private (Bulmer and Burch, 1998). There is a long distance between treaty negotiation and the implementation of a directive. However, this does not mean that this period has been used to prepare for implementation. The underlying lack of transparency in the civil service on these issues is promoted as a need to engage publicly with EU policy only when it is near finalisation. To do so before might create unnecessary uncertainty and costs for civil society. However, this also masks the need for the civil service to remain in control of the agenda and to find time to develop policy narratives that can deliver EU-generated policies for UK politicians. It suggests a culture of denial that relates to loss of policy power.

The civil service guards its role as advisers to ministers. Ministers are largely detached from access to others. Information is prepared by civil servants in briefs that include suggested lines to take and 'elephant traps' – where any statement or indication of a position could lead to further problems in policy and delivery. Foster and Plowden (1996) have identified this closed system as problematic and, as Blair (2010, p 226) found later, 'left to initiate policy, the department will usually produce something useful, but rarely of much originality or deep significance'. Despite the UK having been a member of the EU for over 40 years, the civil service has not found a way to engage with the policy process that is integrated into their daily round. Indeed, research shows that the 'tried and tested' civil service approaches to policy engagement with the EU have remained unchanged during the whole of this period (Bulmer and Burch, 2009). Even post-devolution, the system has been maintained and discussions with Scotland and Wales incorporated (Wright, 2004). Whitehall modes of adaptation have been in the UK tradition rather than the EU style, Whitehall has absorbed Europeanisation rather than been influenced by it (Bulmer and Burch, 1998). Civil servants seek coordinated responses and share information within government, unlike other states, although this coordination may represent central control (O'Riordan and Jager, 1996a). National expert civil servants are sent to United Kingdom Permanent Representation to the EU in Brussels on postings. These are seen as less attractive jobs because rather than being valued for their expertise, civil servants may struggle to find career-enhancing job slots on their return.

The Commission has developed a cultural style that is different from that of the civil service, particularly in England. Despite member states having national interests, staff at the Commission understand and promote EU strategic objectives within their policy domains. Decision-making is collegial in the EU rather than majoritarian (Pollitt and Boukaert, 2000). There is also a socialising effect in policymaking in the EU (Beyers and Trondal, 2004; Goetz and Meyer-Sayling, 2008) that has led to a transformation of executive politics in Europe, although these changes are less apparent in the UK (Egberg and Curtin, 2008). The EU has tried to rebalance this through more informal methods of policy development and decision-making (CEC, 2001) and enhancing the role of domestic Parliaments (Cooper, 2012).

e. Detaching policy from delivery

One of the key outcomes of the UK's membership of the EU has been the increasing detachment between UK policymakers and delivery in central government. The core executive is focused on policy while delivery is regarded as less prestigious. The absence of EU dialogue and narrative in the UK has meant that the process is opaque. Thus, the core executive has focused its efforts on managing the context of delivery before passing on the mechanics to other government departments. In another detaching process, the core executive's response to the exposure of the public sector to competition has led to the agencification agenda, where 'policymaking' and mechanistic delivery are separated into different institutional constructions (see Chapter Six).

Although institutional restructuring has been an intended consequence, the effects of the separation of policy and delivery have been unintended and created problems in practice. The core executive is detached from the policy development process in Brussels and may have little or no ownership of it. This is magnified by the length of time between policy agreement and delivery. This creates a greater detachment in those developing and presenting policies agreed in this way. The frequent movement of civil servants into new postings can camouflage this process. When policies are translated into delivery forms, the core executive has little operational knowledge to draw upon and this detachment creates greater opportunities for blame and institutional displacement if there are subsequent problems.

f. Gold-plating

The opaque approach to negotiation and transposition of EU legislation into UK law has frequently led to the practice of 'gold-plating' (Davidson, 2006; Miller 2011a). In this process, EU legislation is augmented to include additional UK requirements, and EU implementation is used as a carrier for wider policy. This technique of augmentation is well known, is used in a number of member states (Fontana, 2011) and has been criticised by the EU, concerned that additional costs and processes are being attributed to the implementation of EU law. This approach also reduces policy debates on both transposition of EU policies and associated UK policy initiatives as they are difficult to disentangle.

g. Blame culture

Where policies are pooled with the EU, this has frequently led to the development and adoption of a 'blame' culture, where the UK is characterised as a victim. As Cary (1993, p 48) states:

> something called 'Brussels' is credited with the glory or the shame for every European development, as if it were a monolithic technocracy [or, in a lurid picture painted in much of the popular press, a Frankenstein, stinking of garlic and bratwurst, which has broken out of the laboratory and is now lurching about the UK out of control]. This picture is nurtured by some national politicians who are too ready to let Europe take the blame for unpopular policies.

This blame or victim narrative has become a convenient method of demonising policies, but has also acted as a means of distracting attention away from other concerns. The use of the UK's veto against the development of a new EU treaty in December 2011 was attributed to its expected inclusion of restrictions on the financial services industry that would be unwelcome to the UK. In reality, the development of the SEM for financial services was already underway. This was a diversion away from an immediate political issue, where Conservative backbench Members of Parliament were threatening a party leadership contest if the Prime Minister agreed to the 'proposal.'

During the period 1994–97, Europe was a politically divisive issue within the Conservative Party. Although there was a raft of policies to implement following the adoption of the Maastricht Treaty in 1992, civil servants adopted a range of approaches to avoid blame or being an unwelcome messenger of EU policy. Hood (2011) has identified the ways in which blame avoidance strategies are developed and used. These include keeping a low profile and removing the messenger. Blame can also be avoided if the unwelcome messages are attributed to an external 'expert' or 'think tank'. As noted earlier, messages can also be wrapped in narratives that align with current political ideologies.

A blame culture, characterised by risk aversion and diversion, can significantly frame the policy agenda and the interrelationships within the core executive. As EU policy decisions are made some time before they are implemented, there is no shared experience of the negotiation that can bind together ministers and civil servants. Policy handling and implementation cannot always be anchored to the current political ideology. In this case, blame can be transferred to the previous government, but a code of silence on the EU provenance of policy can sublimate this. It can make the implementation of EU legislation a low priority and those responsible for implementing it disengaged.

2. Policy priorities

The EU has shaped key areas of British public policy since its membership, and as the extent of pooled powers has increased, then so has the level of influence. However, this is not an external influence, as frequently characterised, but one where the UK is within the policy development and decision-making processes. Although the Commission has the power of initiation, the policies that are progressed have already been agreed within more strategic contexts, whether these are treaties, European Councils or through Presidency programmes. All of these are developed over long periods of time, well signposted and require engagement from all member states.

This book has considered key policy issues that have been brought to the UK agenda through this policy process but where government has chosen its own delivery methods. In the UK, the characterisation of policy as 'externalised' has provided greater confidence in delivery. Meeting EU compliance gives a clear mandate for new legislation, which is always seen as career-enhancing for civil servants. It also requires the greatest feats of policy ingenuity in translating EU agreements into UK policy. A policy has to be sold to the press and the public without them suspecting the source. This can be a more satisfying approach to policy development than engaging in policy agendas *ab initio* in the EU, where longer negotiation is required. The cult of the generalist and the policy of short-term postings in the civil service are designed to ensure that individuals do not lose their sense of detachment by ensuring that they 'don't go native' and also mitigates against longer-term policy relationships. For civil servants in the core executive, specialism is the antidote to promotion.

3. Policy outcomes

EU policy has direct outcomes, but there are also indirect influences that shape the way in which the state operates, and some of these are discussed here.

a. Administrative law

A key area where the implementation of EU policies has shaped the UK state and its institutions can be exemplified through the development and application of administrative law. The doctrine of Parliamentary sovereignty means that Parliament cannot be applied to for Judicial Review of its laws. However, it is possible to apply for a review where EU law is the basis of a decision. The adoption of the European Human Rights Convention and EU legal principles means that more decisions can be challenged. The creation of the UK Supreme Court in 2003, and implemented in 2009, separate from the House of Lords, has also been part of this wider process. The Supreme Court cannot overturn primary legislation made by Parliament, but it can address claims against secondary legislation and it can find incompatibilities between UK law and the Human Rights Act 1998.

b. Quasi-marketisation of the public sector

The marketisation of the public sector is derived from agreements made in 1975 to embrace full market liberalisation (Crosland, 1976). The approaches to achieve these ends in the UK have been significant in reshaping public institutions and services and, in some cases, unique in their approach. The EU has undertaken the negotiations with the WTO on agreements on behalf of all its members, including the UK. Despite the difficult passage of the Health and Social Care Bill in the UK in 2011–12, neither the EU nor the WTO has been identified as the source of the agreement for open government procurement in this public service. Commentary on the role of the General Agreement on

Tariffs and Trade and WTO Government Procurement Agreement in generating this open procurement process has been silent.

While the EU has been responsible for ensuring compliance through timescales, the UK government has had a significant effect in interpreting these rules. This has been through the UK government's selection of public services for open competition and the contract-selection method based on price rather than criteria, although this has always been included in the EU process. Frequent criticisms of the extent of foreign ownership of public services in the UK as an outcome of these open procurement processes may be explained by the lowest-price approach. In other countries, the use of criteria-based contract selection has allowed other factors, such as training, local sourcing to be taken into account and provided more opportunity for local suppliers. A further issue is the scale of the contract that is set for open procurement. Larger contracts will inevitably attract international companies. Further, entering the market of another member state has considerable entry costs that can be offset by contract scale and length.

The quasi-marketisation of the public sector has also had a significant influence on the culture of delivery in public services. Increased customer focus through different delivery channels, more personalised services and integrated service delivery were all supported by the use of national and local e-government initiatives during 2000–05 (Morphet, 2008). These approaches have been criticised by those who have argued that public service embodies different values from the private sector and that people should be seen as citizens with rights rather than customers (Stewart and Walsh, 1992). The case against this has been a concern to move away from a producer focus in public services, where local monopolistic public supply can disempower the user's influence on quality and delivery (HMG, 2007).

c. Subsidiarity and constitutional reform

'The Conservative government's interpretation of subsidiarity – that power was devolved no further than London – had been out of step with European trends' (Scott et al, 1994, p 46); this gives some indication of the position on the application of subsidiarity in the UK at the time that the Maastricht Treaty was agreed. Although subsidiarity was promoted by the UK during its presidency in 1992, it was regarded as a means of dealing with the EU's democratic deficit and legitimacy rather than having any impact on the UK constitution (Scott et al, 1994). The UK viewed the development of subsidiarity in the Maastricht

Treaty as a 'substantive principle', whereas it has been interpreted and implemented as a procedural criterion.

Implementing subsidiarity has had consequences in the UK. In 1992, other than local authorities, the UK did not have any democratic structures below state level. Further, local authorities were confined in their actions to those activities where the state had given them power to act. The state was in control at all levels. Implementing subsidiarity required the central state to devolve some of its powers. As Scott et al (1994, p 48) stated:

> The Major government is not the only one in the EC which is disinclined to decentralisation, but the intensity of its ideological aversion to 'subsidiarity at home' is unique.... The centralization of the British state [is] an obstacle to the application of the principle of substantive subsidiarity.

Although subsidiarity was introduced in the Single European Act 1986 (SEA), the Maastricht Treaty was drawn up on the principle of subsidiarity. In a division of policymaking, the EU should do only those things that could not be done individually. This was based on the Tindemans Report (CEC, 1975). However, elsewhere, in the Treaty on the European Union (TEU), there is a focus on the distribution of power and the notion of proportionality, where decisions are taken closer to the people.

The outcome of the application of subsidiarity has been considerable (as discussed in Chapter Eight). It has resulted in devolution and changes in local government. It has created a different kind of state, where decisions about delivery are taken closer to the people. Subsidiarity has had implications in other member states, including France, Denmark and the Netherlands. In France, the application of the principle has increased regionalisation. This has been used as a means to overcome issues of nationalism, immigration and differentiation and is also associated with market liberalisation (Ladrech, 1994). Local authorities were reformed in Denmark in 2007 and in Finland in 2005, and in Ireland, a Mayor for Dublin was directly elected in 2010.

4. Policy institutions

Policy institutions within the EU, such as the Commission, member state civil servants, policy networks, territorial groupings and policy communities, all play a key role in developing and internalising policy processes across government institutions. This can extend to policy communities, where issues and agendas can be developed (Peterson, 2009; van der Steeg and Risse, 2010). An issue for the UK is the extent to which it engages in policy communities and networks. The negative and distanced approach to engagement from the core executive suggests that understanding of the interrelationship between UK and EU policy processes is low. The temporal and political separation between negotiation and delivery may mean that policy communities are only effective at the point of policy delivery. Further, policies that are not supported centrally and apparently have no parentage can encourage less formal approaches to flourish. Thus, policy networks may not have power at the point of negotiation (Peterson, 2009), but may have more power subsequently if they are able to problematise, own and deliver the policy in the UK context. This extends to the role of think tanks.

Those engaged in the policy process are frequently seen as playing the same role. However, what is emerging here is that those engaged in policymaking operate in different ways. Policymakers or advisers are seldom policy initiators or deliverers. *Policy initiators* are intermediaries between strategic decision-making and *policy shapers*, who work within this strategic context to manage these constructs into the system. This may include commissioning a 'personality' review, engaging a think tank or encouraging bodies of experts to call for reform. If this is associated in timing with a general election, policy shapers may be able to include any required changes into ideological or 'machinery of government' packages. Policy shapers develop politically acceptable and realist policies that can be translated into national policy by policymakers. *Policymakers* are more likely to be within specialist departments rather than in the core executive. They broker between interests and also have political experience in identifying the role that can be played by the policy in a wider narrative and then finding an opportunity for the policy to be performed. Once set in this context, the *policy deliverers* will transfer the policy to the point of implementation through developing its detail and finding a runway slot for its launch or legislative process. They may create competitions or pilot approaches to encourage wider preparation and to flag up policy shifts. This policy process is mechanised through a chain of policy specialists who each perform a different role in launching policy initiatives. Policy networks will differ at each of these points.

It is difficult to understand how policy development works without recognising these active networks. Conversely, there is a need to recognise that not all networks will work in the same way and they may be culturally defined and/or path-dependent. Networks may also become tighter and looser over time, when issues have more political salience or come to a point of proposed legislation. Networks sit outside formal negotiation processes but will be significant in their contextual and shaping roles. Informal discussions before, between and at the margins of meetings all help in creating a political shorthand that can be understood by the actors in the process. Those with less interest in an issue are sometimes used as 'honest brokers' in providing advice or an opinion on behalf of the network. Policy networks have a role in distanced and displaced policy ownership and can offer a credible substitution for institutions.

5. Policy culture

The influence of the EU on the culture of policy shaping is more nebulous and slippery, but it represents a *zeitgeist* or policy ambiance that is difficult to grasp but is present in decision-making. Policy culture includes the prevailing orthodoxy in approaching policy negotiation and the problematisation of issues, which frame the potential array of solutions and delivery.

a. The EU: an imagined community?

Each member state presents the EU in ways that are politically advantageous within their own domestic setting (Wallace, 1997), while the EU promotes cultural allegiance to the idea of Europe (Citrin and Sides, 2008). Further, the EU has no state apparatus and, as a largely indirect institution, it allows each member state to project and frame its image. The EU promotes citizen engagement and identification through programmes such as 'Citizen's Europe' and specific projects at a sub-national level, but for most people, the EU is an abstract and, in the UK, a negative concept. The EU can be perceived as an 'imagined community' (Anderson, 2006).

Early in the UK's discussions with the EU, at the time of the campaign for membership, a positive relationship was reinforced. Once the political decision was made to join, a campaign was led through Parliament and other organisations. As Kitzinger (1973, p 201) set out:

> there were all sorts of ways in which Whitehall and the publicists, politicians and the organisers of voluntary bodies could be actively useful to each other in promoting the campaign to support the UK's membership.... The Government held weekly meetings for 'group think' and included planning press issues to focus on each week.

Speakers were identified for groups and there was an exchange of intelligence on who was supportive or otherwise. This made the EU tangible and accessible so that people could identify with it. Since then, the EU has become Britain's 'other'.

The development of an EU identity has been stronger in Wales, Scotland and Northern Ireland and at local levels in England. Here, these EU relationships were warmer than those provided by central government, certainly during the Thatcher period. This has encouraged an easier relationship and active engagement. Further, through the increasing incorporation of subsidiarity, the EU has developed an identity that is decentralised and positive for sub-state levels. The UK identity has traditionally been expressed in English terms, but since devolution, this construct is now used more narrowly and the identity of the UK has yet to settle (Risse, 2010). Since devolution, Scotland and Wales have continued to evolve their separate identities, supported by decision-making, institutions and the other machinery of government. This is already the case in Northern Ireland. All three nations have more positive relations and views on the EU than with England, while funding has brought a large range of European contacts and alliances. This was particularly important when Thatcherism was seen to be against Scotland and Wales – it was the EU that funded the economic restructuring that followed. The EU comprises large and small nations and the models created by smaller countries allowed Scotland and Wales to argue an approach to self-government within the UK construct.

While the EU remains as an imagined community, it performs a significant role for the UK as the other. Relations with the US are seen as positive and beneficial, particularly in terms of financial services and military cooperation. The relationship with the EU is primarily silent or negative. As the 1972 campaign for EU membership demonstrated, a strategy of engagement that performs in a variety of contexts is a prerequisite of positive relationships. While this absence remains, the UK responds to the EU through a culture of passive-aggression.

b. Depoliticisation and distance

The temporal separation between policy negotiation and implementation has led to a distancing between the UK and the EU. Politicians are engaged in daily negotiation of policies and legislation, although these will be implemented by another minister, civil servant and possibly government. Meanwhile, the same minister has to implement decisions made by their predecessors, when the politicians may have been from the same or different government and the civil servants will have changed. Politicians are disconnected from their current negotiations and implementation, where they are asked to find post hoc rationalisations for earlier decisions.

This has contributed to the depoliticisation of the EU within the British state. Depoliticisation is defined as a process 'which places at one remove the political character of decision making', which is incorporated within wider ideological concepts and used as a governing strategy (Burnham, 2001, p 128). The discourse of depoliticisation can also incorporate the widening of government to governance, which diffuses responsibility from the core executive and shares it with other parts of civil society. Depoliticisation detaches decision-making from the political context, such as freeing the Bank of England from the Treasury on monetary policy in 1997. Burnham attributes depoliticisation to the need of all governments to maintain a manoeuvrability gap between policy and delivery in order to cope with changes in the global economic system.

Exogenous shocks or external factors contribute to depoliticisation, including the economy (Buller and Flinders, 2005) and foreign policy (Daddow and Gaskarth, 2011). In this context, depoliticisation is an intentional political response, creating a gap between politicians and the issues, by externalising and distancing responsibility for these issues. Agencification is one means to manage external expectations but not lose internal influence or control (Jenkins, 2008; Rutter et al, 2012a). This was used in managing nationalised industries before they were open to competition and described as 'management by luncheon' (Flinders and Buller, 2006, p 301).

However, depoliticisation since the UK's membership of the EU has been unintentional. The gap between the core executive and decisions has been an acquired culture of duty rather than one of choice. Decisions made by the UK in the EU have to be actioned but not owned. As Perri 6 (2011) has shown, the exercise of politics is about judgement focused on solving difficult issues. In the case of implementing previously made decisions, less is required of this judgement and it is focused on detached delivery rather than the implementation of a decision taken by government within the construct of cabinet responsibility. A policy made by the UK within the EU is regarded as a 'done deal'. Whereas positive depoliticisation has been used to manage expectations and risk (Douglas, 1999), unintended depoliticisation is a product of disinterest within the construct of felt powerlessness. This culture goes beyond individual decisions made by the UK within the EU and extends to the overarching narrative of the other member states in their objective of further integration (Hix, 2000)

c. Dependency?

One of the unintended consequences of receiving policies made within the EU rather than engaging with the process (Bulmer and Burch, 2009) has been the creation of a dependency culture. When policy is pooled, agreement is negotiated over an extended time period and requires personal investment. If preferred outcomes cannot be fully achieved, there can be a temptation not to fully engage in the process. In the debate between the two candidates in the French presidential election in 2012, one key criticism made by Sarkozy of his opponent Hollande was that he had never had any significant experience or held a key role in Brussels, with the implication that this lack of experience would be detrimental to France if Hollande were to be elected. This demonstrates the gap with the UK, where experience in the EU may be seen to be a positive disadvantage to a candidate, who may have shown 'divided' loyalties between the EU and the UK.

This is part of the sectarian discourse on the role of the UK in the EU and it is this that has created a dependency culture. If it is difficult to discuss issues without fear of being labelled as 'pro' or 'anti', it is easier, less risky and more politically adroit not to engage at all. Discussing the policies that the UK has agreed within the EU has become an area of 'blame' in public discourse (Hood, 2011) and fatalism in practice, 'where "Why bother?" is the rational ... response' (Verweij et al, 2006, p 820). This behaviour is difficult to break unless there are political or pragmatic incentives for the core executive to change its culture for the development and implementation of UK policy made within the EU.

d. Without a strategy?

The combined influence of a dependency culture and devolution has had the unintended consequence of leaving the UK without an overarching narrative or strategy. The UK's position is characterised as being responsive to others and defensive in its actions, rather than having a clear programme for the future. However, does the absence of a national strategy matter? Are national strategies only expressed in political party manifestos at the time of a general election? Or are national strategies part of the *zeitgeist* of the nation, understood without needing to be expressed?

In the private and voluntary sectors, business or organisational strategies are a key element in the financial health of the organisation. Organisational strategies are the basis of share price and maintaining the confidence of staff and customers. Strategies communicate an organisation's longer-term objectives, goals and future orientation (Cornut et al, 2012) and they have a practical role in framing decision-making and the cultural significance of incorporation inside the organisation. Alternatives to strategising include 'mudding through' and 'disjoined incrementalism' (Lindblom, 1959, 1979), 'clumsy' approaches that incorporate all views in an attempt to arrive at a deliberative solution (Verweij et al, 2006) or fatalism, which is a form of dependency (Putnam and Bayne, 1987).

The absence of strategy or a strategic approach in the UK government has been criticised by a Parliamentary Select Committee Report that identified a 'strategic vacuum' in policy (PASC, 2012a). The Committee concluded with the concern that:

> Government policies are not informed by a clear, coherent strategic approach and that poor strategic thinking also undermines clarity of presentation to the public. PASC also found that an absence of clear and precise definition of terms meant that policy and different levels of strategy became muddled, leading to unintended and unwelcome outcomes. (PASC, 2012b)

This committee, which has no executive power, concluded that there should be an annual statement of national strategy that would frame the Budget and the programme for government. It should also be used ensure cross-departmental working. The committee identified the absence of strategy in those areas that have been the focus of depoliticisation, namely, foreign affairs and finance. The committee identified the content of a UK national strategy as being:

a) How the geopolitical factors shaping the UK strategic environment are identified;

b) how policy is based on perceptions of UK national interests;

c) how such national interests are perceived by different audiences;

d) how public attitudes and aspirations are engaged in the formation of such perceptions; and

e) how perceived national interests are advanced. (PASC, 2012a, §22)

The absence of a national strategy creates an aporia. The committee did not identify the reasons for this gap, although they questioned witnesses on the practice in other countries where national strategies are prepared, including the US, Singapore and some EU member states such as Sweden and Finland, which has a Committee of the Future. There was also a discussion on the way that the UK works with the EU. The evidence presented indicated that there was little or no strategy in the conduct of this relationship (Butler, 2011; Mulgan, 2011).

Strategy can vary in style and timescale. In Europe, the goal of political, economic and social integration has a long time horizon, but each major institutional event marks the renewal of a strategy to achieve it. In the UK, strategy may be more apparent in Wales, Scotland and Northern Ireland than in England. In Scotland and Northern Ireland, separation from the UK is a main driver of strategy for some, whereas in Wales, there is a strategy of survival as a small nation and the challenge of being able to determine domestic affairs. In England, the pooling of policy development and delivery at sub-state level has left an aporia in strategic consideration. As England has no specific identity, a lack of strategy may be an issue in the future as internal and external policy environments change. As Hallsworth and Rutter (2011) demonstrate, policymaking in the UK is short-term, responding to manifestos or crises rather than being bound by long-term strategy.

e. Habituated responses

The relationships between the UK and the EU have become habituated over 50 years and include internal relations and external presentation. As Anastasiou (2007, p 71) suggests, this can result in 'non-communication, shutting down one's mental and political state of being'. Adopting an habituated approach can require no agency (Tarrow, 1994) and can become part of a repertoire that compartmentalises or modularises specific activities or problems to be dealt with in this way' (Krieger, 1999). Over time, these behaviours become stable patterns of interaction. Yesilkagit (2004) uses Berger and Luckmann's (1966, pp 70–1) definition – that 'any action that is repeated frequently becomes cast into a pattern, which can then be reproduced with an economy of effort and which, *ipso facto*, is apprehended by its performers as that pattern' – to underpin institutionalisation. In the UK's relationship with the EU, the core executive's behaviours are endemic and intergenerational, although they may not be genealogical. They are habituated and learned behaviours.

Detecting where the EU shapes British public policy

This book has focused on the way in which Europe has shaped British public policy through the lens of government narratives and policy arenas. The development of EU-pooled policies has been seen to be habitually opaque and under-reported. When policies surface, they are unacknowledged and not contextualised. They are frequently presented in defensive ways, which are epitomised by a 'victim mentality'. EU policy decision processes are pooled but are publicly characterised as imposed. Greater understanding of these processes might open debate and increase engagement, but this is more likely to be conducted through social media than more traditional forms of engagement.

However, is it possible to identify any ways in which existing or future policies could be discussed within their EU provenance? Here, some key factors are identified that might be useful as part of an investigative approach. Given the extent of UK domestic policy that is pooled in full or in part within the EU, it is realistic to start with a presumption that there is an EU link rather than not. In attempting to discover the provenance of policies, those in the UK and particularly in England are at a disadvantage. Literary sleuths solve their mysteries through closely examining unperceived observations. For those interested in the derivation of UK policies in the EU policy process, there are no developed frames of reference in the UK and these observations are lost by default. There is no developed, cumulative awareness of EU policy contexts and current issues. UK policy is immediate and seen as flexible and responsive. When looking at the EU, policy is long-term, and this is critical for the interpretation of the current path. The following questions and tests provide ways in which these investigations can be developed and pursued. They might be regarded as circumstantial or too general, but they are not intended to be used on their own but to enable the development of a more attuned policy consciousness of EU–UK relationships.

1. Intertextuality

The most obvious way to investigate the potential EU provenance of any policy or legislation is to examine the use of common terms. Frequently, the transposition of policy themes and legislation will use phrases or verbal constructions that are more frequently used in EU documents than those in the UK, although, over time, these become embedded in domestic usage. For some time, EU economic policy has been concerned with 'missing links' and 'bottlenecks' in areas of growth and the provision of infrastructure. These phrases are found in documents such as *Europe 2020* (CEC, 2010a) as well as in the Treasury's response to *Europe 2020* (HMT, 2010), the national infrastructure plan and the Department for Transport's policies. Similar intertextuality is identified in the proposals for financial regulation expressed through directives and in the Finance Bill 2012. Although these similarities might be considered to be coincidental, more detailed analysis should identify similarities in policy construction and outcome. In a practical approach, inserting a UK policy initiative name into an internet search engine, prefacing it by the term 'EU', is frequently enough to identify a source or link to explore.

2. Meta-narratives

Meta-narratives such as 'new localism', 'Big Society', 'fairness' or 'deregulation' are frequently used by government when a new set of EU policies has been developed but their final destination is as yet to be agreed or, in the case of the UK, accepted. These meta-narratives provide a mechanism for creating a general public discourse and setting the context for a change in policy direction. However, they are also sufficiently broad to contain both a widening and deepening of policy and its implementation should this be required. Some meta-narratives use specific tropes, and 'fairness' is an example of this. What does it mean? It is one of the three principles in the Coalition's *Programme for government* (HMG, 2010b) and has been used by the Prime Minister in speeches. As the development of a meta-narrative for the extended principle of cohesion set out in the Lisbon Treaty has yet to be found, will 'fairness' be useful in implementing an assessment of UK policies against the principle of achieving economic, social and territorial cohesion?

3. Orphan policies

In the policies considered in this book, there have been a number of examples where contemporaneous commentators have indicated that policy redirections have emerged as if they are the solution to a question that has never been put. These include policies on opening up the public sector to competition, more sustainable transport policies, agencification and the removal of regionalism. As noted earlier, the easiest way for a government to change direction is through cabinet reshuffles, and for the civil service it is through general elections – both using the 'machinery of government' tools. However, changing policy direction when these options are not open may mean the introduction of an orphan policy, which is stated with conviction but appears to have no antecedents. This may also be a sign that the UK has agreed to progress within the EU within a specific time frame, but where none of the meta-narratives are able to cover the agreed action to meet looming deadlines.

4. Continuity

One of the key indicators for investigating where the UK has made policy agreements within the EU is considering which policies are continued following general elections. This can only be reviewed where there is a change in political party, so its potential is limited. However, an example that continued before and after the 1997 general election was competition in the public sector. It was widely assumed by local government that this policy would be dropped after Labour came to power, but, rather, it was extended to include all public services through the application of Best Value. In 2010, the continuity of new localism and the creation of sub-regional institutions are two further examples. The implementation of sub-regional governance approaches in England since 2010 is directly based on the preceding government's sub-national review (HMT et al, 2007). New localism was introduced by the Labour government through Raynsford's (2004) 10-year programme of local government reform, and the Localism Act 2011 has implemented more than local government was anticipating. Devolution is also continuing regardless of the Scottish referendum on independence.

5. Persistence

Although some policies that are unpopular are dropped quickly in the face of public opinion, others are continued despite internal and external political opposition. The development of the HST2 rail line is an example. This has difficult political implications for the Conservative Party as the route mainly traverses party-held Parliamentary constituencies. However, in the application of this policy, there is persistence about the mode of delivery as well as the route, which comes close to being an orphan policy as well as one that is applied persistently. A second example is the application of health reforms despite overt opposition from all the major institutions involved in health delivery. The introduction of competition into health services was developed over the period since the agreement to open health to competition 10 years earlier. Competition was also a key component of the previous Labour government's National Health Service Act 2006. This policy again appears to be an orphan, with no contextual narrative, with no comparisons with other WTO member countries where similar legislative processes were taking place – for example, in

Australia in 2007, New Zealand in 2011 and Canada in 2010 – and with its continuance without extensive political or civil society acceptance.

6. Shadow synchronicity

When investigating the relationship between any domestic policy and one agreed by the UK in the EU, the principle of shadow synchronicity is useful. Each policy has a temporal shadow that can be identified through meetings, speeches, projects and programmes. This approach suggests looking back over a period, particularly since the last major EU treaty, to identify policy sources. For longer-range policy development, it is useful to review projects funded through EU research and development or territorial cooperation programmes. These are frequently the sites of early policy consideration, testing and familiarisation. Shadow synchronicity can have a long tail.

7. Absenting the 'other'

As the UK has pooled much of it domestic policy within the EU, policy that does not refer or relate to EU policies might suggest a closer look. The links between the application of the principle of subsidiarity in the UK for English regional administrative structures, devolution, general powers of competence for local government and greater roles for parish councils has never been overtly made. Yet, these issues were connected and considered in contemporaneous discussions in the UK after the TEU (Maastricht) in 1992. As part of this consideration, Foreign Office discussions on the implications for the UK of subsidiarity and its potential path to internal and pan-EU federalism were considered in 1992 (Denton, 1992). In Financial regulatory reforms, the discussions in Parliament between the legislation and the scrutiny of the implementation of EU financial directives were taken separately in 2011/12.

8. Indirect comparison

Although the use of direct references to the implementation of policies and approaches agreed by the UK within the EU is politically problematic for any government, there has been a rise of the use of indirect policy exemplars from other EU member states. These indirect comparisons, using policy examples from other member states, have been cited by ministers in speeches and television interviews. The examples used have included youth policy from Finland, social security policy from Belgium and planning and housing policy from the Netherlands. This use of examples from other member states' practice is a distanced but reflected EU policy reference.

9. Comparative coincidence

Comparative policy reviews frequently mention serendipitous similarities between policies of individual member states, such as that on transport, cities and governance arrangements, as if they are coincidences and rarely is there any detailed consideration of the application of underlying policies to achieve agreed outcomes. These policies will not be exactly similar in each member state as they will have different contextual and cultural starting points together with different institutional frameworks. However, they will demonstrate similarities if they are derived from the same EU policy process and are deigned to achieve a common outcome.

Conclusions

The arena for much British public policymaking needs to be relocated and refocused, even if the UK continues to adopt a 'receptor' stance for EU policy. There is also potential for the UK to develop greater promotion and projection of a policy stance. The main difficulties and challenges are the habituated cultures, opaque discussions and decisions detached from delivery. These are set within a context of sectarianism, which pervades any discussion of the EU. This makes it difficult for any discussion to progress. The disengagement of the core executive and the tribal competition between government departments also contributes to the operating environment. Without this, legitimate and required discussions about the development of UK policy areas pooled within the EU lies abandoned. The EU is not only an orphan policy sphere, but also an outcast.

However, unless there is considerable policy effort and focus to maintain the status quo, things change. The role of the civil service in England is likely to be challenged through the introduction of contestability in decision-making (Heywood and Kerslake, 2012) and the extension of the application of subsidiarity within the state (O'Donnell, 2009; Heseltine, 2012). The opening of policy advice to ministers would change the role of the civil service established through the principles set out in the Northcote-Trevelyan Report of 1854. The application of subsidiarity in all parts of the UK also introduces contestability into the operation of centralised services and policy leadership (Rutter, 2012). At the point of developing any service for delivery in the UK, there has been little or no discussion about the most appropriate scale for its delivery or institutional responsibility. If more systematic subsidiarity and territorial tests are adopted against which new legislation is measured, and similar challenges are applied to existing services, then the application of the principle of subsidiarity, which the UK promoted as part of the SEA in 1986 and Maastricht Treaty in 1992, will have a profound effect on the structure of the core executive.

If the EU is to remain pre-eminent as a world trading bloc, it has to recognise the benefits and disbenefits of its structure. Other major countries such as China, India or Brazil are single nation states and have the potential to legislate and locate investment. This is less available to the EU, with its composition of individual member states. The US has a federal structure, so the central state does not have control of all decisions, but it is possible for the state to promote national policies and incentives to support the economy and strategic investment. In the adoption and application of the principle of social, economic and territorial cohesion, the EU may be strengthening its role in determining investment locations and types.

On the other hand, smaller states that represent homogeneous markets can be successful in world trade (Alesina and Spolaore, 2003). Morris (2010) argues beyond this that the structure and forms of Eastern countries could teach the West about the alliance between different forms of governance and economic power. Although not advocating the break-up of nation states, the OECD is strongly promoting the role of developed sub-state powers as the mechanism to achieve endogenous growth (Charbit, 2011).

In the EU, the inclusion of territorial cohesion policies within the Lisbon Treaty 2009 suggests that sub-state scales are beginning to have a key role in the development of the EU's economic power and that there has been an internalisation of the OECD's policy advice. The future of structural funding programmes will be brought within territorial cohesion policy from 2014 and this is expected to widen across decisions in all policy areas. Adherence to principles of territorial cohesion is expected to be undertaken through the territorial impact assessments, and these may shape pan-EU investment. Although the EU does not have powers on planning, it has agreed a European Spatial Development Perspective in 1999, and this could be revised and developed further to create an underpinning strategy for development and investment.

Where does this leave the UK? British public policy has been shaped by pooling a range of policies within the EU and these have moulded policy priorities and programmes. Some of this engagement has been intentional, such as the SEM, but much has been the unintended consequence of low engagement and detached delivery of earlier decisions. The EU continues moving towards the objectives set out in the Treaty of Rome 1957, to which the UK is a party. Without a different style of engagement, the policy-shaping process will continue without an active UK debate. In the political climate constructed after the 2010 general election, it is difficult to see how this can be shifted in the short term. Meanwhile, the deepening of national integration between Eurozone states may change this area's relationship with the rest of the EU. Public understanding of the UK's role within pooled EU policy is a first step to internalising these discussions as part of the daily political round and more informed engagement in the debates about the UK's future.

References

6, P. (2011) *Explaining political judgement*, Cambridge: Cambridge University Press.

6, P., Leat, D., Seltzer, K. and Stoker, G. (2002) *Towards holistic government: the new reform agenda*, Basingstoke: Palgrave Macmillan.

6, P., Fletcher-Morgan, C. and Leyland, K. (2010) 'Making people more responsible: the Blair governments' programme for changing citizens' behaviour', *Political Studies*, vol 58, no 3, pp 427–49.

Adam S., H Kriesi (2007) *Theories of the policy process*, Boulder, CO: Westview Press.

Adlung, R. (2009) 'Services negotiations in the Doha Round: lost in flexibility?', *Journal of International Economic Law*, vol 9, no 4, pp 865–93.

Alesina A. and E. Spolaore, (2005) *The size of nations*, Cambridge, Mass: MIT Press.

Alesina A. and R. Wacziarg (1999) 'Is Europe going too far?', Carnegie–Rochester Conference Series on Public Policy, vol 51, December pp 1-42

Alexander, D., Lewis, J.M. and Considine, M. (2011) 'How politicians and bureaucrats network: a comparison across governments', *Public Administration*, vol 89, no 4, pp 1274–92.

Allen, D. (2005) 'The United Kingdom: a Europeanized government in a non-Europeanized polity', in S. Bulmer and C. Lesquesne (eds) *The member states of the European Union*, Oxford: Oxford University Press, pp 119–41.

Allen, D. (2010) 'The structural funds and cohesion policy: extending the bargain to meet new challenges', in H. Wallace, M. Pollack and A.R. Young (eds) *Policy making in the European Union* (6th edn), Oxford: Oxford University Press.

Allen, G. (2012) *Illustrative draft code for central and local government, Political and Constitutional Reform Select Committee*, London: House of Commons.

Allen J. and A. Cochrane, (2007) 'Beyond the territorial fix: regional assemblages, politics and power', *Regional Studies*, vol 41, no 9, pp 1161-75.

Allmendinger, P. (2003) 'Integrating planning in a devolved Scotland', *Planning Practice and Research*, vol 18, no 1, pp 19–36.

Alter, K.J. (2000) 'The European Union's legal system and domestic policy: spillover or backlash?', *International Organization*, vol 54, part 3, pp 489–518.

Anastasiou, Harry, (2007) 'The Communication Imperative in an Era of Globalization: Beyond Conflict-Conditioned Communication', *Global Media Journal: Mediterranean Edition* 2, pp 63-75.

Anderson, B. (2006) *Imagined communities: reflections on the origin and spread of nationalism* (2nd edn), London: Verso.

Andre, C. (2011) *Improving the functioning of the housing market in United Kingdom*, Economic Department Working Papers no 867, Paris: OECD.

Armstrong, K.A. (2002) 'Rediscovering civil society: the European Union and the White Paper on governance', *European Law Journal*, vol 8, no 1, pp 102–32.

Armstrong, K.A. (2004a) 'Implementing the Lisbon Strategy: policy co-ordination through "Open Methods"', ESRC seminar series 'Lisbon', Queen Mary Westfield College, University of London.

Armstrong, K.A. (2004b) 'How open is the United Kingdom to the OMC process on social inclusion?' ESRC seminar series 'Lisbon', Queen Mary Westfield College, University of London.

Armstrong, K.A. and Bulmer, S. (1998) *The governance of the Single European Market*, Manchester: Manchester University Press.

Armstrong, M. and Vickers, J. (1995) 'Competition and regulation in telecommunications', in M. Bishop, J. Kay and C. Mayer (eds) *The regulatory challenge*, Oxford: Oxford University Press, pp 283–308.

Audit Commission (1998) *The competitive council*, Management Papers no 1, London: Audit Commission.

Audit Commission, (2004), *People, places and prosperity*, London: Audit Commission.

Aughey, A. (2007) *The politics of Englishness*, Manchester: Manchester University Press.

Bache, I. (2008) *Europeanization and multilevel governance*, Plymouth: Rowman and Littlefield.

Bache, I. and Flinders, M. (2004a) 'Themes and issues in multi-level governance', in I. Bache and M. Flinders (eds) *Multi-level governance*, Oxford: Oxford University Press, pp 1–11.

Bache, I. and Flinders, M. (2004b) 'Multi-level governance: conclusions and implications', in I. Bache and M. Flinders (eds) *Multi-level governance*, Oxford: Oxford University Press, pp 195–206.

Bache, I. and Jordan, A. (2008) 'Britain in Europe and Europe in Britain', in I. Bache and A. Jordan (eds) *The Europeanization of British politics*, Basingstoke: Macmillan, pp 3–16.

Bache, I., George, S. and Buller, S. (2011) *Politics in the European Union* (3rd edn), Oxford: Oxford University Press.

Bainbridge, T. and Teasdale, A. (1995) *The Penguin companion guide to European Union*, London: Penguin.

Baines, P. (2004) 'Parliamentary scrutiny of the policy and legislation: the procedures of the Lords and Commons', in P. Giddings and G. Drewry (eds) *Britain in the European Union: law, policy and parliament*, Basingstoke: Palgrave Macmillan, pp 60–96.

Balchin, P., Sykora, L. and Bull, G. (1999) *Regional policy and planning in Europe*, London: Routledge.

Banister, D., Stead, D., Steen, P., Akerman, J., Derborg, K., Nijkamp, P. and Schleicher-Tappeser, R. (2000) *European transport policy and sustainable mobility*, London: Spon.

Barca, F. (2009) *An agenda for a reformed cohesion policy*, Brussels: CEC.

Barker K. (2004) *Review of housing supply*, London: HMT.

Barker K. (2006) *Review of land-use planning*, London: HMT.

Barratt, S. and Fudge, C. (1981a) 'Examining the policy–action relationship', in S. Barratt and C. Fudge (eds) *Policy and action*, London: Methuen, pp 3–32.

Barroso, J.M. (2012) 'State of the Union', speech to the European Parliament, 12 September.

Barzelay, M. and Gallego, R. (2006) 'From "new institutionalism" to "institutional processualism": advancing knowledge about public management policy change', *Governance*, vol 19, no 4, pp 531–57.

Baumgartner, F. and Jones, B.D. (2002) *Policy dynamics*, Chicago, IL: University of Chicago Press.

Beardsworth, R. (2011) *Cosmopolitanism and international relations theory*, Cambridge: Polity Press.

Beesley, M. and Laidlaw, B. (1995) 'The development of telecommunications policy in the UK 1981–1991', in M. Bishop, J. Kay and C. Mayer (eds) *The regulatory challenge*, Oxford: Oxford University Press, pp 309–35.

Bennett, C.J. (1991) 'What is policy convergence and who causes it?', *British Journal of Political Science*, vol 21, no 2, pp 215–33.

Benson, D. and Jordan, A. (2011) 'What have we learned from policy transfer research? Dolowitz and Marsh revisited', *Political Studies Review*, vol 9, no 3, pp 366–78.

Berger, J. and Luckmann, T. (1966) *The social construction of reality*, Harmondsworth: Penguin.

Bertelli, A.M. and John, P. (2011) 'Public policy investment: risk and return in British politics', paper for 'Government Agendas' project, 6 July.

Bevir, M. and Rhodes, R. (2003) *Interpreting British government*, London: Routledge.

Beyers, J. and J. Trondal, (2004) 'How Nation States 'Hit' Europe: Ambiguity and Representation in the European Union', Western *European Politics*, vol 27, no 5, pp 919–42.

Bickerton, C.J. (2011) 'Europe's neo-Madisonisans: rethinking the legitimacy of limited power in a multi-level polity', *Political Studies*, vol 59, no 3, pp 659–73.

BIS (Department of Business Industry and Skills) (2007) *Transposition guidance: how to implement European Directives effectively*, London: BIS.

BIS (2012) *Partnership agreement: delivery of structural funds, rural development funds and maritime and fisheries funds in England: informal consultation document*, March, London: BIS.

Bishop, M., Kay, J. and Mayer, C. (1995) 'Introduction', in M. Bishop, J. Kay and C. Mayer (eds) *The regulatory challenge*, Oxford: Oxford University Press, pp 1–17.

Blackstone, T. and Plowden, W. (1990) *Inside the think tank advising the cabinet 1971–1983*, London: Mandarin Press.

Blair T. (2010) *A journey*, London: Hutchinson.

Blanco, I., Lowndes, V. and Pratchett, L. (2011) 'Policy networks and governance networks: towards greater conceptual clarity', *Political Studies Review*, vol 9, no 3, pp 297–308.

Blick, A. (2004) *People who live in the dark: the history of special advisers in British government*, London: Politico's.

Blöchliger, H. and Vammalle, C. (2012) *Reforming fiscal federalism and local government: beyond the zero-sum game*, OECD Fiscal Federalism Studies, Paris: OECD.

Boaz, A., L. Grayson, R. Levitt, and W. Solesbury (2008) 'Does evidence-based policy work? Learning from the UK experience', *Evidence and Policy*, vol 4, no 2, pp 233–53.

Bohme, K., Doucet, P., Komornicki, T., Zaucha, J. and Swiatek, D. (2011) *How to strengthen the territorial cohesion dimension of 'Europe 2020' and the EU cohesion policy: report based on the Territorial Agenda 2020*, Warsaw: CEC/ERDF.

Bomberg, E. (1994) 'Policy networks on the periphery: EU environmental policy and Scotland', *Regional Politics and Policy*, vol 4, no 1, pp 45–61.

Bongers, P. and Chatfield, J. (1993) 'Regions and local authorities in the governance of Europe', in A. Duff (ed) *Subsidiarity within the European Community*, London: The Federal Trust, pp 77–85.

Booth, P. (2009) 'Planning and the culture of governance: local institutions and reform in France', *European Planning Studies*, vol 17, no 5, pp 677–95.

Borras, S. and Jacobsson, K. (2004) 'The open method of co-ordination and new governance patterns in the EU', *Journal of European Public Policy*, vol 11, part 2, pp 185–208.

Borzel, T. (1999) 'Towards convergence in Europe? Institutional adaptation to Europeanization in Germany and Spain', *Journal of Common Market Studies*, vol 37, no 4, pp 573–96.

Borzel, T. (2001) 'Europeanization and territorial institutional change', in M. Cowles, J. Caporaso and T. Risse (eds) *Transforming Europe*, Ithaca, NY: Cornell University Press, pp 137–58.

Borzel, T. (2002) 'Pace-setting, foot-dragging, and fence-sitting: member state responses to Europeanization', *Journal of Common Market Studies*, vol 40, no 2, pp 193–214.

Borzel, T. (2005) 'Europeanization: how the European Union interacts with its member states', in S. Bulmer and C. Lesquesne (eds) *The member states of the European Union*, Oxford: Oxford University Press, pp 45–70.

Borzel, T. (2011) *Comparative regionalism: a new research agenda*, KFG Working Paper no 28, August, Berlin: Free University.

Borzel, T, T. Hofmann and D. Panke (2012), 'Caving in or sitting it out? *Longitudinal* patterns of non-compliance in the European Union', *Journal of European Public Policy*, vol 19, no 4, pp 454–71.

Borzel, T. and Risse, T. (2012) 'When Europeanization meets diffusion. exploring new territory', *West European Politics*, Special Issue, vol 35, no 1, pp 192–207.

Bouckaert, G., Ormond, D. and Peters, B.G. (2000) *A possible governance agenda for Finland*, Helsinki: Ministry of Finance.

Bourne, A.K. (2007) 'Regional Europe', in M. Cini (ed) *European Union politics* (2nd edn), Oxford: Oxford University Press.

Brack, N. and Costa, O. (2012) 'Beyond the pro/anti europe divide: diverging views of Europe within EU institutions', *Journal of European integration*, vol 34, no 2, pp 101–11.

Braconier, H. (2012) *Reforming education in England*, Paris: OECD.

Bradbeer, J. (2001) 'UK environmental policy under Blair', in S. Savage and R. Atkinson (eds) *Public policy under Blair*, Palgrave: Basingstoke, pp 102–22.

Bradbury, J. (2002) 'Conservative governments, Scotland and Wales; perspectives on territorial management', in J. Bradbury and J. Mawson (eds) *British regionalism and devolution: the challenges of state reform and European integration*, Abingdon: Routledge, pp 74–98.

Bretherton C. and J. Vogler, (1999) *The European Union As a Global Actor*, Abingdon: Routledge.

Breton, R. (1964) 'Institutional completeness of ethnic communities and the personal relations of immigrants', *American Journal of Sociology*, vol 70, no 2, pp 193–205.

Breuss, F. and Eller, M. (2004) 'The optimal decentralisation of government activity: normative recommendations for the European constitution', *Constitutional Political Economy*, vol 15, no 1, pp 27–76.

Brigham, C. (2011) *New initiatives with open data*, presentation RGS IBG conference, 31 August, London: World Bank.

Brown, R. (2012) 'Giving government a harder nudge', IPPR original, 28 February. Available at: http://www.ippr.org/articles/56/8788/giving-government-a-harder-nudge

Brundtland, G.H. (1987) *Our common future*, New York, NY: United Nations.

Buller, J. (2000) *National statecraft and European integration: the Conservative government and the European Union, 1979–1997*, London: Pinter.

Buller, J. and Flinders, M. (2005) 'The domestic origins of depoliticisation in the area of British economic policy', *The British Journal of Politics and International Relations*, vol 7, no 4, pp 526–43.

Bulmer, S. and Burch, M. (1998) 'Organizing for Europe: Whitehall, the British state and European Union', *Public Administration*, vol 76, no 4, pp 601–28.

Bulmer, S. and Burch, M. (2005) 'The Europeanization of UK government: from quiet revolution to explicit step-change?', *Public Administration*, vol 83, no 4, pp 861–90.

Bulmer, S. and Burch, M. (2009) *The Europeanisation of Whitehall, UK central government and the European Union*, Manchester: Manchester University Press.

Bulmer, S., Burch, M., Carter, C., Hogwood, P. and Scott, A. (2002) *British devolution and European policy-making*, Basingstoke: Palgrave Macmillan.

Bulmer, S., Dolowitz, D., Humphreys, P. and Padgett, S. (2007) *Policy transfer in European Union governance*, Abingdon: Routledge.

Bulpitt J., (1983) *Territory and power in the United Kingdom* Manchester: Manchester University Press.

Bun, M.J.G. and Klaassen, F. (2002) 'Has the euro increased trade?', Social Science Research Network, 10 October.

Burchell J. and S. Lightfoot (2002) *Greening of the European Union*, London: Continuum.

Burgess, M. (2009) 'Federalism', in A. Wiener and T. Diez (eds) *European integration theory*, Oxford: Oxford University Press, pp 25–44.

Burnham, J. and Pyper, R. (2008) *Britain's modernised civil service*, Basingstoke: Palgrave Macmillan.

Burnham, P. (2001) 'New Labour and the politics of depoliticisation', *The British Journal of Politics and International Relations*, vol 3, no 2, pp 127–49.

Butcher, L. (2012) *Railways: EU policy*, SN 184, 17 February, London: House of Commons Library.

Butler, N. (2011) 'Evidence given to the Public Administration Select Committee', 13 December, London: House of Commons.

Cabinet Office (1999) *Modernising government*, London: Cabinet Office.

Cabinet Office (2003) *Trying it out – the role of 'pilots' in policy-making, report of a review of government pilots*, London: Cabinet Office.

Cabinet Office (2012) Procurement Policy Note 03/12 - European Legislative Proposal on Third Country Access to the EU Public Procurement Market, London: Cabinet Office.

Cable, V. (2010) 'Press release', 15 December, London: BIS.

Cairney, P. (2011) 'The new British policy style: from a British to a Scottish political tradition?', *Political Studies Review*, vol 9, no 2, pp 208–20.

Cairney, P. (2012) *Understanding public policy*, Basingstoke: Macmillan Palgrave.

Camagni, R. (2010) *TIPTAP – Territorial Impact Package for Transport and Agricultural Policies*, ESPON 2013 Programme, Brussels: CEC.

Cameron, D. (2012) Speech at reception for mayors, No 10 Downing Street, 28 March.

Cameron D. (2013) EU speech at Bloomberg (as written not as spoken) 23 January, http://www.number10.gov.uk/news/eu-speech-at-bloomberg/

Camps, M. (1964) *Britain and the European Community 1955–1963*, London: Oxford University Press.

Camps, M. (1967) *European unification in the sixties: from the veto to the crisis*, London: Oxford University Press.

Cannadine, D. (2003) *In Churchill's shadow: confronting the past in modern Britain*, Harmondsworth: Penguin.

Capano, G. (2009) 'Understanding policy change as an epistemological and theoretical problem', *Journal of Comparative Policy Analysis: Research and Practice*, vol 11, no 1, pp 7–31.

Capano, G. and Howlett, M. (2009) 'Introduction: the determinants of policy change: advancing the debate', *Journal of Comparative Policy Analysis: Research and Practice*, vol 11, no 1, pp 1–5.

Carbone, M. (2010a) 'Introduction: understanding the domestic politics of treaty reform', in M. Carbone (ed) *National politics and European integration: from the constitution to the Lisbon Treaty*, Cheltenham: Edward Elgar, pp 1–15.

Carbone, M. (2010b) 'Conclusions: preference formation, inter-state bargaining and the Treaty of Lisbon', in M. Carbone (ed) *National politics and European integration: from the constitution to the Lisbon Treaty*, Cheltenham: Edward Elgar, pp 215–33.

Cardona, F. (1999) *Modernizing the civil service*, Sigma Programme, Paris: OECD.

Carrington, D. (2012) 'Ocean cables to bring green energy to UK', *The Guardian*, 12 April, p 1.

Carswell, D. (2012) 'Worried about the role of Sir Humphrey? It's not only me', Douglas Carswell's blog, 18 April. Available at: http://www.talkcarswell.com/home/all

Carter, C.A. (2002) *The formulation of UK–EU policy post-devolution: a transformative model of governance?*, Manchester Papers in Politics Devolution and European Policy Making Series no 3, Manchester: European Policy Research Unit.

CEC (Commission of the European Communities) 1975 Tindemans Report, Brussels: CEC.

CEC (1977) *Directive 77/62/EEC: coordinating procedures for the award of public supply contracts*, Brussels: CEC.

CEC (1980) *Directive 80/767/EEC 1980: adapting and supplementing in respect of certain contracting authorities*, 22 July, Brussels: CEC.

CEC (1985) *White Paper on the completion of the internal market including technical appendix*, Brussels: CEC.

CEC (1992a *Sustainable mobility*, Brussels: CEC.

CEC (1992b) The Birmingham European Council 16 October, Brussels: CEC.

CEC, 1998 *The Cecchini Report Europe 1992: the overall challenge*, Brussels SEC (88) 524 final, 13 April.

CEC (1993) *Towards Sustainability Fifth environmental action programme*, Brussels: CEC.

CEC (1994) *Growth, competitiveness, employment*, Brussels: CEC.

CEC (1999) *European spatial development perspective*, Brussels: CEC.

CEC (2001) *European governance White Paper*, COM(2001) 428, 25 July, Brussels: CEC.

CEC (2004) *White Paper on services of general interest*, COM(2004) 374, Brussels: CEC.

CEC (2005) *White Paper financial services policy 2005–2010*, Brussels: CEC.

CEC (2006a) 'Directive 2006/123/EU on services in the internal market', *Official Journal of the European Union*, 12 December, L 376, pp 36–68.

CEC (2006b) *European grouping of territorial cohesion*, Regulation (EC) 1082/2006, 5 July, Brussels: CEC.

CEC (2006c) *Keep Europe moving: sustainable mobility for our continent: mid-term review of the European Commission's 2001 transport White Paper*, COM(2006) 314, Brussels: CEC.

CEC (2007) *Towards a new culture for urban mobility*, COM(2007), 25 September, Brussels: CEC.

CEC (2008a) *Green Paper on territorial cohesion: turning territorial diversity into strength*, SEC(2008) 2550, Brussels: CEC.

CEC (2008b) *Commission staff working document accompanying the Green Paper on territorial cohesion: turning territorial diversity into strength*, Brussels: CEC.

CEC (2009a) *What is Europe's trade policy?*, Brussels: CEC.

CEC (2009b) *Territorial cohesion; unleashing the territorial potential*, Kiruna 10–11 December, Brussels: CEC.

CEC (2009c) *Action plan on urban mobility*, COM(2009) 490, 30 September, Brussels: CEC.

CEC (2010a) *Europe 2020*, Brussels: CEC.

CEC (2010b) *North Sea Countries Offshore Grid Initiative*, Brussels: CEC.

CEC (2010c) *Consultation on the future trans European transport network policy*, COM(2010) 212, Brussels: CEC.

CEC (2010d) *New evidence on smart, sustainable and inclusive territories: first ESPON synthesis report*, Brussels: CEC.

CEC (2010e) *Regulating financial services for sustainable growth*, COM(2010) 301, 2 June, Brussels: CEC.

CEC (2011a) *Review of Small Business Act for Europe*, COM (2011) 78 final, 23 February.

CEC (2011b) *Communication on a quality Framework for Services of general Interest,* 20 December Brussels: CEC.)

CEC (2011c) *List of pre-identified projects on the core network in the field of transport*, 19 October, Brussels: CEC.

CEC (2011d) *The sixth Community environment action programme: final assessment*, COM(2011) 531 final, 31 August, Brussels: CEC.

CEC (2011e) *White Paper: roadmap to a single European transport area – towards a competitive and resource efficient transport system*, SEC(2011) 359 final, Brussels: CEC.

CEC (2011f) *Territorial agenda of the European Union 2020 – towards an inclusive, smart and sustainable Europe of diverse regions*, Godollo, HU: CEC.

CEC (2012a) *Consultation document: EU environmental priorities for 2020: towards the seventh environmental action programme*, Brussels: CEC.

CEC (2012b) *Roadmap for the 7th environmental action programme*, Brussels: CEC.

CEC (2012c) *Statistics on environmental infringements 2008 and 2009,* Brussels: CEC.

CEC (2012d) Council Recommendations on the national reform programme 2012 of the United Kingdom, 6th July Brussels: CEC.

Centre for Cities (2012) *Cities outlook 2012*, London: Centre for Cities.

Cerny, P. and Evans, M. (2004) 'Globalisation and public policy under New Labour', *Policy Studies*, vol 25, part 1, pp 51–66.

Chapman, R.A. and O'Toole, B.J. (2010) 'Leadership in the British Civil Service: an interpretation', *Public Policy and Administration*, vol 25, no 02, pp 123-36.

Charbit, C. (2011) *Governance of public policies in decentralised contexts: The multi-level approach,* Regional Development Working Papers, 2011/04. Paris: Organisation for Economic Co-operation and Development.

Cini, M. (2007a) 'Intergovernmentalism', in M. Cini (ed) *European Union politics* (2nd edn), Oxford: Oxford University Press, pp 100–16.

Cini, M. (2008) 'Competition policy', in I. Bache and A. Jordan (eds) *The Europeanization of British politics*, Basingstoke: Macmillan, pp 216–30.

Citrin, J. and Sides, J. (2008) 'Immigration and the imagined community in Europe and the United States', *Political Studies*, vol 56, no 1, pp 33–56.

Clapham, D. (2002) 'Housing pathways: a post modern analytical framework', *Housing Theory and Society*, vol 19, no 2, pp 57–68.

Clark, G. (2012) 'German cities and urban policy' MIPIM World Blog 8th October, http://blog.mipimworld.com/2012/10/german-cities-and-urban-policy/

Clarke, J. (2004) 'Dissolving the public realm? The logics and limits of neoliberalism', *Journal of Social Policy*, vol 33, no 1, pp 27–48.

Clayton, N., Smith, R. and Tochtermann, L. (2011) *Access all areas: linking people to jobs*, London: Centre for Cities.

Clifford, B. (2006) 'Only a town planner would run a toxic-waste pipeline through a recreational area: planning and planners in the British press', *Town Planning Review*, vol 77, no 4, pp 423–56.

Clifford, B. and Morphet, J. (2012) '"Who else would we speak to?" National policy communities in post-devolution Britain: the case of spatial planning', PSA Specialist Group Territorial Politics Biennial Conference, 13–14 September, Scotland House and Wales House, Brussels.

Clift, B. and Woll, C. (2012) 'Economic patriotism: reinventing control over open markets', *Journal of European Public Policy*, vol 19, no 3, pp 307–23.

Cochrane, A. (2011) 'Foreword', in E. McCann and K. Ward (eds) *Mobile urbanism: cities and policymaking in the global age*, London: University of Minnesota Press, pp ix–xi.

Cockfield, A. (1994) *The European Union: creating the single market*, London: Wiley Chancery Law.

Cole, A. and Jones, G. (2005) 'Reshaping the state: administrative reform and new public management in France', *Governance*, vol 18, no 4, pp 567–88.

Cole, M. (1998) 'Globalisation, modernisation and competitiveness: a critique of the New Labour project in education', *International Studies in the Sociology of Education*, vol 8, no 3, pp 315–34.

Collins, P. (2009) 'Successful policy relies on failure and mistakes', *The Times*, 20 July, p 15.

Conant, L. (2001) 'Europeanization and the courts: variable patterns of adaptation in national judiciaries', in M. Cowles, J. Caporaso and T. Risse (eds) *Transforming Europe*, Ithaca, NY: Cornell University Press, pp 97–115.

Conceicao-Heldt, E. (2011) 'Variation in EU member states' preferences and the Commission's discretion in the Doha Round', *Journal of European Public Policy*, vol 18, no 3, pp 403–19.

Cook, R. (1997) Ethical Foreign Policy speech, *The Guardian* 12 May.

Cooper, I. (2012) 'A virtual third chamber for the European Union? National parliaments after the Lisbon Treaty', *West European Politics*, vol 35, no 3, pp 441–65.

Cornut, F., Giroux, H. and Langley, A. (2012) 'The strategic plan as a genre', *Discourse and Communication*, vol 6, no 1, pp 21–54.

Costa, O. and Jorgensen, K.E. (eds) (2012) *When multilateralism hits Brussels: the influence of international institutions on the EU*, Basingstoke: Palgrave Macmillan.

Cowles, M. and Risse, T. (2001) 'Transforming Europe: conclusions', in M. Cowles, J. Caporaso and T. Risse (eds) *Transforming Europe*, Ithaca, NY: Cornell University Press, pp 217–37.

Crosland, A. (1976) *Developments in the European Communities, November 1975–April 1976*, Cabinet meeting 14 May, London: National Archive.

Crossman, R. (1979) *The Crossman diaries: condensed version* (ed A. Howard), London: Magnum Books.

Curran, A. and Williams, I. (2010) 'The role of furniture and appliance re-use organisations in England and Wales', *Resources Conservation and Recycling*, vol 54, no 10, pp 692–703.

Currie, G., Grubnic, S. and Hodges, R. (2011) 'Leadership in public service networks: antecedents, process and outcome', *Public Administration*, vol 89, no 2, pp 242–64.

Cutler, T. and Waine, B. (2002) 'Managerialism reformed? New Labour and public sector management', *Social Policy and Administration*, vol 34, part 3, pp 318–32.

Daddow, O. (2007) 'Playing games with history: Tony Blair's European policy in the press', *The British Journal of Politics and International Relations*, vol 9, no 4, pp 582–98.

Daddow, O. and Gaskarth, J. (2011) 'Introduction: Blair, Brown and New Labour's foreign policy, 1997–2010', in O. Daddow and J. Gaskarth (eds) *British foreign policy: the New Labour years*, Basingstoke: Palgrave Macmillan, pp 1–28.

Damro, C. (2012) 'Market power Europe', *Journal of European Public Policy*, iFirst.

Davidson, N. (2006) *The Davidson review: implementation of EU legislation: final report*, Norwich: HMSO.

Davies, P. (2004) *Is evidence-based government possible?*, London: Cabinet Office.

Davies, E. and Flanders, S. (1995) 'Conflicting regulatory objectives: the supply of gas to UK industry', in M. Bishop, J. Kay and C. Mayer (eds) *The regulatory challenge*, Oxford: Oxford University Press, pp 43–67.

Davis, G., Weller, P., Craswell, E. and Eggins, S. (1999) 'What drives machinery of government change? Australia, Canada and the United Kingdom 1950–1997', *Public Administration*, vol 77, no 1, pp 7–50.

Daviter, F. (2007) 'Policy framing in the European Union', *Journal of European Public Policy*, vol 14, no 4, pp 654–66.

Davoudi, S. and Strange, I. (2008) *Conceptions of space and place in strategic spatial planning*, Abingdon: Routledge.

DCLG (Department for Communities and Local Government) (2012) *National planning policy framework*, London: DCLG.

Deacon, A. (2000) 'Learning from the US? The influence of American ideas upon New Labour thinking on welfare reform', *Policy and Politics*, vol 28, part 1, pp 5–18.

DECC (Department of Energy and Climate Change) (2012) 'Smart meters'. Available at: http://www.decc.gov.uk/en/content/cms/tackling/smart_meters/smart_meters.aspx (accessed 15 April 2012).

DEFRA (Department for Environment and Rural Affairs) (2011) *Government review of waste policy in England*, London: DEFRA.

Delhousse, R. and Thompson, A. (2012a) 'Intergovernmentalists in the Commission: foxes in the henhouse?', *Journal of European Integration*, vol 34, no 2, pp 113–32.

Delhousse, R. and Thompson, A. (forthcoming) The Commission in the EU institution system; a citadel under siege', in H. Kassim, J. Peterson, M. W. Bauer, S. Connolly, R. Dehousse, L. Hooghe, and A. Thompson (eds) *The European Commission in the twenty-first century*, Oxford: Oxford University Press.

Delors, J. (1989) *Report on Economic and Monetary Union in the European Community*, Brussels: CEC.

Denton, G. (1992) *Federalism and European Union after Maastricht*, Wilton Park Paper 67, London: HMSO.

DfT (1989) *Roads for Prosperity*, London: HMSO.

DfT (1991) Transport and the Environment, London: HMSO.

DfT (Department for Transport) (2012a) *Devolving local major transport schemes*, London: DfT.

DfT (2012b) *Consultation of charging heavy goods vehicles*, London: DfT.

DETR (Department of the Environment, Transport and the Regions) (1997) *Criteria for project selection*, London: DETR.

DETR (1998) *Modern local government – in touch with the people*, London: HMSO.

DETR (1998) *A new deal for transport*, London: DETR.

DETR (1999) *Subsidiarity and proportionality in spatial planning activities in the European Union: final report*, London: DETR.

De Ville, F. (2012) 'European Union regulatory politics in the shadow of the WTO: WTO rules as a frame of reference and rhetorical device', *Journal of European Public Policy*, iFirst.

Diez, T. and Wiener, A. (2009) 'Introducing the mosaic of integration theory', in A. Wiener and T. Diez (eds) *European integration theory*, Oxford: Oxford University Press, pp 1–22.

Dilnott, A. (2011) *Fairer funding for all – the Commission's recommendations to government*, London: HMT and DH.

Dimitrakopoulos, D.G. (2001) 'The transposition of EU law: "post-decisional politics and Institutional autonomy"', *European law Journal*, vol 7, no 4, pp 442–58.

Dinan, D. (2010) *Ever closer union: an interdiction to European integration* (4th edn), Boulder, CO: Lynne Reiner Publishers.

DoE (1990) *This common inheritance*, London: HMSO.

Dolan, P., Hallsworth, M., Halpern, D., King, D. and Vlaev, I. (2010) *Influencing behaviour through public policy*, London: Institute for Government.

Dolowitz, D.P. (2003) 'A policy-maker's guide to policy transfer', *The Political Quarterly*, vol 74, no 1, pp 101–8.

Dolowitz, D.P. and Marsh, D. (1996) 'Who learns what from whom: a review of the policy transfer literature', *Political Studies*, vol 44, no 2, pp 343–57.

Douglas, M. (1999) 'The depoliticisation of risk', in M. Douglas *Implicit Meanings*, London: Routledge, pp 218–31.

Dowding, K. and John, P. (2009) 'The value of choice in public policy', *Public Administration*, vol 87, no 2, pp 219–33.

Downey, G. (1986) *The Rayner scrutiny programme, 1979–1983, report of the Comptroller and Auditor General*, London: HMSO.

DRD (Department of Regional Development) (2012) *Regional development strategy RDS 2035: building a better future*, Belfast: DRD.

Drewry, G. and Giddings, P. (2004) 'Introduction', in P. Giddings and G. Drewry (eds) *Britain in the European Union: law, policy and parliament*, Basingstoke: Palgrave Macmillan, pp 1–11.

Duff, A. (1993) 'Towards a definition of subsidiarity', in A. Duff (ed) *Subsidiarity within the European Community*, London: The Federal Trust, pp 7–32.

Duhr, S., Colomb, C. and Nadin, V. (2010) *European spatial planning and territorial cooperation*, Abingdon: Routledge.

Dur, A. and Elsig, M. (2011) 'Principals, agents and the European Union's foreign economic policies', *Journal of European Public Policy*, vol 18, no 3, pp 323–38.

Dur, A. and Zimmermann, H. (2007) 'Introduction: the EU in international trade negotiations', *Journal of Common Market Studies*, vol 45, no 4, pp 771–87.

Dyson, T. (2011) 'Defence policy under the Labour government: operational dynamism and strategic inertia', *British Journal of Politics and International Relations*, vol 13, no 2, pp 206–29.

Eberlein, B. and Kerwer, D. (2004) 'New governance in the European Union: a theoretical perspective', *Journal of Common Market Studies*, vol 42, no 1, pp 121–42.

Eckert, P. (2006) 'Communities of practice', in *Encyclopaedia of language and linguistics*, Amsterdam: Elsevier.

Eddington, R. (2006) *The Eddington transport study*, London: HMT.

Eden, R. and Hyndman, N. (1999) 'Performance measurement in the UK public sector: poisoned chalice or Holy Grail?', *Optimum: The Journal of Public Sector Management*, vol 29, no 1, pp 9–15.

Eden, S. (2003) 'People and the contemporary environment', in R. Johnston and M. Williams (eds) *A century of british geography*, London: The British Academy, pp 213–45.

Edmonds, T. (2012) *Financial Services Bill: committee stage report*, Research paper 12/18, 19 April, London: House of Commons Library.

Efficiency Unit (1988) *Improving management in Government the Next Steps, Report to Prime Minister,* London: HMSO.

Egan, M. (2007) 'The single market', in M. Cini (ed) *European Union politics* (2nd edn), Oxford: Oxford University Press, pp 253–70.

Egberg M. and D. Curtin, (2008) 'Tradition and innovation: Europe's accumulated executive order', *West European Politics*, vol 31, no 4, pp 639–61.

Elkins, Z. (2009) 'Constitutional networks', in M. Kahler (ed) *Networked politics: agency, power and governance*, Ithaca, NY: Cornell University Press, pp 43–63.

Elphicke, C. and Raab, D. (2012) Letter to *The Telegraph* signed by 102 MPs, 5 February.

Evans, B. and Theobald, K. (2003) 'LASALA: evaluating Local Agenda 21 in Europe', *Journal of Environmental Planning and Management*, vol 46, no 5, pp 781–794.

Evers, D., Tennekes, L., Borsboom, J., van den Heiligenberg, H. and Thissen, M. (2009) *A territorial impact assessment of territorial cohesion for the Netherlands*, The Hague, Netherlands Environmental Assessment Agency.

Eyre, S. and Lodge, M. (2000) 'National tunes and a European melody? Competition law reform in the UK and Germany', *Journal of European Public Policy*, vol 7, no 1, pp 63–79.

Fairbrass, J. and Jordan, A. (2001) 'European Union environmental policy and the UK government: a passive observer or a strategic manager?', *Environmental Politics*, vol 10, no 2, pp 1–21.

Fairbrass, J. and Jordan, A. (2004) 'Multi-level governance and environmental policy', in I. Bache and M. Flinders (eds) *Multi-level governance*, Oxford: Oxford University Press, pp 147–64.

Faludi, A. (2010) *Cohesion, coherence, cooperation: European spatial planning coming of age?*, Abingdon: Routledge.

FCO (Foreign and Commonwealth Office) (1970) *Sovereignty and the European Communities*, London: FCO.

Fergusson, M., Coffey, C., Wilkinson, D., Baldock, D., Farmer, A., Kraemer, R.A. and Mazurek, A.-G. (2001) *The effectiveness of EU Council integrations strategies and options for carrying forward the Cardiff process*, London: IEEP/Ecologik.

Ferlie, E., Fitzgerald, L., McGivern, G., Dopson, S. and Bennett, C. (2011) 'Public policy networks and "wicked problems": a nascent solution?', *Public Administration*, vol 89, no 2, pp 307–24.

Flinders M., (2000) 'The Politics of Accountability: A Case Study of Freedom of Information Legislation in the United Kingdom', *Political Quarterly*, vol 71, no 4, pp 422-35.

Flinders, M. (2002) 'Shifting the balance? Parliament, the executive and the British constitution', *Political studies*, vol 50, no 3, pp 23–42.

Flinders, M. and Buller, J. (2006) 'Depoliticisation: principles, tactics and tools', *British Politics*, vol 1, no 3, pp 293–318.

Florida, R. (2009) *Who's your city? How the creative economy is making where you live the most important decision of your life*, New York, NY: Basic Books.

Flowerdew, J. (2004) 'The discursive construction of a world-class city', *Discourse and Society*, vol 15, no 5 pp 575–605.

Flynn, A., Gray, A., Jenkins, W. and Rutherford, B. (1988) 'Implementing the Next Steps', *Public Administration*, vol 66, no 4, pp 439–45.

Flynn, A., Gray, A. and Jenkins, W.I. (1990) 'Taking the Next Steps: the changing management of government', *Parliamentary Affairs*, vol 43, no 2 pp 159–78.

Fontana, M.-C. (2011) 'Europeanization and domestic policy concertation: how actors use Europe to modify domestic patterns of policy-making', *Journal of European Public Policy*, vol 18, no 5, pp 654–71.

Forman, F.N. (2002) *Constitutional change in the United Kingdom*, London: Routledge.

Foster, C.D. and Plowden, F.J. (1996) *The state under stress: can the hollow state be good government?*, Buckingham: Open University Press.

Frankel, B. (1997) 'Beyond labourism and socialism: how the Australian Labor Party developed the model of "New Labour"', *New Left Review*, vol 221, pp 3–33.

Freeden, M. (1999) 'The ideology of New Labour', *Political Quarterly*, vol 70, no 1, pp 42–51.

Freud, D. (2008) *Raising expectations and increasing support: reforming welfare for the future*, London: DWP.

Friedland, J. (2011) *The Guardian*, 6 October, p 1.

Fry, G. (1988a) 'The Thatcher government, the financial management initiative and the "new civil service"', *Public Administration*, vol 66, no 1, pp 1–20.

Fry, G. (1988b) 'Outlining the Next Steps', *Public Administration*, vol 66, no 4, pp 429–39..

Fulton, L.J.S. (1968) *The civil service report of the committee 1966–68*, London: HMSO.

Gains, F. (1999) 'Implementing privatization policies in next steps agencies', *Public Administration*, vol 77, no 4, pp 713-30.

Gains, F. (2004a) '"Hardware, software or network connection?" Theorizing crisis in the UK Next Steps agencies?', *Public Administration*, vol 82, no 3, pp 547–66.

Gains, F. (2004b) 'Adapting the agency concept: variations within "Next Steps"', in C. Pollitt and C. Talbot (eds) *Unbundled government*, Abingdon: Routledge, pp 53–75.

Gamble, A. (2003) *Between Europe and America: the future of British politics*, Basingstoke: Palgrave Macmillan.

Gamble, A. (2004) 'Foreword', in I. Bache and M. Flinders (eds) *Multi-level governance*, Oxford: Oxford University Press, pp v–vii.

Geddes, A. (2004) *The European Union and British politics*, Basingstoke: Palgrave Macmillan.

George, S. (1991) *Politics and policy in the European Community* (2nd edn), Oxford: Oxford University Press.

George, S. (1998) *An awkward partner: Britain in the European Community* (3rd edn), Oxford: Oxford University Press.

George, S. (2004) 'Multi-level governance and the European Union', in I. Bache and M. Flinders (eds) *Multi-level governance*, Oxford: Oxford University Press, pp 107–26.

Gershon. P., (2004) *Releasing Resources for the frontline: Independent Review of Public Sector Efficiency,* London: HMT.

Giddings, P. and Drewry, G. (2004) 'Finding the way forward', in P. Giddings and G. Drewry (eds) *Britain in the European Union: law, policy and parliament*, Basingstoke: Palgrave Macmillan, pp 240–55.

GLA (Greater London Authority) (2011) *Languages spoken at home by pupils in London*, London: GLA Datastore.

Glaister, S., Burnham, J., Stevens, H. and Travers, T. (2006) *Transport policy in Britain* (2nd edn), Basingstoke: Palgrave Macmillan.

Glasson, J. and T. Marshall, (2007) *Regional planning*, Abingdon: Routledge.

Glencross, A. (2009) *What makes the EU viable?*, New York, NY: Palgrave Macmillan.

Glencross, A. (2011) 'A post-national EU? The problems of legitimising the EU without the nation and national representation', *Political Studies*, vol 59, no 2, pp 348–67.

Glennie, A. and Straw, W. (2012) *The third wave of globalisation*, London: IPPR.

Goetz, K.H. (2001) 'European integration and national executive: a cause in search of an effect?', in K.H. Goetz and S. Hix (2001) *Europeanised politics? European integration and national political systems*, London: Frank Cass, pp 211–31.

Goetz, K.H. and Hix, S. (2001) *Europeanised politics? European integration and national political systems*, London: Frank Cass.

Goetz, K.H. and Meyer-Sahling, H.-H. (2008) 'The Europeanisation of national political systems: parliaments and executives', *Living Review of European Government*, no 2. Available at: http://www.livingreviews.org/lreg-2008-2

Goetz, K.H. and Meyer-Sahling H.-H. (2009) 'Political time in the EU: dimensions, perspectives, theories', *Journal of European Public Policy*, vol 16, no 2, pp 180–201.

Goffman, E. (1974) *Frame analysis*, Cambridge, MA: Harvard University Press.

Goleman, D. (1988) *Working with Emotional Intelligence New York*, NY: Bantam.

Golub, J. (1996) 'State power and institutional influence in European integration: lessons from the packaging waste directive', *Journal of Common Market Studies*, vol 34, no 3, pp 313–40.

Goodwin, P. (1999) 'Transformation of transport policy in Great Britain', *Transportation Research Part A*, vol 33, nos 7-8, pp 655–69.

Gorard, S. (2009) 'What are academies the answer to?', *Journal of Education Policy*, vol 24, no 1, pp 101–13.

Graham, S. (2000) 'Constructing premium network spaces: reflections on infrastructure networks and contemporary urban development', *International Journal of Urban and Regional Research*, vol 24, no 1, pp 183–200.

Granovetter, M. (1978) 'Threshold models in collective behaviour', *American Journal of Sociology*, vol 83, pp 1420–43.

Grant, C. (1994) *Delors: inside the house that Jacques built*, London: Nicholas Brealey Publishing.

Graz, J.-C. (2003) 'How powerful are transnational elite clubs? The social myth of the World Economic Forum', *New Political Economy*, vol 8, no 3, pp 321–40.

Greener, I. (2008) 'Choice or voice? Introduction to the themed section', *Social Policy and Society*, vol 7, no 2, pp 197–200.

Green-Cowles, M. (1994). 'Transcending Political Representation: the Mobilization of Big Business in the European Community', *American Political Studies Association Conference, Washington, September 1994*.

Groth, N.B., Smidt-Jensen, S. and Nielsen, T. (2011) 'Polycentricity: an issue in local development strategies? Findings form the Baltic Sea region', *European Planning Studies*, vol 19, no 5, pp 727–51.

Haahr, J.H. (2004) 'Open co-ordination as advanced liberal government', *Journal of European Public Policy*, vol 11, no 2, pp 209–30.

Haas, Ernst B. (1958) *The uniting of Europe*, Stanford: Stanford University Press.

Hachmann, V. (2011) 'From mutual learning to joint working: Europeanization processes in the INTERREG B programmes', *European Planning Studies*, vol 19, no 8, pp 1537–55.

Haddon, C. (2012) *Reforming the Civil Service – The Efficiency Unit*, London: Institute for Government.

Hagemann, S. (2010) 'Voting, statements and coalition-building in the Council from 1999 to 2006', in D. Naurin and H. Wallace (eds) *Unveiling the Council of the European Union: games governments play in Brussels*, Basingstoke: Palgrave Macmillan pp 36–63.

Hahn, J. (2011) 'The future EU cohesion policy: investing in Europe's cities', speech at conference on Effective Instruments for Territorial Development, Brussels, CEC, 24 October.

Haigh, N. (1987) *EEC environmental policy and Britain*, Harlow: Longman.

Haigh, N. (1996) 'Climate change policies and politics in the European Community', in T. O'Riordan and J. Jager (eds) *Politics of climate change: a European perspective*, London: Routledge, pp 155–87.

Hall P. (1993) 'Policy Paradigms, Social Learning and the State', Comparative Politics, vol 23, no 3, pp 275-96.

Hallsworth, M. (2011) *System stewardship: the future of policy making*, Working Paper, London: Institute for Government.

Hallsworth, M. and Rutter, J. (2011) *Making policy better: improving Whitehall's core business*, London: Institute for Government.

Halpern, D. (2004) *Social capital*, Cambridge: The Polity Press.

Halpern, D. (2009) *The wealth of nations*, Cambridge: The Polity Press.

Halpin, D. (2011) 'Explaining policy bandwagons: organised interest mobilization and cascades of attention', *Governance*, vol 24, no 2, pp 205–30.

Hameiri, S. (2009) 'Beyond methodological nationalism, but whereto for the study of regional governance?', *Australian Journal of International Affairs*, vol 63, no 3, pp 430–41.

Hameiri, S. and Jayasuriya, K. (2011) 'Regulatory regionalism and the dynamics of territorial politics', *Political Studies*, vol 59, no 1, pp 20–37.

Happold, M. (2000) 'Independence: in or out? An independent Scotland and the European Union', *International and Comparative Law Quarterly*, vol 49, no 1, pp 15–34.

Harrington, M. (1962) *The other America: poverty in the United States*, Harmondsworth: Penguin.

Harris, P. and Lock, A. (1996) 'Machiavellian marketing: the development of corporate lobbying in the UK', *Journal of Marketing Management*, vol 12, no 4, pp 313–28.

Harrison, S. (2002) 'New Labour, modernisation and the medical labour process', *Journal of Social Policy*, vol 31, part 3, pp 465–86.

Harvie, C. (1994) *The rise of regional Europe*, London: Routledge.

Hatcher, R. (2006) 'Privatization and sponsorship: the re-agenting of the school system in England', *Journal of Education Policy*, vol 21, no 5, pp 599–619.

Hay, C. (1998) 'The tangled webs we weave: the discourse, strategy and practice of networking', in D. Marsh (ed) *Comparing policy networks*, Buckingham: Open University Press.

Hay, C. and Richards, D. (2000) 'The tangled webs of Westminster and Whitehall; the practice of networking within the British core executive', *Public Administration*, vol 78, no 1, pp 1–28.

Hay, C. and Rosamund, B. (2002) 'Globalization, European integration and the discursive construction of economic imperatives', *Journal of European Public Policy*, vol 9, part 2, pp 147–67.

Hayes-Renshaw, F., van Aken, W. and Wallace, H. (2006) 'When and why the EU Council of Ministers votes explicitly', *Journal of Common Market Studies*, vol 44, no 1, pp 161–94.

Hazell, R. (1999a) 'The shape of things to come: what will the UK Constitution look like in the early 21st century?', in R. Hazell (ed) *Constitutional futures: a history of the next ten years*, Oxford: Oxford University Press, pp 7–20.

Hazell, R. (ed) (2006) *The English question*, Manchester: Manchester University Press.

Hazell, R. and Morris, B. (1999) 'Machinery of government: Whitehall', in R. Hazell (ed) *Constitutional futures: a history of the next ten years*, Oxford: Oxford University Press, pp 136–55.

Heclo, H. and Wildavsky, A. (1974) *The private government of public money* (2nd edn), London: Macmillan.

Heidbreder, E.G. (2009) *Structuring the European administrative space: channels of EU penetration and mechanisms of national change*, KFG Working Paper 5, Berlin: Free University.

Held, D. (2006) 'Reframing global governance: apocalypse soon or reform', *New Political Economy*, vol 11, no 2, pp 157–76.

Held, D. (2010) *Cosmopolitanism ideas and realities*, Cambridge: Polity Press.

Helgason, S. (1997) 'International benchmarking: experiences from OECD Countries', paper presented to conference on benchmarking, Copenhagen, 21/22 February.

Henderson, A. (2010a) 'Why regions matter: sub-state polities in comparative perspective', *Regional and Federal Studies*, vol 20, nos 4/5, pp 439–46.

Henderson, A. (2010b) '"Small worlds" as general predictors of political attitudes', *Regional and Federal Studies*, vol 20, nos 4/5, pp 469–86.

Hennessey, P. (2003) *The secret state*, London: Penguin.

Hepburn, E. and McLoughlin, J. (2011) 'Celtic nationalism and supranationalism: comparing Scottish and Northern Ireland party responses to Europe', *The British Journal of Politics and International Relations*, vol 13, no 3, pp 383–99.

Heritier, A. (2001a) 'New modes of governance in Europe: policy-making without legislating?', Renner Institute, Vienna, 10 December.

Heritier, A. (2001b) 'Differential Europe: national administrative response to community policy', in M. Cowles, J. Caporaso and T. Risse (eds) *Transforming Europe*, Ithaca, NY: Cornell University Press, pp 44–59.

Heritier, A., Knill, C. and Mingers, S. (1996) *Ringing the changes in Europe. Regulatory competition and the transformation of the state*, Berlin: de Gruyter.

Heseltine, M., (2012) *No Stone unturned: In pursuit of growth*, London: BIS.

Hewison, G. (2001) 'A power of general competence – should it be granted to local government in New Zealand?', *Auckland University Law Review*, vol 9, no 2, pp 498–528.

Heywood, J. and Kerslake, B. (2012) *Introducing contestability into civil service policy advice*, London: HMG.

Hill, C. and Smith, M. (2005) 'Acting for Europe: reassessing the European Union's place in international relations', in C. Hill and M. Smith (eds) *International relations and the European Union*, Oxford: Oxford University Press, pp 388–406.

Hill, M. (1981) 'The policy–implementation distinction; a quest for rational control?', in S. Barratt and C. Fudge (eds) *Policy and action*, London: Methuen, pp 207–24.

Hill, M. (2006) *The public policy process* (4th edn), Harlow: Pearson Longman.

Hix, S. (1998) 'The study of the European Union II: the new governance agenda and its rival', *Journal of European Public Policy*, vol 5, no 1, pp 38–67.

Hix, S. (2000) 'Britain, EU and the Euro', in P. Dunleavy, A. Gamble, I. Holliday and G. Peele (eds) *Developments in British politics*, Basingstoke: Macmillan, pp 47–68.

HMG (1971) *The United Kingdom and the European Communities*, Cmnd 4715, London: HMSO.

HMG (2007) *Building on progress: public services*, London: Prime Minster's Strategy Unit.

HMG, (2010) *The Coalition: Our Programme for Government*, London: HMG.

HMG (2011a) *Open public services White Paper*, Cm 8145, Norwich: HMSO.

HMG (2011b) *Unlocking growth in cities*, London: HM Government.

HMG (2012) *Open public services 2012*, London: Cabinet Office.

HMSO (Her Majesty's Stationery Office) (1970) *Reorganisation of central government*, Cmnd 4506, London: HMSO.

HMT (Her Majesty's Treasury) (1995) *Public expenditure: statistical supplement to the financial and budget report 1995–96*, Cm 2821, London: HMSO.

HMT (2004) *Devolved decision making: 1 delivering better public services: refining targets and performance management*, London: HMT.

HMT (2005) *Devolved decision making: 3 meeting the regional economic challenge*, London: HMT.

HMT (2010) *National Infrastructure Plan*, London: HMT.

HMT (2011) *National Infrastructure Plan 2*, London: HMT.

HMT (2012) *Construction pipeline, xl*, 26 April, London: HMT. Available at: http://www.hm-treasury.gov.uk/infrastructure_pipeline_data_update.htm

HMT and BIS (Department of Business, Industry and Skills) (2010) *A new approach to financial regulation: consultation on reforming the consumer credit regime*, London: HMT and BIS.

HMT, Department of Business Industry and Skills (BIS) and Department opf Communities and Local Government (DCLG), (2007) Review of sub-national economic development and regeneration, London: HMT

HoC (House of Commons) (2008) *Subsidiarity, national parliaments and the Lisbon Treaty*, Thirty-third report of Session European Scrutiny Committee, 2007–8, 21 October, London: House of Commons.

HoC (2012) *Sulphur emissions by ships*, 9 March, London: House of Commons Transport Select Committee.

Hogwood, B.W. (1992) *Trends in British public policy: do governments make any difference?*, Buckingham: Open University Press.

Hogwood, B.W. (1994) 'A reform beyond compare? The Next Steps restructuring of British central government', *Journal of European Public Policy*, vol 1, no 1, pp 71–94.

Hogwood, B.W. (1995) 'Whitehall families: core departments and agency forms in Britain', *International Review of Administrative Sciences*, vol 61, no 4, pp 511–30.

Hogwood, B.W. and Peters, B.G. (1982) 'The dynamics of policy change; policy succession', *Policy Sciences*, vol 14, no 3, pp 225-45.

Holden, P. (2011) 'Still "leading from the edge"? New Labour and the European Union', in O. Daddow and J. Gaskarth (eds) *British foreign policy: the New Labour years*, Basingstoke: Palgrave Macmillan, pp 157–69.

Holder, J. and Layard, A. (2011) 'Drawing out the elements of territorial cohesion: re-scaling EU spatial governance', *Yearbook of European Law*, vol 30, no 1, pp 358–80.

Hood, C. (1991) 'A public management for all seasons?', *Public Administration*, vol 69, no 1, pp 3–20.

Hood, C. (1995) 'The "new public management" in the 1980s: variations on a theme', *Accounting Organisations and Society*, vol 20, nos 2/3, p 93.

Hood, C. (1998) *The art of the state, culture, rhetoric and public management*, Oxford: Clarendon Press.

Hood, C. (2000) 'Paradoxes of public sector managerialism, old public management and public service bargains', *International Public Management Journal*, vol 3, pp 1–22.

Hood, C. (2002) 'Control, bargains and cheating: the politics of public-service reform', *Journal of Public Administration Research and Theory*, July, pp 309–32.

Hood, C. (2010) *The blame game; spin, bureaucracy and self-preservation in government*, Oxford: Princeton University Press.

Hood, C. (2011) *The blame game; spin, bureaucracy and self-preservation in local government*, Oxford: Princeton University Press.

Hood, C. and Lodge, M. (2005) 'Aesop with variations: civil service competency as a case of German tortoise and British hare?', *Public Administration*, vol 83, no 4, pp 805–22.

Hood, C. and Peters, G. (2004) 'The middle aging of new public management: into the age of paradox?', *Journal of Public Administration Research and Theory*, vol 14, no 3, pp 267–82.

Hooghe, L. (2001) *The European Commission and the integration of Europe*, Cambridge: Cambridge University Press.

Hooghe, L., Marks, G. and Blank, L. (1996) 'European integration since the 1980s', *Journal of Common Market Studies*, vol 34, no 3, pp 341–78.

Hope, C. (2010) Interview with Eric Pickles, *Daily Telegraph*, 13 December 2010, p 1.

Hope, N. and Leslie, C. (2009) *Challenging perspectives: improving Whitehall's spatial awareness*, London: NLGN.

Howlett, M. and Cashore, B. (2009) 'The dependent variable problem in the study of policy change: understanding policy change as a methodological problem', *Journal of Comparative Policy Analysis: Research and Practice*, vol 11, no 1, pp 33–46.

Hutton, J. (2011) *Independent Public Service Pensions Commission final report*, London: HMT.

Huysmans, J. (2000) 'The European Union and the securitization of migration', *Journal of Common Market Studies*, vol 38, no 5, pp 751–78.

Hyman, H. (1989) 'Privatisation: the facts', in C. Veljanovski (ed) *Privatisation and competition*, Hobart Paperback 28, London: Institute of Economic Affairs.

Ianucci, A. (2005) *The thick of it*, London: BBC.

Ibbs, R. (1988) *Improving management in government: the Next Steps*, London: HMSO.

Ilzkovitz, F., Dierx, A., Kovacs, V. and Sousa, N. (2007) *Steps towards deeper economic integration: the single market in the 21st century*, Brussels: CEC.

International Monetary Fund, (2012) *World Economic Outlook Database*, October, Washington DC: IMF.

IPPR (Institute of Public Policy Research) (2012) *Northern prosperity is national prosperity: NEFC interim report*, Newcastle-upon-Tyne: IPPR North.

Iser, W. (1980) *The act of reading: a theory of aesthetic response*, Baltimore, MD: The Johns Hopkins University Press.

James, S. (1988) 'The central policy review staff 1971–1983', *Political Studies*, vol 34, no 3, pp 423–40.

James, S. (1993) 'The idea brokers: the impact of think tanks on British government', *Public Administration*, vol 7, no 4, pp 491–506.

James, S. (2010a) 'The rise and fall of euro preparations: strategic networking and the depoliticisation of Labour's national changeover plan', *British Journal of Politics and International Relations*, vol 12, no 3, pp 368–86.

James, S. (2010b) 'Managing European policy at home: analysis network adaptation within the core executive', *Political Studies*, vol 58, no 5, pp 930–50.

Jamet, J.-F. (2011) 'The optimal assignments of prerogatives to different levels of government in the EU', *Journal of Common Market Studies*, vol 49, no 3, pp 563–84.

Jenkin, B. (2012) Statement on publication of PASC report on strategy, 24 April, London, House of Commons.

Jenkins, E. (1993) 'The reform of local government: the Conservative Party', in A. Duff (ed) *Subsidiarity within the European Community*, London: The Federal Trust, pp 110–11.

Jenkins, K. (2008) *Politicians and public services: implementing change in a clash of cultures*, Cheltenham: Edward Elgar.

Jenkins, K. and Gold, J. (2011) *Unfinished business: where next for executive agencies?*, London: Institute for Government.

Jenkins, S. (2011) *A short history of England*, London: Profile Books.

Jeppesen, T. (2000) 'EU environmental policy in the 1990s: allowing greater national leeway?', *European Environment*, vol 10, pp 96–105.

Jessop, B. (2004) 'Multi-level governance and multi-level metagovernance', in I. Bache and M. Flinders (eds) *Multi-level governance*, Oxford: Oxford University Press, pp 49–74.

Jetschke, A. (2010) *Do regional organizations travel? European integration, diffusion and the case of ASEAN*, KFG Working Paper no 17, October, Berlin: Free University.

John, P. and Bevan, S. (2011) 'What are policy punctuations? Large changes in the legislative agenda of the UK government 1911–2008', Working Paper, School of Social Sciences, University of Manchester.

John, P. and Margetts, H. (2003) 'Policy punctuations in the UK: fluctuations and equilibria in central government expenditure since 1951', *Public Administration*, vol 81, no 3, pp 411–32.

John, P., Cotterill, S., Hanhua, L., Richardson, L., Moseley, A., Nomura, H., Smith, G., Stoker, G. and Wales, C. (2011) *Nudge nudge think think: using experiments to change civic behaviour*, London: Bloomsbury.

Jones, M.D. and McBeth, M.K. (2010) 'A narrative policy framework: clear enough to be wrong?', *Policy Studies Journal*, vol 38, no 2, pp 329–53.

Jordan, A. (1998) 'The impact on UK administration', in P. Lowe and S. Ward (eds) *British environmental policy and Europe*, London: Routledge, pp 173–94.

Jordan, A. (1999) 'The implementation of EU environmental policy: a policy problem without a political solution', *Environment and Planning C*, vol 17, no 1, pp 69–90.

Jordan, A. (2001) 'National environmental ministries: managers or ciphers of European environmental policy', *Public Administration*, vol 79, no 3, pp 643–63.

Jordan, A. (2004) 'The United Kingdom: from policy "taking" to policy "shaping"', in A. Jordan and D. Liefferink (eds) *Environmental policy in Europe: the Europeanization of national environmental policy*, Abingdon: Routledge, pp 205–23.

Jordan, A. (2008) 'Environmental policy', in I. Bache and A. Jordan (eds) *The Europeanization of British politics*, Basingstoke: Macmillan, pp 231–47.

Jordan, A. and Lenschow, A. (2000) '"Greening" the European Union: what can be learned from the "leaders" of EU environmental policy?', *European Environment*, vol 10, pp 109–20.

Jordan, A. and Lenschow, A. (2010) 'Environmental policy integration: a state of the art review', *Environmental Policy and Governance*, vol 20, no 3, pp 147–58.

Jordan, A., Wurzel, R.K.W. and Zito, A.R. (2003) 'Comparative conclusions – "new" environmental policy instruments: an evolution or a revolution in environmental policy?', *Environmental Politics*, vol 12, no 1, pp 201–24.

Jordan, G. (1990) 'Policy community realism versus "new" institutionalist ambiguity', *Political Studies*, vol 38, pp 470–84.

Jordan, G. (1998) 'Towards regulation in the UK: from "general good sense" to "formalised rules"', *Parliamentary Affairs*, vol 51, no 4, pp 524–37.

Jordan, G. (2003) 'Cultivating small business influence in the UK: the Federation of Small Business' journey from outsider to insider', *Journal of Public Affairs*, vol 3, part 4, pp 313–25.

Jordan, G. and Halpin, D. (2006) 'The political costs of policy coherence: constructing a rural policy for Scotland', *Journal of Public Policy*, vol 26, no 1, pp 21–42.

Kahler, M. (2009) 'Networked politics: agency, power and governance', in M. Kahler (ed) *Networked politics: agency, power and governance*, Ithaca, NY: Cornell University Press, pp 1–23.

Kaletsky, A., (2010) *Capitalism 4.0, The birth of a new economy*, London: Bloomsbury.

Kassim, H. (2004) 'The United Kingdom and the future of Europe: winning the battle, losing the war', *Comparative European Politics*, vol 2, pp 261–81.

Kassim, H. (2005) 'The Europeanization of member state institutions', in S. Bulmer and C. Lesquesne (eds) *The member states of the European Union*, Oxford: Oxford University Press, pp 254–82.

Kassim, H., Menon, A., Peters, B.G. and Wright, V. (2000) *Coordination in the European Union: the national dimension*, Oxford: Oxford University Press.

Kay, J. (2011) *Obliquity*, London: Profile Books.

Keating, M., Cairney, P. and Hepburn, E. (2009) 'Territorial policy communities and devolution in the UK', *Cambridge Journal of Regions, Economics and Society*, vol 2, pp 51–66.

Kellner, P. and Crowther-Hunt, N. (1980) *The civil servants*, London: Macdonald.

Keohane R. and Nye J. (1989) Power and Interdependence (2nd edn) Glenview, Ill: Scott, Foresman.

King, S. and Pitchford, R. (1998) 'Privatization in Australia: understanding the incentives in public and private firms', *Australian Economic Review*, vol 31, no 4, pp 313–28.

Kingdon, J.W. (2003) *Agendas, alternatives and public policies* (2nd edn), London: Longman.

Kitzinger, U. (1973) *Diplomacy and persuasion: how Britain joined the Common Market*, London: Thames and Hudson.

Knill, C. (1999) 'Explaining cross-national variance in administrative reform: autonomous versus instrumental bureaucracies', *Journal of Public Policy*, vol 19, no 2, pp 113–40.

Knill, C. and Lenschow, A. (2001) 'Adjusting to EU environmental policy: change and persistence in domestic administrations', in M.G. Cowles, J. Caporaso and T. Risse (eds) *Transforming Europe*, Ithaca, NY: Cornell University Press, pp 116–36.

Knill, C. and Liefferink, D. (2007) *Environmental politics in the European Union: policy making, implementation and patterns of multi-level governance*, Manchester: Manchester University Press.

Korac-Kakabdase, N. and Kakabadse, A. (2002) 'Trends in outsourcing: contrasting USA and Europe', *European Management Journal*, vol 20, no 2, pp 189–98.

Krahmann, E. (2003) 'National, regional, and global governance: one phenomenon or many?', *Global Governance*, vol 9, no 3, pp 323–34.

Krieger, J. (1999) British politics in the global age: can social democracy survive?, Oxford: Oxford University Press.

Krugman, P., (1991) 'Increasing Returns and Economic Geography', *The Journal of Political Economy,* 99:3, pp 483-499.

Kuhn, T. (1962) *The structure of scientific revolutions*, Chicago, IL: University of Chicago Press.

Kuus, M. (2011a) 'Bureaucracy and place: expertise in the European quarter', *Global networks*, vol 11, no 4, pp 421–39.

Kuus, M. (2011b) 'Whose regional expertise? Political geographies of knowledge in the European bureaucracy', *European Urban and Regional Studies*, vol 18, no 3, pp 275–88.

Kuus, M. (2011c) 'Symbolic capital and expert authority in European Union policy-making', plenary lecture at EUGEO, at IBG, London, 30 August.

Kynaston, D. (2007) *Austerity Britain 1945–51*, London: Bloomsbury.

Ladrech, R. (1994) 'Europeanization of domestic politics and institutions: the case of France', *Journal of Common Market Studies*, vol 32, no 1, pp 69–88.

Ladrech, R. (2010) *Europeanization and national politics*, Basingstoke: Palgrave Macmillan.

Laguna, M.I.D. (2010) 'From lesson-drawing to bounded transfer', paper presented to 14 International Research Society for Public Management Conference, Berne, Switzerland, 7 April.

Laredo, P. (1998) 'The networks promoted by the framework programme and the questions they raise about its formulation and implementation', *Research Policy*, vol 27, no 6, p 598.

Larner, W. and Walters, W. (2000) 'Privatisation, governance and identity: the United Kingdom and New Zealand compared', *Policy and Politics*, vol 28, no 1, pp 361–77.

Layard, A. and Holder, J. (2010) 'From territorial to environmental cohesion', *Social Science Research Network*, 21 July.

Lazer, D. (2006) 'Global and domestic governance: modes of interdependence in regulatory policymaking', *European Law Journal*, vol 12, no 4, pp 455–68.

Leblond, P. (2011) 'EU, US and international accounting standards: a delicate balancing act in governing global finance', *Journal of European Public Policy*, vol 18, no 3, pp 443–61.

Lenschow, A. (2010) 'Environmental policy', in H. Wallace, M.A. Pollack and A.R. Young (eds) *Policy-making in the European Union*, Oxford: Oxford University Press, pp 307–30.

Leontitsis, V. (2011) 'Environmental policy', in I. Bache, S. George and S. Bulmer (eds) *Politics in the European Union* (3rd edn), Oxford: Oxford University Press, pp 448–65.

Letwin, O. (2012a) Evidence to PASC, February.

Letwin, O. (2012b) 'Why mandarins matter', speech to Institute for Government, 17 September, London.

Leuning, T. (2012) 'Post-Second World war British railways: the unintended consequences of insufficient government intervention', in H. Margetts, P. 6 and C. Hood (eds) *Paradoxes of modernization: unintended consequences of public policy reform*, Oxford: Oxford University Press, pp 155–81.

Levitt, R. (2012) 'Why are there so many policy tsars?', podcast, Kings College London. Available at: http://www.kcl.ac.uk/sspp/news/newsrecords/tsars. aspx (accessed 3 October 2012).

Lewis, J. (2011) 'The search for coordination: the case of the central policy review staff and social policy making 1971–77', *Social Policy and Administration*, vol 45, no 7, pp 770–87.

LGA (Local Government Association) (2010) *Total place*, London: Local Government Association.

Liefferink, D. and Jordan, A. (2005) 'An "ever closer union" of national policy? The convergence of national environmental policy in the European Union', *European Environment*, vol 15, pp 102–13.

Lindblom, C.E. (1959) 'The science of "muddling through"', *Public Administration Review*, vol 19, no 2, pp 79–88.

Lindblom, C.E. (1979) 'Still muddling: not yet through', *Public Administration Review*, vol 39, no 6, pp 517–26.

Lipson, D.J. (2001) 'The World Trade Agreement's health agenda', *British Medical Journal*, vol 323, p 1139.

Loder, J. (2011) 'The Lisbon Strategy and the politicization of EU policy-making: the case of the Services Directive', *Journal of European Public Policy*, vol 18, no 4, pp 566–83.

Lodge, G., Wincott, D., Henderson, A. and Wyn Jones, R. (2012) *The dog that finally barked: England as an emerging political community*, London: IPPR.

Loughlin, J. (no date) 'Territorial policy communities in Wales'.

Loughlin, J. and Sykes, S. (no date) 'Devolution and policy-making in Wales: restructuring the system and reinforcing identity', Cardiff: Welsh Assembly Government.

Lowe, R. (2005) 'Grit in the oyster or sand in the machine? The evolving role of special advisers in British government', *Twentieth Century British History*, vol 16, no 4, pp 497–505.

Lu, C. (2011) 'The EU as a "fourth branch" of member state governments?', in F. Laursen (ed) *The EU and federalism: polities and policies compared*, Farnham: Ashgate, pp 57–78.

Lynn, J. and Jay, A. (1990a) *Yes minister*, London: Guild Publishing.

Lynn, J. and Jay, A. (1990b) *Yes prime minister*, London: Guild Publishing.

Lyons M., (2007) *Place shaping a shared ambition for local government*, HMT London.

Mabey, C. and Skinner, D. (1998) 'Empowerment in an executive agency? A grass-roots assessment of strategic intent', *International Journal of Public Sector Management*, vol 11, nos 6/7, pp 494–508.

MacCormick, N. (1999) *Questioning sovereignty: law, state and nation in the European commonwealth*, Oxford: Oxford University Press.

Mackay, D. (2011a) 'What does home rule mean for economic policy?', in D. Mackay (ed) *Scotland's economic future*, Edinburgh: Reform Scotland, pp 149–78.

Mackie, P. (1998) 'Developments in transport policy: the UK transport White Paper', *Journal of Transport Economics and Policy*, vol 32, no 3, pp 399–403.

Macrory, R. and M. Hession , (1996) 'The European Community and climate change: the role of law and legal competence' in T. O'Riordan and J. Jager (eds) *Politics and climate change: a European perspective*, London: Routledge, pp 106-54.

Mahon, R. and McBride, S. (2009) 'Standardizing and disseminating knowledge: the role of the OECD in global governance', *European Political Science Review*, vol 1, no 1, pp 83–101.

Mahony, P., Hextall, I. and Menter, I. (2002) 'Threshold assessment: another peculiarity of the English or more McDonaldisation', *International Studies in Sociology of Education*, vol 12, part 2, pp 145–68.

Mair P. (2004) 'The Europeanisation Dimension', *Journal of European Public Policy*, vol 11, no 2, pp 337-48.

Majone, G. (1996) *Regulating Europe*, London: Routledge.

Major, J. (1999) *The autobiography*, London: Harper Collins.

Mandelson, P. (2011) *The third man*, London: Harper Press.

March, J.G. and Olsen, J.P. (1984) 'The new institutionalism: organizational factors in political life', *American Political Science Review*, vol 78, pp 734–49.

Margetts, H. (2010) 'The Internet in political science', in C. Hay (ed) *New directions in political science*, Basingstoke: Palgrave Macmillan, pp 64–87.

Margetts, H., 6, P. and Hood, C. (eds) (2012) *Paradoxes of modernization: unintended consequences of public policy reform*, Oxford: Oxford University Press.

Marks, G. (1992) 'Structural policy in the European Community', in A. Sbragia (ed) *Europolitics: institutions and policymaking in the 'new' European Community*, Washington, DC: The Brookings Institute.

Marks, G. (1993) 'Structural policy and multilevel governance in the EC', in A. Cafruny and G. Rosenthal (eds) *The state of the European Community. Vol. 2: the Maastricht debates and beyond*, Harlow: Longman.

Marks, G. and Hooghe, L. (2004) 'Contrasting visions of multilevel governance', in I. Bache and M. Flinders (eds) *Multi-level governance*, Oxford: Oxford University Press, pp 15–30.

Marks, G. and Wilson, C.J. (2000) 'The past in the present: a cleavage theory of party response to European integration', *British Journal of Political Science*, vol 30, no 3, pp 433–60.

Marks, G., Hooghe, L. and Blank, K. (1996) 'European integration from the 1980s', *Journal of Common Market Studies*, vol 34, no 3, pp 341–78.

Marsh, D. and Rhodes, R.A.W. (1992) *Policy networks in British government*, Oxford: The Clarendon Press.

Martens, K. (2007) *New arenas of education governance: the impact of international organizations and markets on educational policy making*, Basingstoke: Palgrave Macmillan.

Maude, F. (2012) *Creating better public services*, 2 October, London: IfG.

Mazey, S. and Richardson, J. (2000) 'Institutionalising promiscuity: Commission–interest group relations in the EU', in A. Stone Sweet, N. Fligstein and W. Sandholtz (eds) *The institutionalisation of Europe*, Oxford: Oxford University Press. pp 71–93.

McCann, E. (2011) 'Urban policy mobilities and global circuits of knowledge: toward a research agenda', *Annals of the Association of American Geographers*, vol 101, no 1, pp 107–30.

McClory, J. (2011) *The new persuaders II: a global ranking of soft power*, London: Institute for Government.

McCormick, J. (2001) *Environmental policy in the European Union*, Basingstoke: Palgrave Macmillan.

McCourt, D. (2011) 'The New Labour governments and Britain's role in the world', in O. Daddow and J. Gaskarth (eds) *British foreign policy: the New Labour years*, Basingstoke: Palgrave Macmillan, pp 31–47.

McGowan, F. and Seabright, P. (1995) 'Regulation in the European Community and its impact on the UK', in M. Bishop, J. Kay and C. Mayer (eds) *The regulatory challenge*, Oxford: Oxford University Press, pp 227–53.

McGuire, M. and Agranoff, R. (2011) 'The limitations of public management networks', *Public Administration*, vol 89, no 2, pp 265–84.

McLain, I. and McMillan, A. (2003) *New localism new finance*, London: New Local Government Network.

McNutt, K. and Pal, L.A. (2011) '"Modernizing government": mapping global public policy networks', *Governance*, vol 24, no 3, pp 439–67.

McQuaid, R. (2011) Paper presented to RSA Winter Conference, November, London.

MEAP (Manchester Economic Advisory Panel) (2012) *Greater Manchester growth plan*, Manchester: Manchester Economic Advisory Panel.

Merton, R.K. (1968) *Social theory and social structure*, New York, NY: Free Press.

Meunier, S. (2005) *Trading voices: the European Union in international commercial negotiations*, Oxford: Princeton University Press.

Meunier, S. and Nicolaidis, K. (2005) 'The European Union as a trade power', in C. Hill and M. Smith (eds) *International relations and the European Union*, Oxford: Oxford University Press, pp 247–69.

Meunier, S. and Nicolaidis, K. (2006) 'The European Union as a conflicted trade power', *Journal of European Public Policy*, vol 13, no 6, pp 906–25.

Meyer-Sahling, J-H. (2009) *Sustainability of Civil Service Reforms in Central and Eastern Europe Five Years After Accession' Sigma Papers no 44*, Paris: OECD.

Meyer, J.-H. (2011) *Appropriating the environment: how European institutions received the novel idea of the environment and made it their own*, KFG Working Paper 31, September, Berlin: The Free University.

Micheli, P. and Neely, A. (2010) 'Performance management in the public sector in England: searching for the golden thread', *Public Administration Review*, vol 7, no 4, pp 591–600.

Midelfart-Knarvik, K.H. and Overman, H.G. (2002) 'Delocation and European integration: is structural spending justified?', *Economic Policy*, no 35, pp 321–60.

Miles, W. and Trott, W. (2011) *Collaborative working*, London: Institute for Government.

Millar, D. and Scott, A. (1993) 'Subsidiarity and Scotland before the Edinburgh Council', in A. Duff (ed) *Subsidiarity within the European Community*, London: The Federal Trust, pp 87–95.

Miller, L. (2009) 'E-petitions at Westminster the way forward for Democracy', *Parliamentary Affairs*, vol 62, no 1, pp 162–77.

Miller, V. (2010) *How much legislation comes from Europe?*, Research Paper 10/62, 13 October, London: House of Commons Library.

Miller, V. (2011a) *EU legislation: government action on 'gold-plating'*, SN/1A/5943, 19 April, London: House of Commons Library.

Miller, V. (2011b) *Repatriating EU powers to member states*, SNO6153, 7 December, London: House of Commons Library.

Miller, V. (2012) *The Treaty on Stability Coordination and Governance in the Economic and Monetary Union: views in other EU member states*, SN/IA/6286, 3 April, London: House of Commons Library.

Mirwaldt, K., McMaster, I. and Bachtler, J. (2009) *Reconsidering cohesion policy: the contested debate on territorial cohesion*, EPRC Paper 66, Glasgow: Strathclyde University.

Monti, M. (2010) *A new strategy for the single market at the service of Europe's economy and society*, 9 May, Brussels: CEC.

Moore, M.H. (1995) *Creating public value: strategic management in government*, London: Harvard University Press.

Moravcsik, A. and Schimmelfennig, F. (2009) 'Liberal intergovernmentalism', in A. Wiener and T. Diez (eds) *European integration theory*, Oxford: Oxford University Press, pp 67–87.

Morgan, G. (2011) 'Supporting the city: economic patriotism in financial markets', *Journal of European Public Policy*, vol 19, no 3, pp 373–87.

Morphet, J. (1993) A Guide to the Fifth Environmental Action programme, Luton: Local Government Training Board.

Morphet, J. (1994) 'The Committee of the Regions', *Local Government Policy Making*, vol 20, no 5, pp 56–60.

Morphet, J. (1998) 'Local authorities', in P. Lowe and S. Ward (eds) *British environmental policy and Europe*, London: Routledge, pp 138–52.

Morphet, J. (2008) *Modern local government*, London: Sage.

Morphet, J. (2011) *Effective practice in spatial planning*, Abingdon: Routledge.

Morphet, J. and Hams, T. (1994) 'Responding to Rio: a local authority approach', *Journal of Environmental Planning and Management*, vol 37, no 4, pp 479–86.

Morphet, J., Hams, T., Jacobs, M., Lusser, H. and Taylor, D. (1994) *Greening your local authority*, Harlow: Longman.

Morris, I. (2010) *Why the West rules for now*, London: Profile Books.

Moynihan, D.P. (2006) 'Ambiguity in policy lessons: the agencification experience', *Public Administration*, vol 84, no 4, pp 1029–50.

Mugge, D. (2006) 'Reordering the marketplace: competition politics in European finance', *Journal of Common Market Studies*, vol 44, no 5, pp 991–1022.

Mulgan, G. (2007) *Good and bad power: the ideals and betrayals of government*, London: Penguin.

Mulgan, G. (2009) *The art of public strategy*, Oxford: Oxford University Press.

Mulgan, G. (2011) Evidence given to the Public Administration Select Committee, 13 December, London, House of Commons.

Mulholland, H. (2012) 'Michael Gove tells academies they can hire unqualified staff', *The Guardian*, 27 July.

Murphy, M.C. (2011) 'Regional representation in Brussels and multi-level governance: evidence form Northern Ireland', *British Journal of Politics and International Relations*, vol 13, no 4, pp 551–66.

Murphy, P. and Mole, S. (2012) Oral evidence to Committee on Foreign Affairs, 27 March, London, House of Commons.

Nadin, V. (2012) 'International comparative planning methodology', *Planning Practice and Research*, vol 27, no 1, pp 1–5.

Nadin, V. and Cullingworth, B. (2006) *An introduction to town and country planning* (14th edn), Abingdon: Routledge.

Nathan, Lord (1987) *Introduction of the EU 4th environmental action programme*, Hansard col 774-807, 9 July, London: House of Lords.

Naurin, D. (2007) *Network capital and cooperation patterns in the working groups of the Council of the EU*, Working Paper RSCAS 2007/14, Florence: Robert Schumann Centre for Advanced Studies, European University Institute.

Naurin, D. and Wallace, H. (eds) (2010) *Unveiling the Council of the European Union: games governments play in Brussels*, Basingstoke: Palgrave Macmillan.

Newman, J.E. (2001) *Modernising government: New Labour policy and society*, London: Sage.

Newman, J.E. (2005) 'Enter the transformational leader: network governance and the micropolitics of modernization', *Sociology*, vol 39, no 4, pp 717–34.

Nicolaïdis, K. (1992) 'Mutual recognition, regulatory competition, and the globalization of professional services', in Y. Aharoni (ed) *Coalition and competition – the globalization of professional services*, London: Routledge.

Nizzo, C. (2001) *National public administrations and European integration*, Sigma Programme, Paris: OECD.

Northcote, S. and C. Trevelyan (1854) *Report on the organisation of the permanent civil service*, London.

Nugent, N. and Phinnemore, D. (2010) 'United Kingdom: red lines defined', in M. Carbone (ed) *National politics and European integration: from the constitution to the Lisbon Treaty*, Cheltenham: Edward Elgar, pp 71–89.

Nye, J.S. (2004) *Soft power: the means to success in world politics*, New York, NY: Public Affairs.

Oates, W.E. (1999) 'An essay on fiscal federalism', *Journal of Economic Literature*, vol 37, no 3, pp 1120–49.

O'Donnell G. (2009) *Challenging Perspectives: Improving Whitehall spatial awareness*, London: NLGN.

O'Donnell, G. (2011a) *The cabinet manual*, London: HMG.

O'Donnell, G. (2011b) 'UK faces break-up', *Daily Telegraph*, 21 December, p 1.

OECD (Organisation for Economic Co-operation and Development) (1996) *Benchmarking, evaluation and strategic management in the public sector*, OCDE/GD 97(50), Paris: OECD.

OECD (2011a) 'Housing and economy policies for renovation', in *Economic policy reforms 2011: Going for growth*, Paris: OECD.

OECD (2012a) *Towards green growth*, Paris: OECD.

OECD (2012b) *Better regulation in Europe*, Paris: OECD.

O'Higgins, M. (2006) speech to Local Government Association Annual Conference 6th July Bournemouth.

Olsen, J.P. (2002) 'The many faces of Europeanization', *Journal of Common Market Studies*, vol 40, no 5, pp 921–52.

O'Riordan, T. and Jager, J. (1996a) 'Beyond climate change science and politics', in T. O'Riordan and J. Jager (eds) *Politics of climate change: a European perspective*, London: Routledge, pp 346–60.

O'Riordan, T. and Jordan, A. (1996) 'Social institutions and climate change', in T. O'Riordan and J. Jager (eds) *Politics of climate change: a European perspective*, London: Routledge, pp 65–105.

O'Riordan, T. and Rowbotham, E.J. (1996) 'Struggling for credibility: the United Kingdom's response', in T. O'Riordan and J. Jager (eds) *Politics of climate change: a European perspective*, London: Routledge, pp 228–67.

Osborne, D. and Gaebler, T. (1993) *Reinventing government*, London: Penguin.

Osborne, D. and P. Hutchinson, (2004) *The Price of Government*, New York: Basic Books.

Ozga, J. and Lingard, B. (2007) 'Globalization, education politics and education', in B. Lingard and J. Ozga (eds) *The Routledge Falmer reader in education policy and politics*, Abingdon: Routledge, pp 65–82.

Page, A. (2004) 'Balancing supremacy: EU membership and the constitution', in P. Giddings and G. Drewry (eds) *Britain in the European Union: law, policy and parliament*, Basingstoke: Palgrave Macmillan, pp 37–59.

Page, E.C. (2010) 'Has the Whitehall model survived?', *International Review of Administrative Sciences*, vol 76, no 3, pp 407–23.

Page, E.C. and Jenkins, B. (2005) *Policy bureaucracy: government with a cast of thousands*, Oxford: Oxford University Press.

Page, E.C., Hood, C. and Lodge, M. (2005) 'Conclusion: is competency management a passing fad?', *Public Administration*, vol 83, no 4, pp 853–60.

Parker, G. and Pickard, S. (2011) 'Hilton mingles "self-help and laissez-faire"', *Financial Times*, 28 July, p 2.

Parker, M. and Jary, D. (1995) 'The McUniversity: organization, management and academic subjectivity', *Organization*, vol 2, no 2, pp 319–38.

Parker, R. and Bradley, L. (2000) 'Organisational culture in the public sector: evidence from six organisations', *International Journal of Public Sector Management*, vol 13, nos 2/3, pp 125–41.

Parry, R. (2008) 'Changing UK Governance Under Devolution', *Public Policy and Administration*, vol 23, no 1, pp 114–20.

PASC (2011a) *Change in government: the agenda for leadership*, 22 September, London: House of Commons, Public Accounts Select Committee.

PASC (2012) 'Strategic thinking in government: without national strategy can viable government strategy emerge?', 24th Report, Press Statement, 24 April, London: House of Commons.

Paterson, W. (1994) 'Britain and the European Union revisited: some unanswered questions', *Scottish Affairs*, no 9, Autumn, pp 1-12.

Pautz, H. (2011) 'Revisiting the think-tank phenomenon', *Public Policy and Administration*, vol 26, no 4, pp 319–435.

Peele, G. (2000) 'The law and the constitution', in P. Dunleavy, A. Gamble, I. Holliday and G. Peele (eds) *Developments in British politics*, Basingstoke: Macmillan, pp 69–87.

Peters, B.G. (2004) 'Back to the centre? Rebuilding the state', in A. Gamble and T. Wright (eds) *Restating the state?*, Oxford: Blackwell with the Political Quarterly, pp 130–40.

Peters, B.G. and Pierre, J. (2004) 'Multi-level governance and democracy: a Faustian bargain?', in I. Bache and M. Flinders (eds) *Multi-level governance*, Oxford: Oxford University Press, pp 75–89.

Peters, B.G. and Pierre, J. (2009) 'Governance approaches', in A. Wiener and T. Diez (eds) *European integration theory*, Oxford: Oxford University Press, pp 91–104.

Peterson, J. (2009) 'Policy networks', in A. Wiener and T. Diez (eds) *European integration Theory* (2nd edn), Oxford: Oxford University Press.

Phinnemore, D. and Nugent, N. (2010) 'The United Kingdom: red lines defended', in M. Carbone (ed) *National politics and European integration: from the constitution to the Lisbon Treaty*, Cheltenham: Edward Elgar, pp 71–89.

Pick, D. (1993) *War machine: rationalisation of slaughter in the modern age*, London: Yale University Press.

Pickles, E. (2012) 'Over 180 bids to improve or reinstate weekly rubbish collections', DCLG Press Notice, 2 April.

Pierre J. (ed) (1995) *Bureaucracy in the modern state*, Aldershot: Elgar.

Pierre, J. and Stoker, G. (2000) 'Towards multi-level governance', in P. Dunleavy, A. Gamble, I. Holliday and G. Peele (eds) *Developments in British politics*, Basingstoke: Macmillan, pp 29–46.

Pierson, P. (1996) 'The path to European integration: a historical institutionalist analysis', *Comparative Political Studies*, vol 29, no 2, pp 123–63.

Pierson, P. (2000) 'Increasing returns, path dependence and the study of politics', *The American Political Science Review*, vol 94, no 2, pp 251–67.

Piris, J.-C. (2010) *The Lisbon Treaty: a legal and political analysis*, Cambridge: Cambridge University Press.

Pitts, J. (2005) 'Incarcerating young people: an Anglo-Finnish comparison', *Youth Justice*, vol 5, no 3, pp 147–64.

Poirier, J. (2001) 'The functions of intergovernmental agreements: post-devolution concordats in a comparative perspective', *Public Law*, SEAS SPR, July, pp 134–57.

Poletti, A. (2011) 'World Trade Organization judicialization and preference: convergence in EU trade policy: making the agent's life easier', *Journal of European Public Policy*, vol 18, no 3, pp 361–82.

Pollack, M. (1997) 'Delegation, agency, and agenda setting in the European Community', *International Organization*, vol 51, pp 99–134.

Pollack, M. (2010) 'Theorizing EU policy-making', in H. Wallace, M.A. Pollack and A.R. Young (eds) *Policy making in the European Union* (6th edn), Oxford: Oxford University Press, pp 15–44.

Pollitt, C. (1984) *Manipulating the machine: changing the patterns of ministerial departments 1960–83*, London: Allen and Unwin.

Pollitt, C. (2004) 'Theoretical overview', in C. Pollitt and C. Talbot (eds) *Unbundled government: a critical analysis of the global trend to agencies, quangos and contractualisation*, Abingdon: Routledge, pp 319–42.

Pollitt, C. (2006) 'Performance management in practice: a comparative study of executive agencies', *Journal of Public Administration Research and Theory*, vol 16, no 1, pp 25–44.

Pollitt, C. and Bouckaert, G. (2000) *Public management reform: a comparative analysis*, Oxford: Oxford University Press.

Pollitt, C., Bathgate, K., Caulfield, J., Smullen, A. and Talbot, C. (2001) 'Agency fever? Analysis of an international policy fashion', *Journal of Comparative Policy Analysis*, vol 3, no 3, pp 271–90.

Pollock, A.M. and Price, D. (2007) 'The WTO and privatisation of health care systems', *The Lancet*, no 356, pp 1995–2000.

Popper, K. (1944) *The poverty of historicism*, London: Routledge.

Price, D., Pollock, A. and Shaol, J. (2000) 'How the World Trade Organisation is shaping domestic policies in health care', *The Lancet*, vol 354, no 9193, pp 1889–92.

Prince, R. (2010) 'Policy transfer as policy assemblage: making policy for the creative industries in New Zealand', *Environment and Planning A*, vol 42, no 1, pp 169–86.

Princen, S. and Rhinard, M. (2006) 'Crashing and creeping: agenda setting dynamics in the European Union', *Journal of European Public Policy*, vol 13, no 7, pp 1119–32.

Prodi, R. (2010) 'A big step towards fiscal federalism in Europe', *Financial Times*, 20 May.

Puetter, U. (2012) 'Europe's deliberative intergovernmentalism: the role of the Council and the European Council in EU economic governance', *Journal of European Public Policy*, vol 19, no 2, pp 161–78.

Pugalis, L. (2010) 'Looking back in order to move forward: the politics of evolving sub-national economic policy architecture', *Local Economy*, vol 25, nos 5/6, pp 397–405.

Putnam, R. (1988) 'Diplomacy and domestic politics: the logic of two-level games', *International Organization*, vol 42, no 2, pp 427–60.

Putnam, R.D. and Bayne, N. (1987) *Hanging together: cooperation and conflict in the seven-power summits* (revised and enlarged edn), London: Sage.

Pyper, R. and Burnham, J. (2011) 'The British civil service: perspectives on "decline" and "modernisation"', *The British Journal of Politics and International Relations*, vol 13, no 2, pp 189–205.

Radaelli, C. (1998) *Policy narratives in the European Union: the case of harmful tax competition*, RSC Working Paper No 98/34, Florence: European University Institute.

Radaelli, C. (2000) 'Whither Europeanization? Concept stretching and substantive change', *European Integration online papers*, vol 4, no 8. Available at: http://ideas.repec.org/a/erp/eiopxx/p0051.html, http://papers.ssrn.com/sol3/papers.cfm?abstract_id=302761

Radaelli, C. (2003) *The Open Method of Coordination: A new governance architecture for the European Union?*, Stockholm: Swedish Institute for European Policy Studies.

Radaelli, C. (2004b) 'Who learns what? Policy learning and the Open Method of Coordination', European Research Institute, University of Birmingham, 26 November.

Raynsford, N. (2004) *Consultation on local government reform*, London: ODPM.

Real-Dato, J. (2009) 'Mechanisms of policy change', *Journal of Comparative Policy Analysis: Research and Practice*, vol 11, no 1, pp 117–43.

Redcliffe-Maud, J. (1969) *Royal Commission on Local Government in England*, Cmnd 4040, London: HMSO.

Reynolds, P. (2011) 'UK taken to court over the "prohibitive expense" of challenges to environmental projects'. Available at: www.richardbuxton.co.uk

Rhinard, M. (2010) *Framing Europe: shaping strategies of the European Commission*, Boston, MA: Martinus Nijhoff.

Rhodes, R.A.W. (1994) 'The hollowing out of the state: the changing nature of the public service in Britain', *Political Quarterly*, vol 65, no 2, p 138-51.

Rhodes, R.A.W. (1995) 'From prime ministerial power to core executive', in R.A.W. Rhodes and P. Dunleavy (eds) *Prime minster, cabinet and core executive*, London: Macmillan, pp 11–37.

Rhodes, R.A.W., Carmichael, P., McMillan, J. and Massey, A. (2003) *Decentralising the civil service: from unitary state to differentiated policy in the United Kingdom*, Buckingham: Open University Press.

Richardson, H. (2005) 'Consuming passions in the global knowledge economy', in D. Howcroft and E.M. Trauth (eds) *Handbook of critical information systems research*, Cheltenham: Edward Elgar, pp 272–98.

Richardson, J. (1996) 'Introduction', in G. Majone (ed) *Regulating Europe*, London: Routledge.

Richardson, J. (2000) 'Government interest groups and policy change', *Political Studies*, vol 48, no 5, pp 1006–25.

Richardson J. and Jordan, G. (1979) *The policy process in a post-parliamentary democracy*, Oxford: Robertson.

Riddell, P. and Haddon, C. (2009) *Transitions: preparing for changes in government*, London: Institute for Government.

Risse, T. (2003) 'The Euro between national and European identity', *Journal of European Public Policy*, vol 10, no 4, pp 487–505.

Risse, T. (2010) *A community of Europeans? Transnational identities and public spheres*, London: Cornell University Press.

Risse, T., Cowles, M.G. and Caporaso, J. (2001) 'Europeanization and domestic change: introduction', in M.G. Cowles, J. Caporaso and T. Risse (eds) *Transforming Europe*, Ithaca, NY: Cornell University Press, pp 1–20.

Robinson, J. (2011) 'The spaces of circulating knowledge: city strategies and global urban governmentality', in E. McCann and K. Ward (eds) *Mobile urbanism: cities and policymaking in the global age*, London: University of Minnesota Press, pp 15–40.

Rochefort, D.A. and Cobb, R.W. (1994) 'Problem definition: an emerging perspective', in D.A. Rochefort and R.W. Cobb (eds) *The politics of problem definition: shaping the policy agenda*, Lawrence, KA: University of Kansas Press, pp 3–31.

Rodriguez-Pose, A. and Fratesi, U. (2004) 'Between development and social policies: the impact of European structural funds in objective 1 regions', *regional Studies*, vol 38, part 1, pp 97–114.

Rosamund, B. (2000) *Theories of European integration*, Basingstoke: Palgrave.

Rosamund, B. (2007) 'New theories of European integration', in M. Cini (ed) *European Union politics* (2nd edn), Oxford: Oxford University Press, pp 118–36.

Rosamund, B. (2012) 'Supranational governance as economic patriotism? The European Union, legitimacy and the reconstruction of state space', *Journal of European Public Policy*, vol 19, no 3, pp 324–41.

Rose, N. and Miller, P. (2010) 'Political power beyond the state: problematics of government', *British Journal of Sociology*, vol 61, pp 271–33.

Rosenau, J.N. (2004) 'Strong demand, huge supply; governance in an emerging epoch', in I. Bache and M. Flinders (eds) *Multi-level governance*, Oxford: Oxford University Press, pp 31–48.

Rotmans, J., Kemp, R. and Van Asselt, M. (2001) 'More evolution than revolution: transition management in public policy', *Foresight*, vol 3, no 1, pp 15–32.

Russell, J. (2012) 'Cameron's guru has lost patience with the status quo', *Evening Standard*, 5 March, p 14.

Russel, D., and A. Jordan, (2009) "Joining up or pulling apart? The use of appraisal to coordinate policy making for sustainable development." *Environment and planning. A* 41:5, 1201-16.

Rutter, J. (2012) *Opening up policy making*, London: Institute for Government.

Rutter, J., Parker, S. and Hallsworth, M. (2011) *Policy making in the real world*, London: Institute for Government.

Rutter, J., Marshall, E. and Sims, S. (2012a) *The 'S' factors: lessons from IfG's policy success reunions*, London: Institute for Government.

Rutter, J., Malley, R., Noonan, A. and Knighton, W. (2012b) *It takes two: how to create effective relationships between government and arm's length bodies*, London: Institute for Government.

Sabatier, P. and Jenkins-Smith, H. (eds) (1993) *Policy learning and policy change: an advocacy coalition approach*, Boulder, CO: Westview.

Saint-Martin, D. (1998) 'The new managerialism and the policy influence of consultants in government: an historical-institutionalist analysis of Britain, Canada and France', *Governance*, vol 11, no 3, pp 319–56.

Salmond, A. (2012) 'On devolution in Scotland'. Speech to Foreign Press association on possibilities for the first written constitution of an independent Scotland, 16th January https://soundcloud.com#scotgov/fm-foreign-press-association

Salomonsen, H.H. and Knudsen, T. (2011) 'Changes in public service bargains: ministers and civil servants in Denmark', *Public Administration*, vol 89, no 3, pp 1015–35.

Sandbrook, D. (2012) *Seasons in the sun: the Battle for Britain 1974–1979*, London: Allen Lane.

Sanders, D. (1990) *Losing an empire, finding a role*, Basingstoke: Macmillan.

Sandholtz, W. and Zysman, J. (1989) '1992: recasting the European bargain', *World Politics*, vol 42, pp 95–128.

Sbragia, A. (2010) 'Foreword', in M. Carbone (ed) *National politics and European integration: from the constitution to the Lisbon Treaty*, Cheltenham: Edward Elgar, pp x–xii.

Schnapper, P. (2011) 'New Labour, devolution and British identity: the foreign policy consequences', in O. Daddow and J. Gaskarth (eds) *British foreign policy: the New Labour years*, Basingstoke: Palgrave Macmillan, pp 48–62.

Schout, A. and Jordan, A. (2005) 'Coordinated European governance: self-organizing or centrally steered?', *Public Administration*, vol 83, no 1, pp 201–20.

Scott, A. (2001) 'The role of concordats in the new governance of Britain: taking subsidiarity seriously?', *Edinburgh Law Review*, vol 5, pp 21–48.

Scott, A., Peterson, J. and Millar, D. (1994) 'Subsidiarity: a "Europe of the regions" v. the British Constitution?', *Journal of Common Market Studies*, vol 32, no 1, pp 47–67.

Scottish Government (2012) *Scotland's cities delivering for Scotland*, Edinburgh: Scottish Government.

Sear, C. (2012) *Local authorities: the general power of competence*, SN/PC/05687, 23 February, London: House of Commons Library.

Seldon A. and G. Lodge, (2010), *Brown at No 10*, London: Biteback Publishing.

Senior, D. (1969) *Memorandum of dissent to the report of the Royal Commission on Local Government in England*, Cmnd 4040-1, London: HMSO.

Shanahan, E., Jones, M.D. and McBeth, M.K. (2011) 'Policy narratives and policy processes', *Policy Studies Journal*, vol 39, no 3, pp 535–61.

Shapiro, M. (2004) *The institutionalisation of European administrative space*, Berkeley, CA: UC Berkeley, Centre for Culture Organizations and Politics.

Sharp, L. and Luckin, D. (2006) 'The community waste sector and waste services in the UK: current state and future prospects', *Resources, Conservation and Recycling*, vol 47, no 3, pp 277–94.

Sharp, R. (1998) 'Responding to Europeanisation: a governmental perspective', in P. Lowe and S. Ward (eds) *British environmental policy and Europe*, London: Routledge, pp 33–56.

Shaw, D., Nadin, V. and Seaton, K. (2000) 'The application of subsidiarity in the making of European environmental law', *European Environment*, vol 10, pp 85–95.

Shaw, K., Fenwick, J. and Foreman, A. (1995) 'Compulsory competition for local government services in the UK: a case of market rhetoric and camouflaged centralism', *Public Policy and Administration*, vol 10, no 1, p 63-75.

Shirky, C. (2011) *Cognitive surplus*, London: Allen Lane.

Simmons, R.H., Davis, B.W., Chapman, R.J.K. and Sager, D.D. (1974) 'Policy flow analysis: a conceptual model for comparative public policy research', *The Western Political Quarterly*, vol 27, no 3, pp 457–68.

Slater, R., Frederickson, J. and Yoxon, M. (2010) *Unlocking the potential of community composting*, full project report for DEFRA, Milton Keynes: the Open University.

Smith, A. (1997) 'Studying multi-level governance. Examples from French translations of the structural funds', *Public Administration*, vol 75, no 4, pp 711–30.

Smith, A. (2000) 'Policy networks and advocacy coalitions: explaining policy change and stability in UK industrial pollution policy?', *Environment and Planning C*, vol 18, no 1, pp 95–114.

Smith, A. (2006) 'Organisational culture change: before and after the public–private partnership of a civil service department', paper presented at the Current Trends in Ethnographic Research in the Social and Management Sciences Conference, The University of Liverpool Management School, 13–14 September.

Smith, M.J. (1999) *The core executive in Britain*, London: Macmillan.

Smith, M. (2007) 'European Union external relations', in M. Cini (ed) *European Union politics* (2nd edn), Oxford: Oxford University Press, pp 225–36.

Smith, P. (1995) 'On the unintended consequences of publishing performance data in the public sector', *International Journal of Public Administration*, vol 18, nos 2/3, pp 277–310.

Stead, D. (2012) 'Best practices and policy transfer in spatial planning', *Planning Practice and Research*, vol 27, no 1, pp 103–16.

Steer, J. (1995) 'The formulation of transport policies in British conurbation, 1990–1995', *Proceedings of the ICE – Transport*, vol 111, no 3, pp 198–204.

Steinmo, S., Thelen, K. and Longstreth, F. (1992) *Structuring politics: Historical institutionalism in comparative analysis*, Cambridge: Cambridge University Press.

Stephens, P. (2001) 'The Blair government and Europe', *The Political Quarterly*, vol 72, no 1, pp 67–75.

Stevens, H. (2004) *Transport policy in the European Union*, Basingstoke: Palgrave Macmillan.

Stewart, J. and Walsh, K. (1992) 'Change in the management of public services', *Public Administration*, vol 7, no 4, pp 499–518.

Stone, D. (2000) 'Think tank transnationalisation and non-profit analysis advice and advocacy', *Global Society*, vol 14, no 2, pp 153–72.

Stone, D. (2008) 'Global public policy, transnational policy communities, and their networks', *Policy Studies Journal*, vol 36, no 1, pp 19–38.

Straw, W. and Glennie, A. (2012) *The third wave of globalisation*, London: IPPR.

Swann, G.P. (2010) *International standards and trade: a review of the empirical literature*, Trade Policy Working Papers no 97, Paris: OECD.

Sweeting, D. and Ball, H. (2002) 'Overview and scrutiny of leadership: the experience of Bristol City Council', *Local Governance*, vol 28, part 3, pp 201–12.

Symonds, G. (2012) 'From Surrey to Finland: lessons in decentralisation', *The Guardian*, 23 January.

Talbot, C. (2004b) 'The agency idea: sometimes old, sometimes new, sometimes borrowed sometimes untrue', in C. Pollitt and C. Talbot (eds) *Unbundled Government*, Abingdon: Routledge, pp 3–21.

Taleb, N.N. (2007) *Black swan*, London: Random House.

Tallberg, J. (2003) 'The agenda-shaping powers of the EU Council Presidency', *Journal of European Policy Making*, vol 10, part 1, pp 1–19.

Tarrow, S. (1994) *Power in movement: collective action, social movements and politics*, Cambridge: Cambridge University Press.

Taylor, P. (2008) *The end of European integration anti-Europeanism examined*, Abingdon: Routledge.

Taylor, R. (1994) 'Employment and industrial relations policy', in D. Kavagnah and A. Seldon (eds) *The Major effect*, London: Macmillan, pp 246–65.

Tayplan, (2012) *Strategic development plan*, Dundee: Tayplan.

Tett, G. (2009) *Fool's gold*, London: Little Brown.

Tews, K., Busch, P.-O. and Jorgens, H. (2003) 'The diffusion of new environmental policy instruments', *European Journal of Political Research*, vol 42, no 4, pp 569–600.

Thaler, R.H. and Sunstein, C.R. (2008) *Nudge*, London: Penguin.

Thatcher, M. (1986) *In defence of freedom: speeches on Britain's relations with the world 1976–1986*, London: Aurum Press.

Thatcher, M. (1995) *The Downing Street years*, London: Harper Collins.

Thatcher, M. and Coen, D. (2008) 'Reshaping European regulatory space: an evolutionary analysis', *Western European Politics*, vol 31, no 4, pp 806–36.

Thelen, K. (2004) *How institutions evolve: the political economy of skills in Germany, Britain, the United States and Japan*, New York, NY: Cambridge University Press.

Thielemann, E.R. (2000) *Europeanisation and institutional compatibility: implementing European regional policy in Germany*, Queen's Papers on Europeanisation no 4, Belfast: Queen's University.

Thompson, G. (2011) *In brief: UK–EU economic relations – key statistics*, SN/EP/6091, 20 October, London: House of Commons Library.

Thorp, A. (2011) *Switzerland's relationship with the EU*, SN 6090, 20 October, London: House of Commons Library.

Thorp, A. and Thompson, G. (2011) 'Scotland, independence and the EU', Standard Note 6110, 8 November, House of Commons Library.

Thurber, J.A. (2004) 'Foreword', in J. Kingdon (ed) *Agendas, alternatives and public policies* (2nd edn), New York, NY: Longman, pp vii–xi.

Tommel, I. (2011) 'The European Union – a federation *sui generis*?', in F. Laursen (ed) *The EU and federalism: polities and policies compared*, Farnham: Ashgate, pp 41–56.

Traghardh, L. (2012) 'The Swedish model is the opposite of the big society, David Cameron, Cameron admires Sweden's strong economy, yet it is based on a social compact that would be his worst nightmare', *The Guardian*, 10 February.

Trench, A. (2001a) 'Intergovernmental relations a year on: Whitehall still rules OK?', in A. Trench (ed) *The state of the nations 2001*, Exeter: Imprint Academic, pp 153–74.

Trusswell, E. and Atkinson, D. (2011) *Supporting heads of government: a comparison across six countries*, London: Institute for Government.

Tsebelis, G. (2002) 'Veto players and institutional analysis', *Governance*, vol 13, no 4, pp 441-74.

Tsoukalis, L. (2005) 'Managing interdependence: the EU in the world economy', in C. Hill and M. Smith (eds) *International relations and the European Union*, Oxford: Oxford University Press, pp 225–46.

Turok, I. and Bailey, N. (2004) 'The theory of polynuclear urban regions and its application to Central Scotland', *European Planning Studies*, vol 13, no 3, pp 371–89.

Van de Steeg, M. and Risse, T. (2010) *The emergence of a European community of communication*, KFG Working Paper no 15, August, Berlin: The Free University.

Van Thiel, S. and Leeuw, F. (2002) 'The performance paradox in the public sector', *Public Performance and Management Review*, vol 25, no 3, pp 267–81.

S. D. Varney (2006) *Service Transformation- a better service for citizens*, London: HMT.

Verweij, M., Douglas, M., Ellis, R., Engle, C., Hendriks, F., Lohmann, S., Ney, S., Rayner, S. and Thompson, M. (2006) 'Clumsy solutions for a complex world: the case of climate change', *Public Administration*, vol 84, no 4, pp 817–43.

Vigar, G. (2001) 'Reappraising UK transport policy 1950–99: the myth of "mono-modality" and the nature of "paradigm shifts"', *Planning Perspectives*, vol 16, no 3, pp 269–91.

Villiers, T. (2012) *EU transport council report*, 27 March, London: DfT.

Von Homeyer, I. and Withana, S. (2011) *Final report for the assessment of the 6th environmental action programme*, Berlin: Ecologic Institute with IEEP.

Wall, S. (2008) *A stranger in Europe*, Oxford: Oxford University Press.

Wallace, H. (1997) 'Pan-European integration: a real or imagined community?', *Government and Opposition*, vol 32, no 2, pp 215–33.

Walsh, K. (1995a) 'Competition and public service delivery', in J. Stewart and G. Stoker (eds) *Local government in the 1990s*, Basingstoke: Macmillan, pp 28–48.

Walsh, K. (1995b) *Public services and market mechanisms: competition, contracting and the new public management*, Basingstoke: Macmillan.

Walsh, K. and H. Davis (1993) *Competiton and Service: the impact of the Local Government Act 1988*, London: HMSO.

Walsh, K., Deakin, N., Smith, P., Spurgeon, P. and Thomas, N. (1995) *Contracting for change: contracts in health, social care and other local government services*, Oxford: Oxford University Press.

Ward, K. (2011) 'Policies in motion and in place: the case of business improvement districts', in E. McCann and K. Ward (eds) *Mobile urbanism: cities and policymaking in the global age*, London: University of Minnesota Press, pp 71–96.

Ward, K. and McCann, E. (2011) 'Conclusion; cities assembled: space, neoliberalization, (re)territorialzation, and comparison', in E. McCann and K. Ward (eds) *Mobile urbanism: cities and policymaking in the global age*, London: University of Minnesota Press, pp 147–84.

Weale, A. (1992) *The new politics of pollution*, Manchester: Manchester University Press.

Webster, R. (1998) 'Environmental collective action: stable patterns of cooperation and issue alliances at the European level', in J. Greenwood and M. Aspinwall (eds) *Collective action in the European Union*, London: Routledge, pp 176–95.

Welch, S. and Kennedy-Pipe, C. (2004) 'Multi-level governance and international relations', in I. Bache and M. Flinders (eds) *Multi-level governance*, Oxford: Oxford University Press, pp 127–44.

Welsh Assembly Government (2012) *City regions: group terms of reference*, Cardiff: Welsh Government.

Wenger, E. (2000) 'Communities of practice and social learning systems', *Organization*, vol 7, no 2, pp 225–46.

Wheatley, J. (1969) *Royal Commission on Local Government in Scotland*, Cmnd 4150, London: HMSO.

Wicks, M. (2009), Security of International Energy Review , London: HMG.

Wiener, A. and Diez, T. (eds) (2009) *European integration theory*, Oxford: Oxford University Press.

Wilkinson, D. (1997) 'Towards sustainability in the European Union? Steps within the European Commission towards integrating the environment into other European Union policy sectors', *Environmental Politics*, vol 6, no 1, pp 153–73.

Wilkinson, R. and Pickett, K. (2010) *The spirit level*, London: Penguin.

Williams, P. (2012) *Collaboration in public policy and practice: perspectives on boundary spanners*, Bristol: The Policy Press.

Willman, J. (1994) 'The civil service', in D. Kavagnah and A. Seldon (eds) *The Major effect*, London: Macmillan.

Wilson, D. and Game, C. (2002) *Local government in the United Kingdom* (3rd edn), Basingstoke: Palgrave Macmillan.

Wolinetz, S. (2011) 'Comparing the incomparable: treating the EU in a comparative context', in F. Laursen (ed) *The EU and federalism: polities and policies compared*, Farnham: Ashgate, pp 27–40.

Wolman, H. (2000) 'Local government systems: from historic divergence towards convergence? Great Britain, France, and Germany as comparative cases in point', *Environment and Planning C*, vol 18, part 1, pp 33–56.

Wolman H. and Page, E. (2002) 'Policy transfer among local governments: an information–theory approach', *Governance*, vol 15, no 4, pp 577-601.

Woolcock, S. (2010) 'Trade policy', in H. Wallace, M.A. Pollack and A.R. Young (eds) *Policy making in the European Union* (6th edn), Oxford: Oxford University Press, pp 381–99.

Wooldridge, A. (2012) 'The visible hand', *Economist*, Special Report, 21 January.

Wright, A. (2004) 'Devolution, Westminster and the EU', in P. Giddings and G. Drewry (eds) *Britain in the European Union: law, policy and parliament,* Basingstoke: Palgrave Macmillan, pp 218–39.

WRR (Netherlands Scientific Council for Government Policy) (2007) *Rediscovering Europe in the Netherlands, Scientific Council for Government Policy,* Amsterdam: Amsterdam University Press.

Yesilkagit, K. (2004) 'Bureaucratic autonomy, organizational culture, and habituation: politicians and independent administrative bodies in the Netherlands', *Administration & Society,* vol 36, no 5, pp 528–52.

Young, A.R. (2004) 'The incidental fortress: the single European market and world trade', *Journal of Common Market Studies,* vol 42, no 2, pp 393–414.

Young, A.R. (2007) 'Trade politics ain't what it used to be: The European Union in the Doha Round', *Journal of Common Market Studies,* vol 45, no 4, pp 789–811.

Young, A.R. (2010) 'The single market: deregulation, reregulation and integration', in H. Wallace, M.A. Pollack and A.R. Young (eds) *Policy making in the European Union* (6th edn), Oxford: Oxford University Press, pp 107–32.

Young, A.R. (2012) 'Less than you might think: the impact of WTO rules on EU policies', in O. Costa and K.E. Jorgensen (eds) *When multilateralism hits Brussels: the influence of international institutions on the EU,* Basingstoke: Palgrave Macmillan.

Young, H. (1998) *This blessed plot,* Basingstoke: Macmillan.

Young, K. and Garside, P. (1982) *Metropolitan London: politics of urban change 1837–1981,* London: Edward Arnold.

Young, S.Z. (1973) *Terms of entry: Britain's negotiations with the European Community, 1970–1972,* London: Heinemann.

Zittoun, P. (2009) 'Understanding policy change as a discursive problem', *Journal of Comparative Policy Analysis: Research and Practice,* vol 11, no 1, pp 65–82.

Zohlnhofer, R. (2009) 'How politics matter when policies change: understanding policy change as a political problem', *Journal of Comparative Policy Analysis: Research and Practice,* vol 11, no 1, pp 97–115.

Zubek, R. (2011) 'Core executives and coordination of EU law transposition: evidence from new member states', *Public Administration,* vol 89, no 2, pp 433–50.

Index

Note: The letter t following a page number indicates a table